THEORETICAL ISSUES
IN
POLICY ANALYSIS

Suny Series in Political Theory:
Contemporary Issues
John G. Gunnell, Editor

THEORETICAL ISSUES

in

POLICY ANALYSIS

M. E. Hawkesworth

STATE UNIVERSITY OF NEW YORK PRESS

Published by
State University of New York Press, Albany

Printed in the United States of America

For information, address State University of New York
Press, State University Plaza, Albany, N.Y., 12246

Library of Congress Cataloging-in-Publication Data

Hawkesworth, M. E., 1952–
    Theoretical issues in policy analysis.
    (SUNY series in political theory. Contemporary
issues)
    Bibliography: p.
    Includes index.
    1. Policy sciences. I. Title. II. Series.
H97.H38   1988   361.6'1   87-33629
ISBN 0-88706-840-5
ISBN 0-88706-841-3 (pbk.)

10   9   8   7   6   5   4   3   2

For
F. M. H.

Contents

Acknowledgements

The approach to policy analysis developed in this book owes a great deal to a number of scholars who have helped to shape my thinking about the theoretical constitution of political events. For introducing me to the formative role of theory in mediating experience, I am greatly indebted to William Connolly, R. Bruce Douglass, and José Sorzano. For prompting me to think more systematically about the issues raised in this volume, I am grateful to Michele Martin, John Gunnell, Fred Dallmayr, and Rita Mae Kelly. Thanks are also due to Edward Portis, Kathleen Shortridge, James O'Sullivan and Edward Thompson for their helpful comments on individual chapters of this volume. I am especially indebted to John Nelson for his thorough consideration of the entire manuscript and for his insightful suggestions for improvement. Finally, I would like to thank Philip Alperson for the extraordinary care with which he reviewed the manuscript in its various incarnations, for his incisive criticisms and constructive suggestions, and for the daily sustenance he afforded throughout the long writing process.

Research for this book was conducted under the auspices of grants from the Commission on Academic Excellence and the College of Arts and Sciences of the University of Louisville. Their support is gratefully acknowledged.

1

Introduction: Unresolved Problems of an Unacknowledged Tradition

THE contemporary field of policy analysis is the product of a long history of inquiry concerning the process of political decision-making and the crucial determinants of specific substantive policies. Although it is typical to situate the discipline of policy studies in the context of twentieth-century social science and to relate current debates on the definition, scope, and techniques of the field to methodological debates which have occupied social scientists for the past century, the intellectual ancestry of policy science is much richer than this focus suggests.[1] The conception of politics which informs most policy inquiry is heavily indebted to the views of Aristotle, Machiavelli and Smith;[2] the methodological commitments of policy analysis reflect conceptions of science which can be traced to Galileo, Newton, and Bacon, and conceptions of knowledge advanced by Hobbes, Pascal, and Hume.[3] Failure to comprehend the intellectual origins of policy inquiry is understandable, given the increasing specialization of policy scientists and the vast proliferation of research materials within substantive areas. But neglecting the genesis of particular political, epistemological, and methodological commitments has a number of important implications for the discipline of policy studies. In the absence of an awareness of the origins of the discipline's commitments, there can be little understanding of the problems which specific ideas were devised to solve. And if the relation between a problem and its solution is not fully understood, it is difficult to assess the adequacy of specific solutions. Thus the discipline becomes, in important respects, the captive of a tradition which is imperfectly understood.

This book explores some of the traditional commitments of policy analysis, empiricist commitments which are incorporated in the methodology of the discipline and which are seldom scrutinized. It will examine beliefs concerning the nature of facts and values, the powers of reason, the structure of science, and the possibilities for scientific knowledge—beliefs so widely accepted by practitioners in the field that they are no longer perceived as issues. Indeed, so entrenched are these beliefs in the practices of the discipline that their examination is likely to be deemed unnecessary. But examining the epistemological assumptions which shape disciplinary objectives and research techniques is crucial, for the empiricist assumptions which sustain contemporary approaches to policy analysis are fundamentally flawed. The task of the following chapters is to elucidate the character of these assumptions and the nature of their defects, to situate these beliefs within a larger tradition in order to explicate their strengths and their weaknesses, and to demonstrate that these empiricist precepts not only fail to accomplish their designated tasks, but also render policy analysis incapable of resolving some basic issues concerning its nature and its role in democratic political systems. In addition, this book will examine an alternative conception of science and explore its implications for policy analysis.

Empiricist Principles and Policy Pursuits

That the legitimate sphere of policy inquiry involves description, explanation, and prediction of issues pertaining to public policy will likely be granted by every practitioner in the field. Whether the focus of research is policy-making, policy implementation, or policy assessment,[4] a commitment to empirical inquiry is virtually a defining characteristic of the discipline. Indeed, so pervasive are empiricist commitments within the profession that few practitioners are aware that there might be anything contestable about them.

That empiricism[5] provides contentious accounts of the nature of reality, the senses, rationality, science, and the possibilities for human knowledge, is not typically noted in methodology courses in policy analysis. Nor is it often explained that these contentious empiricist accounts were developed in a specific historical context as part of an effort to undermine the intellectual hegemony of Aristotelianism and medieval scholasticism. Methodology texts seldom acknowledge that crucial methodological precepts concerning the nature of facts, the separation of facts and values, the importance of quantification and measurement in scientific studies, and the appropriateness of mechanistic explanations of social events, were developed as part of a thoroughly political battle against church and crown.[6]

This neglect of the political genesis of empiricist principles is not accidental. On the contrary, such matters are rendered irrelevant by fundamental empiricist premises that scientific methods are neutral, and that specific strategies of empirical inquiry rooted in observation are value-free. Three beliefs—that systematic observation is the appropriate method for gaining truth about the world; that in the process of observation, the observer's subjectivity can be controlled by rigid adherence to neutral procedures designed to produce identical measurements of the real properties of objects; and that empirical techniques can produce scientific laws that identify the necessary and sufficient conditions of observed phenomena—combine to discredit claims that methodological commitments are contentious and that their origins may shed light upon their political cast. The belief in the neutrality of the scientific method itself provides an immunity against claims concerning the history and politics of the empiricist tradition.[7]

Mutually reinforcing empiricist assumptions dispel questions concerning the political cast of empiricist commitments by providing a formula for preserving the objectivity of scientific investigations and for insulating scientific research from the taint of politics. That formula requires a dichotomous division of the world into the realm of the empirical and the non-empirical. Structured in accordance with the belief that knowledge depends upon the evidence of the senses, the empirical realm comprises all that can be corroborated by the senses; as a residual category, the non-empirical comprises everything else. On this view, as long as scientific investigations operate within the realm of the empirical, eschewing speculative and valuative discourse, objectivity lies within reach. The division of the world into separate spheres and the restriction of scientific endeavors to the sphere of facts provides a means for the maintenance of objectivity and the attainment of truth.

The separate spheres doctrine surfaces in the methodology of policy analysis in the fact/value dichotomy. As an organizational tool, the fact/value dichotomy demarcates between the legitimate sphere of scientific inquiry and the legitimate sphere of politics. Available for observation and amenable to corroboration by intersubjective testing, the realm of facts constitutes the appropriate sphere of scientific policy analysis. Restricted to the activities of description, explanation, and prediction, empirical policy analysis is committed to the development of objective knowledge about the policy-making process, the key determinants of policy decisions, the necessary means for achieving policy objectives, and the predictable consequences of various strategies of policy implementation. The realm of values, of questions of right and wrong, of good and bad, of what ought and what ought not be done, falls beyond the legitimate sphere of scientific policy investigation. Undiscernible by the senses, unresolvable by scientific techniques, and dependent on subjective assessments, questions of value constitute the agenda of the political process. Because resolving these questions involves a contest of personal preferences in which reason plays little role, political criteria rather than scientific principles govern the determination of value disputes. Thus the fact/value dichotomy identifies not only the appropriate focus for policy inquiry and the methods necessary for attaining objective knowledge, but also the line of demarcation between legitimate scientific authority and inescapable political engagement. The fact/value dichotomy sanctions a clear division of labor between the policy analyst and the political decision-maker.

Imbued with empiricist assumptions concerning the substance of their investigations, the scope of their responsibilities, the objectives of their research and the limits of their authority, policy analysts have little reason to question the merits of empiricism. The character of the research endorsed by empiricist precepts appears eminently reasonable, perfectly feasible, and rich in potential. Adherence to the strictures of empirical policy analysis promises to generate scientific knowledge of the policy process, which may facilitate improved decision-making, enhance the efficiency of service delivery, heighten the level of technical sophistication in substantive policy areas, contribute to the success of policy initiatives, and produce benefits for the political community.

The pervasiveness of empiricist commitments, the apparent reasonableness of empiricist principles, and the potential utility of empirical research might explain the dearth of attention to the contentious character of empiricist conceptions of reality, the senses, reason, science, and knowledge within contemporary policy studies. Yet the very centrality of empiricist commitments to the definition and direction of policy analysis makes an examination of empiricist presuppositions all the more important. For the legitimacy of empirical policy analysis as a scientific endeavor is inextricably linked to the validity of the empiricist project.

Theoretical Issues in Policy Analysis

The task of this volume is to consider the nature of policy analysis in detail, to explore the theoretical assumptions which sustain policy inquiry, and to subject the contentious precepts which define the discipline to critical scrutiny. In particular, questions concerning the nature of facts and values, of perception and observation, of reason and cognition, of science and objective knowledge will be examined and the adequacy of empiricist conceptions of these phenomena will be assessed.

The next three chapters advance arguments to demonstrate that the empiricist foundation of policy analysis is fundamentally flawed. Chapter 2 investigates issues pertaining to definitions of, models for, and methods appropriate to policy analysis which have been the focus of intense debate within the discipline in the past several decades. The central objective of the chapter is to move beyond the vitriol of antagonistic rhetoric in order to discern the central theoretical issues that policy analysis must confront. Toward this end, two markedly different images of policy inquiry—an image of policy science in service to democracy and an image of depoliticizing scientism in service to technocracy—will be examined. The juxtaposition of these opposing conceptions of policy science helps illuminate fundamental theoretical issues confronting policy analysts. What is the nature of policy inquiry? Is policy analysis scientific or scientistic? Do extensive empiricist policy investigations generate usable knowledge or ideological obfuscations? Is the policy expert a handmaiden of democracy or an agent of depoliticization? This chapter will also suggest, however, that empiricist conceptions of facts, values, and the limits of rational inquiry produce a unique problem for the discipline of policy studies. Although they allow the identification of the central theoretical questions pertinent to the nature of policy inquiry, empiricist commitments preclude the possibility that such questions could be rationally resolved.

In order to challenge the conclusion that the nature of policy inquiry cannot be determined by rational analysis, chapter 3 considers the problem of the scientific status of policy analysis in the context of debates within the philosophy of science. Through an explication of the criticisms of empiricism and positivism advanced by post-positivist theories of science, the chapter details the defects in the presuppositions of empirical policy inquiry. It explores problems related to induction, verificationism and falsificationism; the hypothetico-deductive model of explanation and prediction; the correspondence theory of truth; the fact/value dichotomy; and the instrumental conception of rationality; which constitute the foundation of empirical policy science. In addition, this chapter delineates an alternative conception of science that avoids the defects of positivism and empiricism and that can provide guidance for more sophisticated approaches to policy inquiry. But after examining recent developments in policy analysis, the chapter concludes that the insights of this revised conception of science have not yet penetrated the discipline of policy studies.

Recognizing the power of the fact/value dichotomy to insulate policy analysis from the force of the criticisms advanced by post-positivist theories of science, chapter 4 subjects the arguments advanced in support of the fact/value dichotomy to direct, critical scrutiny. Investigating the uses to which the fact/value dichotomy is put in the policy literature suggests that rather than promote the acquisition of objective knowledge, the deployment of the fact/value dichotomy truncates systematic inquiry by circumventing critical investigation of a range of questions and by uncritically accrediting contentious claims. Chapter 4 demonstrates that the institutionalization of the fact/value dichotomy within policy studies impairs rather than facilitates the acquisition of knowledge. Thus, a commitment to systematic inquiry requires the abandonment of the fact/value dichotomy. The final sections of the chapter consider the implications of such a development for the future of policy analysis. In particular, it considers changes in the conception of theory, the understanding of the empirical realm, and the comprehension of cognitive practices which would be necessary if the discipline of policy studies were to take advantage of the insights of post-positivist theories of science.

Chapters 5 through 8 continue to explore the implications of post-positivist theories of science for policy analysis in the context of specific domestic and foreign policy questions and in light of particular objectives (prediction, explanation, evaluation) of policy research. Chapter 5 considers issues raised by a revised conception of theory which recognizes and capitalizes on the essentially contestable character of theoretical presuppositions. In the context of issues pertaining to discrimination, affirmative action, and preferential treatment, the chapter investigates the means by which contentious theoretical presuppositions shape what is perceived as a fact, what is conceived as a political problem, and what is accepted as a legitimate policy option. The chapter demonstrates the manner in which contentious assumptions about individual identity and freedom structure the capacity to perceive discrimination in the contemporary United States, and thereby influence assessments of the need for a remedy for discrimination, as well as the appropriateness of affirmative action as such a remedy. After identifying competing theoretical assumptions which structure the perceptions and policy prescriptions of opponents on these issues, the chapter examines the manner in which reason can be brought to bear upon theoretically constituted conceptions of the world in order to facilitate the resolution of intractable policy disputes. It considers various ways in which rational assessment of policy presuppositions can contribute to a reconsideration of policy options and a reconception of political possibilities in terms of collective action and social justice.

Explanation of events pertaining to policy-making, to the success of policy initiatives, to the consequences of various policy options, and to the causes of policy failure remains a primary objective of policy inquiry. Indeed, the explanation of relevant political events remains a crucial precondition for forming any policy proposals whatsoever. But what counts as an adequate explanation? Chapter 6 considers the implications of post-positivist theories of science for the model of explanation appropriate to policy inquiry.

Taking a foreign policy context as its point of departure, this chapter investigates competing explanations of two decades of political violence in Kampuchea. In the final phases of the Vietnam war, Cambodia became a microcosm of political violence, experiencing invasions of foreign armies, systematic aerial bombing, coups d'etat, civil war, revolutionary transformation, purges, summary executions, and continuing guerilla activity. How to explain these complex events is an important question, whether the objective is to understand these decades of devastation, to form policy responses toward this besieged nation, or to cull lessons from this experience for later use in other contexts. This chapter examines five alternative explanations of Kampuchea's experience in order to identify and criticize the theoretical presuppositions which structure these divergent explanatory accounts. Moving from the specifics of the Kampuchean case to the more general problem of explanation, the chapter suggests that neither the hypothetico-deductive model nor the interpretive model of scientific explanation deals adequately with the role of contentious theoretical presuppositions in generating explanatory accounts. In order to overcome this deficiency, the chapter concludes by advancing an alternative model of explanation grounded in an understanding of the formative role of theoretical assumptions in human cognition and in political analysis.

The conception of prediction which has dominated the discipline of policy studies acquires its meaning in relation to a host of positivist assumptions concerning the nature of science. In challenging those positivist commitments, anti-positivist critics have discredited the covering law model of prediction. Chapter 7 considers the possibility that there may be grounds other than the illusory laws of social physics upon which policy predictions may be predicated. Taking policy questions related to issues of human rights as a case in point, the chapter suggests that a sophisticated understanding of the operation of divergent theoretical presuppositions upon the constitution of political beliefs and upon the construction of policy options may afford policy analysts an alternative foundation for policy predictions.

In recent years, appeals to human rights have surfaced with increasing regularity in the international arena in the rhetoric of the oppressed, in the language of international accords, and in the legitimations of the foreign policy ventures of particular nations. Claims concerning the universal, inalienable, and absolute character of human rights provide a foundation for arguments that enforcing rights cannot be restricted to the internal affairs of individual states, that each state must prevent abuses of rights and must punish abusers throughout the world. Yet the appeal to a universal code of human rights as a justification for foreign policy initiatives is challenged by charges that international human rights policies promote ideological, hegemonial, and propagandistic purposes. Can human rights be defined neutrally? Can the United States devise policies to protect the rights of the oppressed in other nations?

Chapter 7 considers the extent to which the rhetoric of universal human rights masks markedly different conceptions of rights and of the fundamental human interests which rights are devised to protect and promote. Moreover, the chapter suggests that a thorough understanding of the discordant theoretical assumptions which inform divergent conceptions of rights can afford policy analysts a remarkably reliable mechanism for predicting the outcomes of human rights initiatives.

The revised focus of policy inquiry suggested by post-positivist theories of science is premised upon an understanding of the theoretical constitution of *facticity*. Through the perceptions they engender, the valuations they sanction, the evidence they accredit, and the explanations they warrant, theoretical assumptions endorse a substantive conception of reality, a set of ontological commitments with a determinate political cast. Moreover, whether their influence is manifested at the level of beliefs and perceptions, or in the political actions and policy options which follow from them, theoretical presuppositions are essentially contentious. For this reason, systematic policy inquiry must engage in sustained, critical examination of the political implications of contestable policy presuppositions. It must consider not only the internal consistency of policy objectives, the adequacy of designated means to achieve policy goals, and the efficiency of implementation strategies, but also the contours of the world and the character of life which would be created if specific policy presuppositions were consistently acted upon and actualized in a determinate political community.

Chapter 8 illuminates the importance of and the possibilities for such inquiry by analyzing recent changes in welfare policy and examining the presuppositions sustaining "workfare" programs. Characterized as the welfare reform of the 1980's, workfare requires public assistance recipients to "work off" the value of their benefits through unpaid labor in community service projects. This chapter explores the conception of poverty which sustains the workfare program, considers the internal consistency of program objectives, and investigates the adequacy of the means established to achieve workfare's goals. In addition, the chapter examines the implications of institutionalizing workfare programs in the contemporary United States. In contrast to the benign descriptions of the program advanced by advocates, a detailed analysis suggests that the assumptions underlying workfare support social relations which intensify the imposition of discipline, diminish individual freedom, and legitimize increasing use of a range of subtle mechanisms of social control. By identifying the underside of the commitments which inform workfare, this chapter illuminates the means by which a theoretically sophisticated policy analysis can expand the terms of political debate by elucidating the contentious dimensions of policy prescriptions.

Having considered the problems of policy analysis created by unreflective adherence to empiricist and positivist principles, having detailed the serious flaws in the conceptions of perception, cognition, facts, values, truth, and science which are taken for granted by most policy analysts, and having illuminated the contours of a post-positivist model of policy inquiry, the book concludes with a recon-sideration of the issues raised in the debate concerning the contrast-ing images of policy inquiry. The final chapter returns to the funda-mental question: Is policy analysis a democratic science or is it a form of depoliticizing scientism? Using the tools of rational analysis freed from unwarranted restrictions imposed by positivist commitments, chapter 9 assesses the merits of the evidence and arguments related to the charge of scientism and considers the implications of this charge for the nature and future of policy analysis.

Policy Analysis:
Images and Issues

EVEN the most cursory review of the recent literature in policy analysis suggests a field in ferment. Questions concerning an appropriate definition of the endeavor, adequate models and methods of research, acceptable roles and responsibilities for analysts, and an accurate conceptualization of the relationship between policy analysis and democratic decision-making have been debated at length. Yet the critical issues and the significant differences among positions advanced on each of these questions are often difficult to discern, in part because the systems of classification used in the debate are not standardized. It is not uncommon to encounter similar arguments concerning problems of definition, as well as advocacy of particular research tools and techniques, and practical stances for policy analysts cast in markedly different terminology. The long-standing antagonism between the rational comprehensive model and the incrementalist model for decision-making which figures prominently in these debates, for example, resurfaces in oppositions between the 'Harvard School' and the 'Berkeley School' approaches, between 'empirico-analytic' and 'neopluralist' strategies, between the 'Management Sciences Model of ASPA' (American Society for Public Administration) and the 'Power and Value Conflict Model of the APSA' (American

Political Science Association), and between 'synoptic' and 'antisynoptic' theories of policy analysis.[1] Beyond the lack of standardized terminology, the intense antagonism among proponents of alternative policy analysis models tends to mask important commonalities among them.

Divergent conceptions of decision-making have fueled the debate over the nature of policy inquiry. Arguments concerning the possibility of rational, comprehensive decision-making sustain claims concerning the development of a highly technical 'policy science' devoted to problem identification, goal articulation, assessment of alternative means for goal attainment, and selection of preferred implementation strategies in order to heighten the rationality of the policy process.[2] At the same time, an understanding of incremental decision-making related to an intensive process of interest accommodation generates a conception of policy analysis as a 'craft' attuned to the multiple dimensions of politics in order to facilitate problem-solving.[3]

The opposition between the *applied social science model* of policy analysis advanced by proponents of a comprehensive planning approach to decision-making, and an *applied pluralist model* of policy inquiry derived from an incrementalist approach to decision-making has focused attention on questions concerning the scientific status of policy analysis. Although the dominant theme within this exchange has been the possibility and the desirability of value-free research,[4] fundamental issues have also been raised about the precise model of science which should inform policy studies. Positivist conceptions of science have been advanced and attacked, post-positivist alternatives have been formed and subjected to counter-attack. *Empiricist models* (which envision the generation of accurate data as their *raison d'être*) have been juxtaposed against *Engineering models* (which focus upon the application of scientific theories to practical problems), as well as *Enlightenment models* (which emphasize the deployment of knowledge for human emancipation).[5] Alternative conceptions of science have also raised questions about the appropriate role of the policy scientist in the policy making process. The scientific credentials of policy analysts have been said to require conformity to a 'handmaiden' or 'hired gun' role (providing information according to the specifications of government contracts) or, alternatively, to necessitate adherence to an 'ivory tower' role (maintaining scientific autonomy by pursuing research within academic institutions in accordance with disciplinary interests rather than government grants).[6]

Arguments concerning the demands of scientific policy analysis have also generated heated debates about the techniques necessary for scientific policy studies. Questions concerning quantitative versus qualitative techniques, univariate versus multivariate causal models, exhaustive versus limited data sets, positivist versus multiplist strategies, cost-benefit analysis versus risk-benefit analysis, case studies versus comparative studies, verificationist versus falsificationist standards of assessment, and efficiency versus equity as decision criteria have all figured in these discussions.

The significance of these debates is often cast in terms of their implications for training future policy analysts, for developing curricula for graduate programs in policy analysis, and for consolidating the identity and integrity of the newly emergent and interdisciplinary field of policy studies. Yet the debates are also related to a larger and more important issue, the role of the policy 'expert' in a democratic polity. On this point, many of the oppositions between hostile opponents dissolve. Rational comprehensive strategists and incrementalist satisficers, value-free and value-committed analysts, proponents of economic factors and political forces tend to concur that the trained expert has an important and legitimate role to play in the policy process of contemporary liberal democratic systems. Despite marked differences on questions of models, methods, and approaches, the received view among those writing in the field of policy analysis suggests that the techniques of policy analysis can contribute to democracy by generating usable knowledge for decision-makers.

The received view does not have unanimous support. A darker image of policy analysis emerges in the works of a small group of contemporary scholars. In contrast to the optimism of the received view, which affirms a compatibility between expertise and democratic decision-making, the alternative image of policy analysis suggests a fundamental incompatibility between technocratic and democratic decision-making. Indeed, the darker image suggests that the scientistic commitments of policy analysts may themselves be complicitous in a process of depoliticization which undermines the possibility of meaningful democracy.

This chapter will explore the issues raised by these contrasting images of policy analysis, an image of science in service to democracy versus an image of depoliticizing scientism. This focus will help to illuminate common assumptions which underlie many antagonisms between applied social science and applied pluralist models of policy analysis. Exploring the dimensions of consensus which unite these opposing conceptions of policy inquiry will allow a more accurate assessment of the differences between them. And by contrasting the shared assumptions which inform the received view of policy studies against the charges advanced by critics of scientism, it will be possible to identify the central theoretical issues which confront the field of policy analysis.

Science in Service to Democracy

That policy analysis can promote social amelioration by heightening human control over the social environment and increasing rationality and efficiency in the delivery of human services is a recurrent theme in the policy literature. The vision which inspired the founding of the policy sciences emphasized an interdisciplinary effort to "make full use of science and democracy in planning for the expansion of national production, for justice, for the fair distribution of national gains, for far higher standards of living, for liberty, for the recognition of the dignity of man, and for his right to participate fully in the civilization he has helped to create".[7] From Charles Merriam's model of 'democratic engineering' to Harold Lasswell's conception of the policy scientist as 'social therapist' who manifests "lively concern for the problem of overcoming the divisive tendencies of modern life and of bringing into existence a more thorough integration of the goals and methods of public and private action,"[8] the emphasis has been on using scientific knowledge to facilitate "enlightened decision in the context of public and civic order."[9]

More recent works in policy analysis have retained this commitment to problem-solving in a democratic polity. Characterizing policy analysis as "public science,"Erve Chambers has noted that "science enters politics on the basis of its authority—to discover 'facts', to generate useful hypotheses, to develop theoretical and data based statements, and to solve the problems presented to it,"[10] and that its legitimacy in a democratic system is inseparable from these activities. Stuart Nagel has defined policy analysis as "the evaluation of alternative government policies or decisions in order to arrive at the best (or a good) policy or decision in light of given goals, constraints, and conditions" of the liberal democratic political order.[11] Randall Ripley has suggested that policy analysts develop a "clinical relationship" with political decision-makers precisely "to solve practical problems in the short run and to establish the basis for good theory in the future."[12] Arguing that the fundamental goal of policy science is the promotion of social welfare, Duncan MacRae has insisted that the social function of social science is "not simply to serve the interests

of any particular class, it is to provide guidance to society, through research, reasoned discourse and education as to what interests should
be served in particular circumstances and as to the means to do so."[13]
Similarly, Aaron Wildavsky has charged the policy analyst with the responsibility "to think about ways to enhance citizens' capacity for
moral development on public purposes"[14] for it is only through the
cultivation of autonomy and reciprocity that better policies can be
promoted. And Michael McPherson has suggested that the policy
analyst has a three-sided obligation in a democracy: "to serve his/her
superiors, to promote better policies and to respect and improve the
democratic process by which decisions are made."[15]

Widespread agreement that policy analysts use their professional expertise to promote democratic objectives is matched by a
good deal of disagreement concerning the best means to achieve this
end. Much of the argument on this point reflects varying degrees of
skepticism about the nature and content of 'usable knowledge' in the
field of policy analysis. Yet, even these differences of opinion on epistemological issues arise within a larger context of consensus. Indeed,
it could be said that the range of differences operative in this debate is
fairly small when considered against the background of shared assumptions which sustain the discourse. Thus it is helpful to consider
the dimensions of consensus which unite opponents in order to gauge
their differences accurately.

Contemporary policy science is the heir to a mixed legacy of optimism and skepticism toward the possibilities of human knowledge.
In contrast to classical conceptions of rationality premised upon the
conviction that humans could attain certain knowledge of theology
and metaphysics, as well as of human affairs, modern approaches to
epistemological questions are marked by a measure of skepticism.
Whether the constriction of the human capacity for knowledge is
traced to Hobbes' instrumental conception of rationality,[16] to Hume's
demolition of the foundations of the rationalist tradition,[17] to
Comte's confident assertion of the arrival of the age of positivism,[18] or
to the Vienna Circle's development of the verificationist criterion of
meaning,[19] the scope accorded to reason has diminished drastically in
the modern era. With the arrival of the twentieth century, the received
view in epistemology suggested that the faculty of human reason was
limited and fallible, that it could be trusted only in the realm of the
empirically observable, and that even then, problems of limited and
incomplete evidence necessitated caution in accepting claims about
the world. Only adherence to strict canons of scientific observation
and testing in conjunction with intersubjective verification through

replication could afford a measure of security to the conclusions reached by fragile human reason.

Texts in policy analysis routinely note that the appropriate sphere for scientific investigations is the empirical realm. Since reason can operate reliably only at the empirical level, policy analysts must restrict their attention to questions of fact, defined as empirically verifiable propositions. Description and explanation constitute the legitimate activities of the policy analyst as applied social scientist. Speculative philosophy, normative theory, and evaluative discourses must all be eschewed not only because they fall outside the purview of science, but because they operate at the level of irrational speculation or emotional expression. From Max Weber's image of the individual confronting an ultimate and ungrounded choice of irreconcilably conflicting values akin to a "death struggle like that between 'God' and the 'Devil'"[20] to Eugene Meehan's stern warning: "With some relatively minor exceptions, those involved in the study of public policy will find little or nothing in philosophy, either substantive or procedural, that can be used productively in their work and much that is actually misleading and counter-productive;"[21] the message has been clear. Policy analysts must strive for value-neutrality as a regulative ideal. Since any excursus beyond the realm of the empirically verifiable involves either emotional preferences or arbitrary decisions immune to rational adjudication, policy analysts must confine their contributions to the observable and intersubjectively verifiable realm of the empirical.

Within the bounds of such an empiricist consensus, disagreements arise in the policy literature concerning the particular models and methods most amenable to scientific policy studies. The skepticism with respect to the power of reason, which distinguishes opponents from proponents of rational comprehensive decision-making, emerges in a larger context of agreement concerning a theory of knowledge (empiricism), a conception of science (positivist),[22] and the fact/value dichotomy which both entail. A commitment to objectivity, understood in terms of the application of impartial scientific procedures and use of a public methodology that allows the validity of findings to be verified through examination or replication, is characteristic of all parties in the debate. At issue in this exchange is the precise nature of *objective knowledge*, which can be deployed in policy analysis. Whether objective knowledge should be conceived in terms of *technical knowledge* derived from the general laws of social science and used to identify the most efficient means to pre-established ends, or in terms of *political knowledge*, derived from an understanding of the actual processes of decision-making and used to enable decision-makers to attain their objectives, constitutes the principal source of antagonism between these two camps.

Technical Knowledge

The conception of technical knowledge advanced by proponents of the rational comprehensive model of policy analysis is heavily indebted to the views of Max Weber, drawing upon both Weber's conceptions of rationalization and bureaucratization, and upon his conception of the appropriate function of social science. The twin processes of rationalization and bureaucratization, which, according to Weber, characterize the development of political systems in the twentieth century, have important implications for both the policy-making process and for the task of policy analysis: The growth of bureaucracy and the gradual rationalization of administrative decision-making transform the central features of policy determination. Policy-making develops from a process dominated by politics to a process in which expertise plays an increasingly significant role. Formalization of decision criteria and institutionalization of bureaucratic norms increase the demand for impartial policy inquiry. As society becomes more fully rationalized, partisan politics gives way to scientific investigation of the most efficient means to realize policy objectives.[23] Thus, the model of policy science is informed by an image of future possibility, an image of the gradual displacement of power struggles over policy options by rational determination of the best means to achieve social objectives. It is an image of the future which policy science may help to create, for the proliferation of scientific policy inquiry contributes to the process of rationalization itself: The more often the scientific counsel of policy experts is heeded in the policy process, the smaller will be the role played by irrational political forces.

On Weber's view, the appropriate balance between scientific expertise and political considerations in the policy process is set by the limits of human reason. Since questions of value fall beyond the scope of scientific investigation, politics will continue to provide a mechanism for decisions involving values. Granting that the choice of ultimate values for a polity, as well as the choice of particular goals, must be determined through the political process, Weber was confident that science could "render inestimable service to persons engaged in political activity."[24] Weber maintained that logic and empirical inquiry, the fundamental tools of the social scientist, had an important role to play in the policy process.[25] Given politically-determined ends, social science could identify the "indispensable means" to achieve those ends, the "inevitable repercussions" of pursuing them, and the "practical consequences" of alternative courses of action.[26] Moreover, harnessing the power of logic, social science could clarify the meaning of particular social values, elaborate and explicate internally consistent value axioms, and deduce the empirical consequences which might follow from the institutionalizaion of certain values.[27] Thus, by combining the power of logic and empirical inquiry, social science could provide information essential to the achievement of political objectives. It could reveal that specific goals are impossible to achieve, even in an approximate way, because their realization demands a degree of technical proficiency which exceeds existing capabilities. It could indicate the probability of success of various implementation strategies related to particular policy questions, as well as the probabilities of intended and unintended consequences associated with particular policy options. Social science could also identify undesirable side-effects of attaining designated ends, and thereby provide information essential to informed policy choices. And social science could identify mutual incompatibility among competing values that would render their simultaneous achievement impossible.[28]

Weber's vision of the possibilities for social science is incorporated in both the rational comprehensive model of decision-making and the analytical technique of cost-benefit analysis. The rational comprehensive model of decision-making suggests that decision-making can be rationalized if Weberian precepts are followed: The decision-maker begins by identifying all values pertinent to a particular decision situation; then ranks those values according to their salience in the existing context; identifies the necessary means for realizing those values; considers the likely consequences (intended and unintended) of adopting alternative means; and chooses the course of action which will maximize the preferred value. Cost-benefit analysis modifies and adapts these principles to fit the needs of policy analysts working within the parameters of quantitative techniques. Thus the cost-benefit analyst accepts politically-determined values as givens and focuses on means-ends relations: identifying the available alternatives for attaining stipulated ends; calculating the full range of costs and benefits associated with each alternative; and indicating the alternative that would yield the greatest net benefit, maximize efficiency, or achieve Pareto optimality.[29]

That technical knowledge conceived in terms of using logic and empirical inquiry to facilitate rational decision-making is parasitic upon systematic and causal theory developed within social science is granted by all proponents of the Weberian paradigm. It is precisely this dependence upon a larger body of social scientific knowledge that sustains the image of the policy analyst as applied social scientist and demarcates the legitimate role of the policy expert within the policy process. The rough distinction between *pure* and *applied* social science suggests that there exists cumulative social science knowledge and sophisticated methodological techniques which an individual must master in order to warrant the title *'policy expert'*. Once initiated into the discipline, the policy analyst, like the pure social scientist, must use the theories, models, and concepts that structure scientific activity; engage in causal explanation to illuminate the relations which hold between independent and dependent variables; identify patterns or regularities in social and political life that can generate testable predictions; and systematically test such predictions against the contingencies of empirical events.[30] What differentiates pure social science from applied policy analysis then, is more a matter of degree than a difference in a kind of endeavor: Pure social science emphasizes the quest for universal generalizations, definitive causal explanations, and theoretical explications of the socio-political world; applied policy analysis uses this general knowledge in particular contexts to provide useful information to decision-makers who need solutions to problems.[31]

What drives the social scientist as policy analyst is the quest for technical knowledge, a quest for "descriptive and analytic tools enabling us to do the following: make a rapid survey of the predispositions found everywhere in the world, 'predict' (retrospectively) the conditioning factors accounting for the direction and intensity of these predispositions; predict the way in which these predispositions would express themselves under the impact of any conceivable constellation of future conditioning factors; predict the probable occurrence of future constellations; outline the strategies by which the probability of future constellations can be modified (at stated cost in terms of values); and connect past and future sequences of events with specifications of goal."[32] Proponents of the applied social science model of policy analysis suggest that through the systematic development of quantitative research techniques, social science has created the tools necessary for the attainment of such knowledge. The task of the policy analyst is to use this technical knowledge to resolve the policy questions raised by political decision-makers.

Within the literature pertaining to the applied social science model of policy analysis there is an unresolved tension between com-

mitment to the rationalization of the policy process and resignation
to the limits of scientific authority established by the fact/value
dichotomy. This tension is manifested in expressions of acute frus-
tration that scientific policy prescriptions continue to be superceded
by political considerations at critical points in the decision-making
process. Professional policy scientists have repeatedly decried the irrationality and the intrigue which produce particular policy decisions.[33] Policy texts have identified strategies to increase the likeli-
hood that technical knowledge will be used in decision-making.[34]
And a great deal of attention has been devoted to a variety of mechanisms for increasing the relevance of policy science in the contemporary policy process. The proponents of the applied social science
model of policy analysis do not doubt that existing canons of social
science afford the technical base necessary for rational policy prescription. Convinced that the technical knowledge essential to sound
decision-making exists, policy scientists confront a practical question: how to create opportunities for deploying policy expertise
within the prevailing system. They accept that their role is limited to
empirical investigations bearing on policy questions, but they seek to
increase the use of the technical knowledge available in order to promote more rational public policy.

Political Knowledge

A review of training programs for policy analysts conducted in the late
1970s suggested that the only agreement to be found amidst the diverse curricula was "apparent agreement on rational-comprehensive
approaches to resource allocation."[35] In the political arena during
roughly the same period, the Ford Administration issued Executive
Order 11821, which required federal agencies to publish "Inflationary
Impact Statements," preliminary cost-benefit studies, for any proposed regulations which might affect "costs, productivity, energy supply and demand, critical materials, employment or market structure."[36] This order was reauthorized by the Carter Administration
and expanded in 1981 by the Reagan Administration with Executive
Order 12291, which required a cost-benefit analysis before any proposed federal regulation was implemented.[37] But just as it appeared
that a consensus concerning the appropriateness of the Weberian
model of the policy analyst as applied social scientist was emerging in
the discipline and being ratified by the political system, skepticism
arose in the ranks. Doubts were aired about the adequacy of the social

science theories, models, and concepts upon which applied policy science depended.

Despite the Weberian model's promise of rationality, objectivity, and certitude in the scientific analyses of empirical affairs, suspicions were aroused by the conclusions of particular studies.[38] Questions concerning research design, outcome measures, sampling techniques, data gathering procedures, causal models, and theoretical presuppositions gave way to more general skepticism concerning the "maturity of social science" and its ability to sustain applied research.[39] Senior scholars began to suggest that the central problem was not merely the time constraints and pressured conditions under which most policy studies were conducted, but rather that "the technical base of policy analysis is weak due to the limitations of social science: innumerable discrete propositions of varying validity and uncertain applicability."[40] Moreover, it was argued that the rational comprehensive model of decision-making "misunderstands the politics of the policy-making process."[41] Afflicted with "hyper-rationalism,"[42] the applied social science model was said to overload decision-makers with irrelevant data, to demand a degree of systematicity in decision-making wholly at odds with real life situations, to investigate an excessive range of alternatives and possible consequences, which both increased costs and prolonged the decision-making process, to impose arbitrary constraints on problem-solving, to demand a staggering loss of information with respect to nonquantifiable factors, and to distract attention from 'real,' i.e., 'political' solutions to society's problems.[43]

As the litany of criticisms grew, opponents of the rational comprehensive decision-making model converged on a number of fundamental charges: the findings of cost-benefit analyses lacked the degree of conclusiveness which practitioners claimed for them under the rubric of scientific knowledge; the demands for systematic appraisal of alternatives and possible outcomes insured that cost-benefit analysis was neither efficient nor cost-effective, and the methodological limitations of contemporary social science, in conjunction with the foibles of contemporary decision-making, rendered it likely that applied social science would function either as a *post hoc* rationalization of political decisions, or as a positive obstruction to problem-solving. In short, opponents claimed that practical applications of the Weberian paradigm obstructed rather than enhanced the generation of usable knowledge for the policy process. The focus on technical knowledge detracted from political knowledge.

The conception of political knowledge operative in the works of critics of the rational comprehensive model of decision-making might best be characterized as *applied pluralism*.[44] In contrast to efforts to introduce rational calculations into the decision-making process through cost-benefit analyses, applied pluralism advocates a brand of hard-headed political realism. On this view, if social science can contribute anything to contemporary politicians, it must be detailed knowledge of the actual processes of interest accommodation that dictate "who gets what, when, and how" in the existing polity.[45] Expert advice concerning the pragmatic aspects of "partisan mutual adjustment" could equip policy-makers with the necessary tools to accomplish their political objectives. Usable political knowledge then, should culminate in political successes.[46]

The applied pluralist model of the policy 'craft' suggests that policy analysts may acquire political knowledge from the systematic study of the political system. In contrast to the overly rationalistic models of the synoptic tradition, specialized training in practical politics reveals that political decision-making is remarkably similar to the processes of bargaining characteristic of market transactions. Thus marshaling the insights derived from applying the market model to political interactions, applied pluralist policy analysts can provide expert information essential to success in the processes of political bargaining and compromise. Moreover, they can help perfect the bargaining process by representing the interests of relevant 'stakeholders,' filling the void created by citizen apathy and ignorance.[47] Following the tradition of consumer advocacy, they can generate materials useful to politicians' endeavors to "improve citizen preferences for the policies they—the people—ought to prefer."[48] And as a last resort, in instances where "we can neither mobilize the masses for necessary political initiatives nor change their political attitudes, we must rely on increasing the capacities of elites not only to innovate in the realm of policy, but equally to contain and neutralize reactive responses to disturbing emergencies."[49] In short, the pragmatic political knowledge of the applied pluralist policy analyst can enable the politician to manage the political system successfully.

The art of political management may not be reducible to a system of scientific principles, nor encapsulated in simple methodological rules; nevertheless, those knowledgeable in the craft may make significant contributions to the resolution of the conflicts which confront contemporary democratic polities. Proponents of applied pluralism are careful to insist that their art affords no absolute guarantees of success. They operate in the medium of politics which is notoriously fickle, structured upon contingencies, and guided by unrelenting conflicts. Their credentials in a democratic system rest on their ability to facilitate the achievement of creative resolutions of intractable disputes. Like the 'Invisible Hand',[50] their genius lies in their capacity to produce unintended public benefits from the raw materials of competing private vices. The realities of contemporary political life constitute the stern taskmaster which serves as the ground of their experience, the source of their expertise, the stimulus for their creativity, and ultimately, the measure of their usefulness.

Pragmatic pluralist policy analysts accept the existing political system, replete with its unwritten rules, norms of operation, and casts of characters as given. Their task is to facilitate the system's operation and maintain its equilibrium. They recognize that the legitimacy of their role in democratic systems turns on the adequacy of the results they produce. Yet, even in the absence of scientific guarantees for their work, they remain confident that the application of their political knowledge will generate policy results far preferable to those which would emerge from the "hyper-rationalist" prescriptions of their opponents, who operate in accordance with the dictates of the rational comprehensive model of decision-making.

Technical Knowledge and Political Knowledge: The Common Ground

Although skepticism toward some of the more expansive claims of proponents of rational comprehensive decision-making sustains much of the pluralist attack, it is clearly a mitigated skepticism.[51] Pluralists are not Pyrrhonists committed to a belief that all knowledge is unattainable. On the contrary, they are committed to the empiricist principle "that there is a real world and that we can know it to an imperfect but useful degree through observation based upon multiplist procedures that have been critically selected after considering multiple perspectives of what the purposes of research should be, what prior research indicates is known and what the preferred methods of study might be."[52] Thus, those who advocate an applied pluralist approach to policy analysis, as well as those who advocate a Weberian approach to policy science, share a commitment to a range of empirical techniques for the study of political affairs. In addition to a common commitment to empiricism, both sides conceive knowledge in terms of the strictures established by the instrumental conception of rationality. Proponents of technical knowledge suggest that by harnessing the laws of social science, reason can illuminate the best means to politically-determined ends. Proponents of political knowledge suggest that a sophisticated understanding of the process of partisan mutual adjustment itself constitutes the esential means to achieve political objectives. In arguing that expert knowledge can make important contributions to the policy process, both sides of this debate accept the limitations imposed by the fact/value dichotomy. They accept that the scope of their potential contribution is restricted to the empirical sphere, for they believe that questions of value lie beyond the range of scientific investigation and rational deliberation.

The rancor of the pluralist attack upon scientific policy studies and the vitriol of the counter-attack by proponents of the rational comprehensive model of decision-making[53] tend to mask remarkable similarities in the opponents' vision of the role for the policy expert in a democratic polity. Both sides believe that the social scientist can make significant contributions to the formation of public policy. Whether conceived in terms of technical knowledge which brings logic and the laws of social science to bear on policy choices, or in terms of political knowledge which brings pragmatic lessons of political experience to bear on decision-makers' strategies, expert knowledge acquired through advanced (inter)disciplinary training is believed capable of providing valuable insights for democratic decision-makers. Thus, arguments pertaining to improving decision-making, stabilizing the system, heightening effectiveness, achieving objectives, facilitating outcomes, increasing efficiency, and optimizing management capabilities play a central role on both sides of the debate.

In addition, both proponents of applied social science and applied pluralist models of policy analysis operate largely within the parameters of the same conception of political 'realism:' both accept that the only feasible democracy is a form of democratic elitism and that usable knowledge must be structured in accordance with that realization. Moreover, both sides use models for analyzing political relations which depend heavily on economic assumptions in general and the market model in particular. The rational comprehensive model of decision-making and the method of cost-benefit analysis depend not only on quantitative techniques developed in economics, but also on a conception of human nature and a theory of individual motivation typically characterized as that of *homo economicus*.[54] The conception of the individual as a self-interested maximizer which provides a foundation for claims concerning market behavior has been incorporated uncritically into applied social science accounts of policy-making and methods of policy evaluation.[55] Pluralists share the same assumptions concerning human nature, deriving a model of political behavior from the inherent traits of *homo economicus*; and in addition, they argue that Adam Smith's conception of the competitive market guided by the 'Invisible Hand' constitutes the most appropriate model for comprehending politics in contemporary liberal democracies.[56]

G. David Garson has characterized the antagonism between applied social science and applied pluralist approaches to public policy analysis as an opposition between the synoptic and anti-synoptic traditions. In the synoptic tradition, systems analysis constitutes the meta-theory, statistical empiricism constitutes the methodology; and optimization of values constitutes the decision criterion. In the anti-synoptic tradition, pluralism constitutes the meta-theory, contextual/case analysis constitutes the methodology, and integration of interests constitutes the decision criterion.[57] This characterization helps to illuminate the extensive commonalities which underline the differences between these antagonists. At the level of meta-theory, the opposites converge: systems analysis and pluralism are virtually identical. Both are simple variations on the equilibrium model of the market.[58] Within this shared set of assumptions concerning the nature and operation of political life, the methodological disputes about usable knowledge acquire their meaning. A common understanding of democratic elitism and the imperatives of equilibrium maintenance in contemporary political systems constitute the foundation for the role of policy expert envisioned by both approaches. The image of the policy analyst providing expert knowledge in service to democracy operates within the parameters established by a political 'realism' tacitly or explicitly informed by analogies drawn from the competitive market. Whether conceived as 'science' or 'craft', whether characterized as 'technical' or 'political', the knowledge which the policy analyst deploys to facilitate democratic decision-making has a common origin in Adam Smith's economic and political theory. Policy analysis as science in service to democracy promotes forms of human freedom and social amelioration consistent with the market model of a democratic polity; applying instrumental reason to particular problems provides the means to promote those ends.

Depoliticizing Scientism

In contrast to the received view's benign self-description of policy analysis as science in service to democracy, a darker image of policy analysis has surfaced with some regularity over the past two decades. Taking issue with characterizations of policy analysis cast in terms of such self-accrediting notions as neutrality, objectivity, technical expertise, scientific management, and political knowledge, critics have suggested that the rhetoric of science deployed by policy analysts is a form of ideological mystification best understood as *scientism*.[59] In the words of physicist Gerald Holton, ". . . scientism may be described as an addiction to science. Among the signs of scientism are the habit of dividing all thought into two categories, up-to-date scientific knowledge and nonsense; the view that the mathematical sciences and the large nuclear laboratory offer the only permissible models for successfully employing the mind or organizing effort. . . One main source of this attitude is evidently the persuasive success of recent technical work . . . The danger—and this is the point where scientism enters—is that the fascination with the mechanism of this successful enterprise may change the scientist and society."[60]

Within the literature on policy analysis, the charge of scientism has taken several forms. Richard Weaver has pointed out that the very notion of policy 'science' is a rhetorical, not an analytical, expression, advanced to capitalize upon the prestige of the natural sciences. He has also suggested that extensive use of quantitative data in policy analysis can be understood in terms of a rhetorical strategy designed to disarm the reader: for the aura of realism exuded by quantitative measures undermines non-experts' critical responses ("they can't argue with the 'facts'"), while simultaneously validating highly implausible claims.[61] Laurence Tribe has identified multiple means by which policy analysis merges with a technical rhetoric in which "passion learns to pose as reason" by proclaiming its strategies for formulating questions, organizing information, and developing answers to be value-free, despite their commitments to substantive conclusions.[62] Similarly, Fred Kramer has suggested that policy prescriptions founded on partial (and often partisan) analyses, validated by quantitative techniques which generate an "appearance of value-free rationality at work," function as ideological masks, used to legitimate decisions based on political predilections.[63] Theodore Lowi has argued that academics' fascination with social engineering has produced a "technocratization of the intelligentsia" through which policy scientists have become slaves to the regimes they serve, losing all capacity to deal critically with political issues and problems.[64] John Ladd has suggested that policy science's emphasis upon cost-benefit calculations sacrifices citizen participation for the putative authority of scientific expertise, supports a restrictive conception of politics un-

derstood chiefly in terms of the production and distribution of consumer goods, and sustains a paternalistic political division of labor between the technical producers and the citizen consumers of public
policy.[65] And David Paris and James Reynolds have noted that policy
analysts aspire to science, but lacking adequate causal theories to sustain their endeavors, produce ideology. Thus, they become a "technical cadre of national governance" which helps to manage society by
manipulating the poor and discontented without solving any fundamental social problems.[66]

These critical discussions of policy science's excessive optimism concerning the possibilities of scientific knowledge and of its
failure to realize its ideal of value-neutrality have much in common
with the pluralist critique of the applied social science model of technical knowledge. They differ, however, in varying degrees of adherence to the belief that even in principle, scientific investigations cannot be neutral, that human knowledge always advances some human
interests, and hence, any claim of value-neutrality must necessarily
be an ideological obfuscation.[67] Where the applied pluralists' adopt
the restrained language of a craft and prescribe the pragmatic use of
political knowledge to facilitate system management as an alternative to the excessive promises of technical knowledge, the critics of
scientism reject this solution as simply one more manifestation of
the problem. On this view, applied pluralists continue to be implicated in scientism for they perpetuate the notion that they possess an
objective expertise, characterized as a form of instrumental knowledge, which can facilitate problem-solving in a liberal democracy.
Applied pluralism continues to embrace two principles central to scientistic ideology: *technocratism*, or the belief that policy objectives
are best promoted by the deployment of expert knowledge; and *de-
cisionism*, or the belief that all political, *qua* normative, decisions ultimately rest upon irrational choice.[68] Operating in accordance with
these precepts, the applied pluralist prescription changes the rhetoric
but not the role of the policy analyst in contemporary political systems.

The critique of policy analysis as a form of depoliticizing scientism begins with epistemological issues, with a challenge to the conflation of all knowledge with instrumental reason. Through an examination of alternative forms of knowledge, it attempts to demonstrate
that the "belief that what science cannot tell us, humanity cannot
know is itself the dominant ideology of our time,[69] an ideology premised upon an arbitrary stipulative definition of knowledge,[70] and an
ideology which must itself be understood as "a special form of

idealism, for it puts one form of human understanding in charge of the universe and what can be said about it."[71] It begins with the critique of epistemological issues in order to illuminate the manifold ways in which scientism impoverishes both the "intellectual landscape by inhibiting the serious expression of certain questions"[72] and social and political life by disseminating notions which reinforce privatization and undermine the possibility of public discourse.[73] It begins with the critique of scientism as an ideology in order to reveal that "it is the scientism of our age and the false idolatry of the expert that pose the threat to practical and political reason" and hence to democratic decision-making.[74]

In moving from the critique of ideology to the critique of politics, critics of scientism suggest that beliefs about the political world play an important role in the political process. Central to their attack on scientistic models of policy analysis is the rejection of the conception of the social scientist as a passive observer of contemporary events, as one who merely describes and explains what is already given in the political world. Critics of scientism conceive of social science as an active political force, a force engaged in an effort to create the world in its own image, even as it shrouds itself in passivity, neutrality, detachment, and objectivity to disguise and conceal its role (for its power depends on its success at disguise and concealment).[75] To sustain this image of policy science as a depoliticizing force, critics of scientism adduce the following evidence.

A number of studies have suggested that while the immediate and direct influence of policy research upon decision-making is rare, social science "does generate concepts, generalizations and ideas which come to permeate policy discussions."[76] The conceptualizations and terms of art developed in social science establish the parameters for contemporary consideration of political questions. The fact/value dichotomy in conjunction with an emotivist conception of values is perhaps social science's most powerful contribution to this process of knowledge-creep. As a version of noncognitivism, emotivism is a meta-ethical theory which is committed to the view that facts and values are ontologically distinct and to the view that evaluative judgments involve questions concerning subjective emotions, sentiments, or feelings rather than questions of knowledge or rational deliberation.[77] Applied to the political realm, emotivism suggests that moral and political choices are a matter of subjective preference or irrational whim about which there can be no reasoned debate.

Although emotivism has been discredited as an altogether defective account of morality and has been repudiated by philosophers for decades, emotivism continues to be advanced as unproblematic truth by social scientists.[78] And there is a good deal of evidence to suggest that "to a large degree, people now think, talk and act as if emotivism were true."[79] Promulgated in the texts of social science and incorporated in pop culture, emotivist assumptions permeate discussions of the self, of freedom, and of social relations. Contemporary conceptions of the self are deeply infused with emotivist and individualist premises: the "unsituated self" who chooses an identity in isolation and on the basis of arbitrary preferences has become an American cultural ideal.[80] The freedom, so highly prized in the American imagination, is conceived in terms of the unrestrained pursuit of idiosyncratic preferences in personal, economic, moral, and political realms.[81] Moral issues are understood in terms of maximizing one's preferred idiosyncratic values, and moral dilemmas are treated as strategic or technical problems related to zero-sum conditions under which the satisfaction of one preference may obstruct the satisfaction of another preference.[82] Respect for other individuals is equated with recognition of their rights to choose and to pursue their own preferences without interference. Condemnation of the immoral actions of others is supplanted by the non-judgmental response of "walking away, if you don't like what others are doing."[83] Emotivism coupled with individualism encourages people to find meaning exclusively in the private sphere, thereby intensifying the privatization of the self and heightening doubts that individuals have enough in common to sustain a discussion of their interests or anxieties.[84]

Any widespread acceptance of emotivism has important ramifications for political life. At its best, emotivism engenders a relativism which strives "to take views, outlooks and beliefs which apparently conflict and treat them in such a way that they do not conflict: each of them turns out to be acceptable in its own place."[85] The suspension of valuative judgment which accompanies privatization aims at conflict reduction by conflict avoidance.[86] By walking away from those whose subjective preferences are different, individuals avoid unpleasant confrontations. By accepting that values are ultimately arbitrary and hence altogether beyond rational justification, citizens devise a way of life which permits coexistence amidst diversity. Yet this coexistence is fragile and the promise of conflict avoidance largely illusory. For the underside of emotivism is cynicism, the "obliteration of any genuine distinction between manipulative and nonmanipulative social relations" and the consequent reduction of politics to a contest of wiles and wills untimately decided by force.[87] Thus, when intractable

conflicts arise because avoidance strategies fail, they cannot be resolved through reasoned discourse, for on this view, rational discussion is simply a facade which masks arbitrary manipulation. Thus the
options for political life are reduced by cynical definition either to the
intense competition of conflicting interests depicted in the pluralist
paradigm, or to the resort to violence.

The political legacy of emotivism, the corollary of scientism, is
radical privatization, the destruction of the public realm, "the disin-
tegration of public deliberation and discourse among members of the
political community."[88] For widespread acceptance of the central
tenets of emotivism renders public discussion undesirable (for it
might provoke violence), unnecessary (for the real outcomes of decisions will be dictated by force of will), and irrational (for nothing rational can be said in defense of arbitrary preferences). Privatization
produces a world in which individuals are free to act on whim and to
realize their arbitrary desires, but it is a world in which collective action is prohibited by a constellation of beliefs which render public deliberation impotent, if not impossible.[89] By convincing members of
the polity that deliberation on public values is unnecessary, undersir-
able, and irrational, scientism "banishes citizens from the public
realm into the privacy of their households and demands of them that
they mind their own business."[90]

Critics of scientism suggest that the progressive dissemination
of concepts drawn from the social sciences in general and the policy
sciences in particular render public discussion obsolete. Validation of
the role of the policy expert on the basis of either technical or political
knowledge depoliticizes: it contributes to the citizen's sense of ignorance and powerlessness and it erodes the citizen's desire to participate
in decision-making.[91] Under the rubric of realism, it reduces the role
of citizens to the periodic ritual acclamation of alternative administration teams.[92] Under the guise of increasing rationalization, it
"erects a social barrier between the knowledgeable and the untutored
segments of society"[93] which validates technocratic decision-making
while it simultaneously diminishes individual freedom by undermining belief in the capacity to deliberate and rationally define a course of
action and by serverely limiting the grounds for non-compliance with
technocratic edicts. Under the precept of scientific objectivity, it reduces reason to "the slave of the passions,"[94] constricting its operation to instrumental calculations designed to facilitate the achievement of desire. Under the principle of pragmatism, it restricts politics
to the play of interests and policy to the product of power alignments
which bring it about.[95] And in pursuit of efficient management, it

launches a concerted attack on dysfunctional and destabilizing forces such as citizen participation, which would prolong or preclude technocratic decision-making.[96]

Critics of scientism do not suggest that policy scientists intentionally promote privatization and depoliticization. On the contrary, they suggest that these are the unintentional consequences of the promulgation of sincere but mistaken beliefs about the nature of facts and values and the limits of human reason. Thus the solution advanced by the critics of scientism involves developing "theoretical self-consciousness"[97] on the part of policy analysts, cultivating greater understanding of the dimensions of human reason, recognizing the ideological implications of the instrumental conception of rationality and the emotivist conception of values, and stimulating critical reflection on the tacit normative presuppositions of specific policy prescriptions. Such a strategy acknowledges that "there is no way to expunge ideology from political analysis but we must take off the mask of objectivity that often covers the face of analytic work."[98] Elimination of the scientistic pretenses of policy analysis, then, might break the hold of pseudo-science on decision-making, restore the public to its legitimate participatory role in the policy-making process, and liberate options for problem-solving precluded by the rigid restrictions of technical rationality.[99]

In this form, the critique of scientism in policy analysis is somewhat optimistic. It suggests that models of policy analysis grounded in a conception of instrumental knowledge are fundamentally flawed, that diagnosis of the problem generates a feasible remedy, and that implementation of the remedy can produce a cure because the democratic polity has not yet reached a terminal stage of the disease. Whether depicted in terms of an 'enlightenment model,' a 'value critical approach,' or a 'post-positivist paradigm' for policy analysis, the image of the policy analyst sustained by these prescriptions is similar.[100] Imbued with theoretical self-consciousness, the analyst refuses the roles of social technician and Machiavellian political manager in order to challenge and subvert preexisting policy premises.[101] Committed to an educative rather than an engineering model for policy analysis, the analyst attempts to provide information which will illuminate alternative interpretations and multiple dimensions of political problems. The provision of alternative conceptual frameworks through which to view pending problems is designed to contribute to emancipatory objectives "by weakening myths, refuting distortions, and preventing an imbalanced view of social reality from dominating collective decisions."[102] By providing citizens with detailed information about their situation and the conditions which affect it in order to enable them to make more informed choices about future developments,[103] the policy analyst adopts a methodological posture designed to promote greater citizen participation while simultaneously dispelling the 'technocratic mystique.'[104] The image of the policy analyst in these prescriptions is not altogether new, for once again the policy expert is accorded the role of facilitating democracy. What changes in the postpositivist paradigm is the model of democracy endorsed: participatory democracy supplants democratic elitism as the model deemed worthy of the policy analyst's allegiance. Commitment to the creation of a participatory, egalitarian polity displaces the commitment to political realism characteristic of both the applied social science and applied pluralist approaches to policy analysis.

The familiarity of the role of the policy expert, revised to accommodate the enlightened policy analyst who uses knowledge to encourage emancipatory democratic politics, might evoke a cynical response. The cynical critic might point out that the move from critique of scientistic ideology to a prescription for critical reflection in service to participatory decision-making manages to preserve a central role for the trained policy expert in the decision-making process. The cynic might note ironically that the rhetoric of egalitarian democracy appears to coexist comfortably with the anticipation of significant contributions to decision-making from an intellectual elite. In order to dispel any doubt concerning this interpretation, the cynic might invoke the 'iron law of oligarchy' as proof that egalitarian commitments always deteriorate into elitist enterprises. Or the cynic might cite a number of historical precedents in which emancipatory rhetoric simply masked the will to power of the manipulative emancipators. Or the cynic might introduce a number of pragmatic considerations to discredit the very notion of an egalitiarian participatory democracy as hopelessly idealistic and naive. Regardless of the specific strategy of reinforcement, the cynical critic would very likely juxtapose an understanding of contemporary political reality against the optimistic or utopian vision of emancipatory democratic politics in order to demonstrate either the total impossibility of the latter or the dearth of any feasible means to attain such an end in the immediate or forseeable future.

By structuring the options in terms of an opposition between realism and idealism, or between pragmatism and naïveté, the cynical response uses the insights of social science to fight what it sees as futile, and potentially dangerous, utopian aspirations. Yet in so doing, the cynical response sustains a conservative political prescription: it endorses resignation to the status quo. The argument that the prevailing political system constitutes the only viable form of democracy is advanced as the only belief consonant with a scientific understanding of political life. For this reason, critics of scientism might retort that by disseminating this pragmatic message, the cynic not only commits the *naturalistic fallacy*, mistaking what currently exists for all that might exist, but also provides an example of the manner in which social science succumbs to depoliticizing scientism. In conflating what currently exists with the scope of the politically possible, the cynical response instantiates depoliticization, for it denies that people might choose to alter their political life.

In the context of an ongoing struggle over the intelligibility of the notion of participatory democracy, critics of scientism advance their conception of an emancipatory role for the policy analyst. Their vision is not intended as a prescription for the function of the analyst in an egalitarian polity, but rather as a posture for policy analysts in contemporary technocratic systems. In advocating an alternative to the roles of the social technician and the Machiavellian political manager, critics of scientism search for strategies to dispel the 'myth of the given,' and the cynical resignation which it breeds. They seek to stimulate an understanding of politics which encompasses the creation, perpetuation, and reconstitution of social relations through collective deliberation. They strive to prevent the occlusion of participatory politics by ascendent technocratism, by triggering a recognition that the reality at stake is one of our own making. Indeed, they hope to reveal the extent to which the policy sciences are complicitous in the processes of privatization and depoliticization that threaten to destroy the possibility of public discourse. Theirs is a subversive vision, but it is not the vision of a self-validating vanguard. Their goal is to illuminate depoliticizing scientism as an ideological (but not inevitable) force, not to eliminate participatory politics.

Issues

The contrasting images of policy analysis which surface in the policy literature and which have been summarized above raise a number of important issues. Chief among them is the difficult question concerning which image is correct. Which view adequately captures the essence of policy analysis and which is in error? Is policy analysis scientific or scientistic? Do extensive empirical policy investigations generate usable knowledge or ideological legitimations? Is the policy expert a handmaiden of democracy or an agent of depoliticization?

Questions concerning the nature of policy analysis are theoretical questions. They aspire to answers which reflect more than what has been said about policy analysis and more than what a majority believes about policy analysis; they seek answers which reveal the nature of the thing in itself. For this reason, attempts to settle the dispute by recourse to stipulative definition (e.g., 'We shall call policy analysis any research, quantitative or qualitative, bearing on policy questions, conducted by trained professionals employed by, or under contract to, existing governments.') are inadequate because they beg the question, assuming precisely what needs to be proven. Attempts to provide a resolution of the debate by surveying the views of policy analysts are similarly inadequate. For even assuming that some consensus concerning the nature of the endeavor might emerge from the survey responses,[105] to accept policy analysts' description of their activity as the truth would be to confuse what is believed to be the case with what is the case, a confusion which fails to acknowledge the influence of fallibility, misunderstanding, self-deception, and willful distortion upon human affairs.

Empirical analysis is crucial to the discovery of the nature of policy analysis and its role in contemporary political systems, for the claims advanced by proponents of both images involve assertions about existing affairs. But in order to adjudicate the empirical evidence introduced in support of the alternative views, a number of subsidiary issues must be resolved: What criteria of meaning will be employed? What standards of relevance will apply? What theory of knowledge will be invoked? What conception of truth will be operative? What model of explanation will be sufficient to resolve the dispute? The notion of the empirical is not unequivocal, and the decisions made with respect to each of these issues will have an enormous influence upon the resolution of the debate. Indeed, certain conceptions of empirical analysis will render this debate unresolvable.

A conception of empirical analysis which imposes a stringent demarcation between facts and values, repudiating evaluative judgments as arbitrary and irrational, will preclude any resolution of the dispute. Descriptions of a wide range of facts and explanations of intricate relationships must play an integral role in any attempt to adjudicate this issue, but descriptions and explanations alone will be insufficient. Central to the debate is not simply a question of what the facts are, but what these facts mean. The question is not simply, "what role does the analyst play," but, "what is its significance for democratic politics?" To answer theoretical questions about the nature of policy analysis, reason must be brought to bear upon issues pertaining to description, explanation, and evaluation. To resolve the dispute between science and scientism, rational judgment must operate effectively at the level of evaluation as well as at the levels of description and explanation.

If contemporary social science and policy science are correct in their depiction of the restricted scope of reason, no resolution to the debate between science and scientism is possible. If all evaluation is merely a matter of subjective preference, then there can be no objective answer to the questions raised by these conflicting images of policy analysis. Policy analysts might prefer to be seen as scientists rather than as ideologues, and may feel strongly that the charge of depoliticizing scientism is keenly unfair, but there is no objective reason to defer to their preferences or to respect their feelings. Indeed, if emotivism is true, the only conceivable resolution to this conflict will be political. The correct image of policy analysis will be decided through a contest of wits and wills in which the 'truth' will be proclaimed as the prerogative of the victor.

Although this conclusion follows from the central precepts of contemporary social science, many will find it decidedly unsatisfactory. That the nature of policy analysis should be determined by a political contest rather than by rational investigation does not fit well with an image of a profession, much less with an image of science. To avoid this unhappy conclusion, however, it is necessary to reconsider the adequacy of some of the central tenets of contemporary social science. It is this task which will be taken up in the next several chapters. Only after the conceptual issues which circumscribe this debate have been resolved will it be possible to assess the evidence concerning the alternative images of policy analysis.

Separate Spheres: On the Institutionalization of a Dichotomy

> In an age of science, we are
> all positivists to some extent.[1]

THE scientific status coveted by both the applied social science and applied pluralist models of policy analysis depends upon the existence of a particular form of expertise. Whether characterized as technical knowledge or as political knowledge, this expertise must be grounded in a systematic comprehension of social and political events which can issue in diagnoses of the causes of particular problems, and predictions of the consequences of alternative courses of action. For this expertise to be genuine, it must be founded upon a grasp of the necessary and sufficient conditions of political events. Does such expertise exist? By what methods could its existence be demonstrated?

Discussion of the issues related to the possibility of such genuine knowledge and the means by which it could be attained and demonstrated has been a major concern of the philosophy of science. Thus, it is not surprising that many dimensions of the debate between the applied social science model and the applied pluralist model of policy analysis reflect issues which have been the subject of extensive consideration in the philosophy of science.[2] Nor is it surprising that a good deal of the argument advanced in support of *post-behavioral* strategies for policy analysis is drawn from recent work in the *post-positivist* philosophy of science. Situating the problem of the scientific status of policy analysis in the more general context of problems of scientific knowledge, then, may help to shed light upon the central issues in the dispute concerning the nature of policy analysis, as well as upon the common assumptions which inform the antagonists' views. It may also illuminate the limitations of traditional social science assumptions about values, and in so doing, it may indicate an appropriate strategy for resolving the larger issues raised by the conflicting images of policy analysis as science or scientism.

This chapter will examine several assumptions of the applied social science and the applied pluralist models of policy analysis in the context of arguments derived from positivist and Popperian philosophy of science. It will then explore the critique of these positivist assumptions advanced by post-positivist theories of science. In the final sections of the chapter, the implications of post-positivist theories of science will be considered in relation to recent developments in post-behavioral policy analysis.

The Positivist Presuppositions of Policy Analysis

It has been suggested that the core literature of the discipline is committed to the principle that "scientific policy analysis is and ought to be value neutral, ethically detached and confined to predicting the consequences of alternative policy actions."[3] Indeed it has been argued that "to be judged proper, all research must—at least officially—pay its respects to the principle of value neutrality."[4] The strictures imposed by adopting value-neutrality as a regulative ideal are intended to free policy research from bias, distortion, and the willful manipulation of "prophets who preach not in the streets, or in churches or in public places or sectarian conventions, but who enunciate their evaluations on ultimate questions 'in the name of science,' under conditions in which they are neither controlled, checked by discussion, nor subject to refutation.[5] Thus, the fact/value dichotomy is introduced to demarcate science from non-science (whether conceived in terms of philosophy, ethics, politics, metaphysics, or religion) and thereby to keep each in its legitimate sphere. Its function is to differentiate that which can be known from that which cannot be known in order to preserve the purity of science, understood as valid knowledge, from contamination by error or deceit.

The fallibility of human knowers renders the effort to identify valid knowledge both important and extremely difficult. The history of the philosophy of science can be read as a continuing struggle to isolate procedures by which knowledge claims could be warranted as valid, to isolate from a wide range of possibilities those scientific techniques capable of certifying beliefs as justified. The particular strategies for knowledge acquisition and validation incorporated in the applied social science model of policy analysis reflect arguments developed in the early twentieth century by positivist philosophers of science.[6] Because these positivist strategies are typically presented only in fragmentary form in the policy literature, a brief consideration of the central tenets of positivism will help clarify the precise problems which these strategies are designed to solve, and clarify the implications of such positivist precepts for policy science.

Committed to the search for a method which would determine the truth once and for all, positivist philosophers of science restricted the sphere of their investigations to the empirically observable. Arguing that only those knowledge claims founded directly upon observable experience could be genuine, positivists advanced the *verification criterion of meaning*, which stipulated that a contingent proposition is meaningful if, and only if, it could be empirically verified. Thus the verification criterion was used to differentiate not only between science and non-science, but between science and 'nonsense.' On the positivist view, any statement which could not be verified by reference to experience constituted nonsense: it was literally meaningless.

The implications of the verificationist criterion for a model of science were manifold. All knowledge was believed to depend on observation, thus any claims, whether theological, metaphysical, philosophical, ethical, normative, or aesthetic, which were not rooted in empirical observation, were rejected as meaningless. The sphere of science was thereby narrowly circumscribed and scientific knowledge was accredited as the only valid knowledge. In addition, induction, a method of knowledge acquisition grounded upon observation of particulars as the foundation for empirical generalizations, was taken to provide the essential logic of science. The task of science was understood to consist in the inductive discovery of regularities which existed in the external world. Scientific research sought to organize in economical fashion those regularities which experience presented in order to facilitate explanation and prediction. To promote this objective, positivists endorsed and employed a technical vocabulary comprising *facts* (empirically verifiable propositions), *hypotheses* (empirically verifiable propositions asserting the existence of relationships among observed phenomena), *laws* (empirically confirmed propositions asserting an invariable sequence or association among observed phenomena) and *theories* (interrelated systems of laws possessing explanatory power). Moreover, the logic of scientific inquiry was believed to be integrally related to a sequence of activities characterized as *the scientific method*.

According to the positivist model, the scientific method began with the carefully controlled, neutral observation of empirical events. Sustained observation over time would enable the regularities or patterns of relationships in observed events to be revealed, and thereby would provide for the formulation of hypotheses. Once formulated, hypotheses were to be subjected to systematic empirical tests. Those hypotheses which received external confirmation through this process of rigorous testing could be elevated to the status of scientific laws. Once identified, scientific laws provided the foundation for scientific explanation, which according to the precepts of the *Covering Law* model, consisted in demonstrating that the events to be explained could have been expected, given certain initial conditions (C_1, C_2, C_3, . . .) and the general laws of the field (L_1, L_2, L_3 . . .). Within the framework of the positivist conception of science, the discovery of scientific laws also provided the foundation for prediction which consisted in demonstrating that an event would occur given the future occurrence of certain initial conditions and the operation of the general laws of the field. Under the covering law model, then, explanation and prediction have the same logical form, only the time factor differs: explanation pertains to past events; prediction pertains to future events.

Positivists were also committed to the principle of the *unity of science*, i.e., to the belief that the logic of scientific inquiry was the same for all fields. Whether natural phenomena or social phenomena were the objects of study, the method for acquiring valid knowledge and the requirements for explanation and prediction remained the same.[7] Once a science had progressed sufficiently to accumulate a body of scientific laws organized in a coherent system of theories, it could be said to have achieved a state of maturity that made explanation and prediction possible. Although the logic of mature science remained inductive with respect to the generation of new knowledge, the logic of scientific explanation was deductive. Under the covering law model, causal explanation, or the demonstration of the necessary and sufficient conditions of an event, involved the deductive subsumption of particular observations under a general law. In addition, deduction also played a central role in efforts to explain laws and theories: the explanation of a law involved its deductive subsumption under a theory; and explanation of one theory involved its deductive subsumption under wider theories.

The legacy of positivism is apparent in the policy literature in many of the arguments and assumptions of the applied social science model of policy analysis. It is manifest in definitions of the field which emphasize "data collection, hypothesis formulation and testing, and other formal aspects of systematic empirical enterprise,"[8] as well as in approaches which stress scientific method, statistical models, and quantitative research designs.[9] It surfaces in conceptions of explanation defined in deductive terms and in commitments to the equivalence of explanation and prediction.[10] It emerges in claims that the policy sciences must be molded upon the methods of the natural sciences, for those alone are capable of generating valid knowledge. It is unmistakable in the assumption that facts are unproblematic, that they are immediately observable, or given, and hence, their apprehension requires no interpretation. It is embodied in the presumption that confirmation or verification provides a criterion of proof of the validity of empirical claims. And it is conspicuous in the repudiation of values as arbitrary preferences, irrational commitments, or meaningless propositions which lie altogether beyond the realm of rational analysis.

The Popperian Emendation

The primary postulates of positivism which provide the foundation for the applied social science model of policy analysis have been subjected to rigorous and devastating critiques. In a series of important works, Karl Popper launched a systematic attack upon the positivist conceptions of observation, induction, and verification, i.e., upon the central assumptions pertaining to the logic of scientific investigation.[11] He also argued that the positivist conception of science rested on a faulty psychology of perception, erroneous assumptions concerning the historical practice of science, and a logically flawed notion of scientific theory. In the wake of his critique of positivism, Popper developed a revised conception of science—one which is echoed in many of the pluralist criticisms of the applied social science model of policy analysis.

Popper advanced an extremely powerful internal critique of positivism designed to show that neither the logic of induction nor the verification criterion of meaning could accomplish positivist objectives, neither could guarantee the acquisition of truth. Drawing on Hume's analysis of the problem of induction, Popper demonstrated that an inductive method was incapable of guaranteeing the validity of scientific knowledge. The problem of induction emphasized that because empirical events are contingent, i.e., because the future could always be different from the past, generalizations based on limited observations are necessarily incomplete and, as such, highly fallible. Thus inductive generalizations could not be presumed to be true. Nor could *confirmation* or *verification* of such generalizations by reference to additional cases provide proof of their universal validity. For the notion of universal validity invokes all future, as well as all past and present occurrences of a phenomenon; yet no matter how many confirming instances of a phenomenon could be found in the past or in the present, these could never alter the logical possibility that the future could be different, that the future could disprove an inductively derived empirical generalization. For this reason, a demonstration of the truth of an empirical generalization must turn upon the identification of a necessary connection establishing a causal relation among observed phenomena.

Unfortunately, the notion of necessary connection also encounters serious problems. If the notion of necessity invoked is logical necessity, then the empirical nature of science is jeopardized. If, on the other hand, positivism appeals to an empirical demonstration of necessity, it runs afoul of the standard established by the verification criterion of meaning, for the necessity required as proof of any causal claim cannot be empirically observed. As Hume pointed out, empirical observation reveals *constant conjunction* (a 'correlation' in the language of contemporary social science); it does not and cannot reveal necessary connection.[12] As a positivist logic of scientific inquiry, then, induction encounters two serious problems: it is incapable of providing validation for the truth of its generalizations, and it is internally inconsistent, for any attempt to demonstrate the validity of a causal claim invokes a conception of necessary connection which violates the verification criterion of meaning.

Popper also argued that the positivist conception of the scientific method rested on a flawed psychology of perception. The positivist conception of the scientific method begins with neutral observation. Tracing the intellectual lineage of this notion to a conception of *manifest truth*, which attempts to reduce the problem of the validity of knowledge to an appeal to the authority of the source of the knowledge (e.g., "the facts speak for themselves"), Popper suggested that the belief that the unmediated apprehension of the given by a passive or receptive observer is possible, misconstrues both the nature of perception and the nature of the world. On Popper's view, the human mind is not passive but active; it does not merely receive an image of the given, but rather imposes order upon the external world through a process of selection, interpretation, and imagination. Observation involves the creative imposition of expectations, anticipations, and conjectures upon external events. Neutral observation, or *immaculate perception*, is impossible; but even if it were possible, deciphering the truth about nature is not a matter of concentrated perception. The truth is neither manifest nor easily available for all who choose to look. Grasping the truth about the world is far more like deciphering a dense mystery than reading a primer.

According to Popper, greater attention to the historical practice of science and the logic of scientific discovery could illuminate the impossibility of positivism's image of the scientic method. Popper argued that scientific observation is always theory-laden. It begins not from nothing, nor from the neutral perception of given relations, but rather from immersion in a scientific tradition which provides frames of reference or conceptual schemes which organize reality and shape the problems for further investigation. In short, scientific observation commences with and proceeds from theory. But, contrary to the positivist notion that theory is the result of observation, the result of the systematization of a series of inductive generalizations, the result of the cumulation of an interrelated set of scientific laws, Popper argued that theory is logically prior to the observation of any similarities or regularities in the world, indeed, that theory is precisely that which makes the identification of regularities possible. Moreover, scientific theories involve risk to an extent that is altogether incompatible with the positivist view of theories as summaries of empirical generalizations. Scientific theories involve risky predictions of things which have never been seen and hence, which cannot be deduced logically from observation statements. Thus Popper suggested not only that theories structure scientific observation in a manner altogether incompatible with the positivist requirement of neutral perception, but also that theories involve unobservable propositions which violate the verification criterion of meaning: abstract theoretical entities cannot be verified by reference to empirical observation.

Popper's attack on positivism also challenged the verification criterion of meaning on a number of grounds. As a mechanism for the validation of empirical generalizations, the verification criterion failed because of the problem of induction. As a scientific principle for the demarcation of the 'meaningful' from the 'meaningless,' the verification criterion was self-referentially destructive. By repudiating all that was not empirically verifiable as nonsense, the verification criterion repudiated itself, for it was not a statement derived from empirical observation, nor was it a tautology. Rigid adherence to the verification criterion then would mandate that it be rejected as metaphysical nonsense. By means of this internal critique, Popper illustrated that the positivist conflation of that which is not amenable to empirical observation with nonsense would not withstand scrutiny. Much (including the verification criterion itself) that cannot be empirically verified can be understood and all that can be understood is meaningful.

Popper's emendation of positivism, which he called *critical rationalism*, included a reformulated theory of perception, a revised criterion of demarcation between science and non-science, and alternative conceptions of science, scientific theory, and the scientific method. Drawing heavily on Hume's psychology of perception, Popper suggested that the human propensity to see patterns or regularities in the world is related to an inborn expectation of regularity which impels people to impose order on external events. Because of this unyielding propensity to anticipate repetition in events, to search for similarities in markedly different contexts, people confront the world with conjectures, with bold hypotheses which they attempt to impose upon external events. Scientific theories have a common origin in this psychological propensity to impose order on nature. But where this propensity can lead the ordinary observer to dogmatism, expecting regularities where none exist and clinging to the comforting familiarity of these expectations, however inappropriate they may be, the scientist trades on the fallibility of conjectures as a technique for the acquisition of knowledge.

Scientific theories, on Popper's view, are bold conjectures which the scientist imposes on the world. Drawing insights from manifold sources in order to solve particular problems, scientific theories involve abstract and unobservable propositions which predict what may happen as well as what may not happen. Thus scientific theories generate predictions which are incompatible with certain possible results of observation; in other words, they 'prohibit' certain occurrences by proclaiming that some things could not happen. As such, scientific theories put the world to the test and demand a reply. Precisely because scientific theories identify a range of conditions which must hold, a series of events which must occur, and a set of occurrences which are in principle impossible, they can clash with observation; they are empirically testable. While no number of confirming instances could ever prove a theory to be true due to the problem of induction, one disconfirming instance is sufficient to disprove a theory. If scientific laws are construed as statements of prohibitions, forbidding the occurrence of certain empirical events, then they can be definitively refuted by the occurrence of one such event.

Thus *falsification* provides a mechanism by which scientists can test their conjectures against reality and learn from their mistakes; it provides a means for preserving a commitment to the correspondence theory of truth,[13] despite the difficulties raised by the problem of induction. According to Popper, an unrelenting quest for falsification is characteristic of the scientific endeavor. In contrast to ordinary observers who often preserve erroneous beliefs for the comfort they provide, scientists are distinguished by their critical attitude which commits them to a method of "trial and error," a method of "conjecture and refutation" which enables science to progress. For it is by identifying error, by recognizing what is false and why it is false, that knowledge advances. Scientific progress, then, consists in the systematic elimination of error made possible by the unrelenting efforts to falsify scientific theories.

Popper's conception of a scientific theory as a conjecture devised to provide solutions to particular problems preserves the rational character of theory even as it recognizes that good theory is not and cannot be wholly empirical. It sustains an image of science as a rational, problem-solving endeavor which proceeds incrementally by testing and falsifying old theories and replacing them with new and better theories which are in turn subjected to new and better tests. Indeed, on Popper's view, the critical, non-dogmatic, experimental nature of science makes it a paradigm for all human rationality. As the only activity in which error is systematically criticized and corrected, science affords an unparalleled model for the progressive acquisition of knowledge, for it transforms human fallibility from an inescapable human vice into a mechanism for untold human benefits.

Arguing that the history of science is a history of irresponsible dreams, errors, and obstinacies, Popper suggested that the virtue of science lies in its ability to transform these ignominious beginnings into progressive solutions to a vast array of problems. The key to this transformation is the scientific method. According to Popper's *hypothetico-deductive model*, the scientist always begins with a problem. To resolve the problem, the scientist generates a theory, a conjecture, or a hypothesis, which can be tested by deducing its empirical consequences and measuring them against the world. Once the logical implications of a theory have been deduced and converted into predictions concerning empirical events, the task of science is falsification. In putting theories to the test of experience, scientists seek to falsify predictions, for that alone enables them to learn from their mistakes. The rationality of science is embodied in the method of trial and error, a method that allows error to be purged by eliminating false theories.

Falsifiability plays a crucial role in Popper's account of science. Replacing the defective verification principle, it provides a criterion for the demarcation of science from non-science. Science pertains to the realm of the testable, the realm of the falsifiable, to that which is susceptible to refutation by experience. Non-science encompasses myth, metaphysics, ideology, dogma, pseudo-science, all that is irrefutable, untestable. In advancing falsifiability as a criterion of demarcation, Popper insisted that it distinguishes between what can and what cannot be refuted by experience. It does not constitute a distinction between meaningful and meaningless propositions or between true and false propositions. Popper noted that irrefutability does not imply truth, nor does unfalsifiability constitute falsity. Identifying a proposition as irrefutable simply recognizes that there is no conceivble human experience which could contradict it. Since unfalsifiable propositions cannot be submitted to the arbitration of experience, they fall outside of science, which consists precisely in putting propositions to the test of experience.

In mandating that all scientific theories be tested, in stipulating that the goal of science is to falsify erroneous views, the criterion of falsifiability provides a means by which to reconcile the fallibility of human knowers with a conception of objective knowledge. The validity of scientific claims does not turn on a demand for an impossible neutrality on the part of individual scientists, on the equally impossible requirement that all prejudice, bias, prejudgment, expectation, or value be purged from the process of observation, or on the implausible assumption that the truth is manifest. The adequacy of a scientific theory is judged in concrete problem contexts in terms of its ability to solve problems and its ability to withstand increasingly difficult empirical tests. Those theories which withstand multiple intersubjective efforts to falsify them are 'corroborated,' identified as 'laws' that, with varying degrees of verisimilitude, capture the structure of reality, and for that reason are tentatively accepted as 'true.' But in keeping with the critical attitude of science, even the strongest corroboration for a theory is not accepted as conclusive proof. For Popperian critical rationalism posits that truth lies beyond human reach. As a regulative ideal which guides scientific activity, truth may be approximated, but it can never be established by human authority. Nevertheless, error can be objectively identified. Thus informed by a conception of truth as a regulative ideal and operating in accordance with the requirements of the criterion of falsifiability, science can progress by the incremental correction of errors and the gradual accretion of objective problem-solving knowledge.

Although Popper noted that the role of intentionality in human action created problems for the social sciences quite different from those confronted by the natural sciences, he suggested that the hypothetico-deductive model could serve social science in several ways. Depicting the main task of social science to be the analysis of the unintentional social repercussions of intentional human action, Popper carved out a sphere particularly suited to the capacities of the hypothetico-deductive model. For on this view, the principle task of social science was not to discover human intentions, to identify what people aspired to achieve through their actions; rather, it involved analyzing the forseeable consequences of their actions regardless of particular intentions. The task for social science involved predicting events which would occur at a system-wide level as the result of thousands of uncoordinated decisions and discrete actions by individuals.[14] Since the question of individual intentions is not at issue in such investigations, social scientists could proceed in accordance with the precepts of the hypothetico-deductive model, inventing theories, deducing the consequences of such theories, and measuring their predictions against actual social outcomes. Like their colleagues in the natural sciences, social scientists could strive to falsify their theories, invest their energy in developing new and tougher empirical tests for their views, and preserve a commitment to a critical, undogmatic scientific attitude. Moreover, those theories which consistently withstood intersubjective efforts at falsification, could be taken as corroborated, could be understood as 'sociological laws' which, with varying degrees of verisimilitude, approximated the invariant structures of social reality.

Popper also suggested that the hypothetico-deductive model could provide an analogy for dealing with the problem of irrefutable values, ideologies, and philosophical claims. Granting that the questions raised by non-science could not be definitively proven or disproven by rational analysis, Popper nevertheless argued that they were not immune to rational discussion. Reason could be brought to bear on such questions by treating their central claims as hypotheses, or assumptions subject to criticism. Treating value systems as alternative hypotheses on analogy with the hypothetico-deductive model in science would facilitate the deduction of the logical implications of the adoption of competing values. These implications could then be compared in order to discern the value system which produced the least harm. Within such a comparison, the notion of the 'Good' could serve as a regulative ideal in the same way that 'Truth' constitutes the regulative ideal in scientific investigations. By means of such hypothetico-deductive assessments in the realm of values, those principles likely to produce more harm could be rejected, just as error is eliminated in science. Bringing reason to bear upon value questions through such systematic comparative assessments could provide a means to avoid major human tragedies. Minimizing potential harm could constitute a criterion for choice in normative evaluations analagous to the criterion of falsifiability in scientific investigations. Through such a "conscious attempt to make our theories, our conjectures, suffer in our stead," humans could be spared the evils of actual implementation of policies derived from destructive value systems.[15]

Although Popper subjected many of the central tenets of logical positivism to systematic critique, his conception of critical rationalism shares sufficient ground with positivist approaches to the philosophy of science that it is typically considered to be a qualified modification of, rather than a comprehensive alternative to, positivism.[16] Indeed, Popper's conception of the hypothetico-deductive model has been depicted as the orthodox positivist conception of scientific theory.[17] Both positivist and Popperian approaches to science share a belief in the centrality of logical deduction to scientific analysis; both conceive scientific theories to be deductively related systems of propositions; both accept a deductive account of scientific explanation; both treat explanation and prediction as equivalent concepts; and both are committed to a conception of scientific progress dependent upon the use of the hypothetico-deductive method of testing scientific claims.[18] In addition, both positivist and Popperian conceptions of science are committed to the correspondence theory of truth and its corollary assumption that the objectivity of science ultimately rests upon an appeal to the facts. Both are committed to the institutionalization of the fact/value dichotomy in order to establish the determinate ground of science. Both accept that once safely ensconced within the bounds of the empirical realm, science is grounded upon a sufficiently firm foundation to provide for the accumulation of knowledge, the progressive elimination of error, and the gradual accretion of useful solutions to technical problems.

And although Popper suggested that reason could be brought to bear upon evaluative questions, he accepted the fundamental positivist principle that, ultimately, value choices rested upon non-rational factors.

Given Popper's insistence upon the centrality of problem-solving and incrementalism in scientific activity and upon pluralism as the essential ingredient for an open, undogmatic society, it is not surprising to find his work frequently invoked by those committed to an applied pluralist approach to policy analysis. Popperian assumptions appear in the applied pluralists' conception of policy analysis as a problem-solving activity.[19] They surface in the recognition that observation and analysis are necessarily theory-laden, as well as in their commitment to intersubjective testing as the appropriate means by which to deflect the influence of individual bias from substantive policy studies.[20] They are manifest in the substitution of testability for verifiability as the appropriate criterion for the demarcation of scientific hypotheses, and in the invocation of falsification and the elimination of error as the strategy for accumulating political knowledge.[21] They are reflected in commitments to a correspondence theory of truth and to the pragmatic notion that the existing political system constitutes the appropriate reality against which to test policy prescriptions.[22] They are obvious in the critique of excessive optimism concerning the possibility of securing truth by deploying inductive, quantitative techniques, in the less pretentious quest for useful knowledge, and in the insistence that truth constitutes a regulative ideal rather than a current possession of policy science. They are conspicuous in arguments that the hypothetico-deductive model is applicable to the policy sciences and in appeals for the development of a critical, undogmatic attitude among policy analysts.[23] Moreover, Popperian assumptions are apparent in a variety of strategies devised to bring reason to bear on normative issues (e.g., modeling normative discourse after scientific methods of analysis, incorporating debate about alternative value-laden prescriptions into the process of policy analysis, assessing the empirical implications of value prescriptions), while simultaneously accepting that there can be no ultimate rational justification of value precepts.[24] And Popperian presuppositions about the fundamental task of social science are manifest in the applied pluralists' commitment to a conception of politics premised on a model of the market which focuses research on the unintended consequences of the actions of multiple actors, rather than on the particular intentions of political agents.[25]

The Post-Positivist Critique

The most serious challenge to positivism has been raised not by Popper, but by what can perhaps best be characterized as *post-positivist presupposition theories of science.*[26] The challenge raised by presupposition theories is radical precisely because it casts doubt upon the validity of the fact/value dichotomy upon which positivist science depends; it raises suspicions about the presumed giveness of events, which is the cornerstone of empirical analysis; it reconsiders the plausibility of the correspondence theory of truth; it impugns the conflation of explanation and prediction; it questions the adequacy of formal logic as the paradigm of scientific rationality; and it disputes positivist accounts of the nature of scientific practices and of the logic of scientific investigations.

Presupposition theories of science concur with Popper's depiction of observation as *theory-laden.* They agree that "there is more to seeing than meets the eye,"[27] that perception involves more than the passive reception of allegedly manifest sense-data. They suggest that perception depends on a constellation of theoretical presuppositions that structure observation, accrediting particular stimuli as significant and specific configurations as meaningful. According to presupposition theories, observation is not only theory-laden, but théory is essential to, indeed, constitutive of, all human knowledge.[28]

As a form of human knowledge, science depends on theory in multiple and complex ways. Presupposition theories of science suggest that the notions of perception, meaning, relevance, explanation, knowledge, and method, central of the practice of science, are all theoretically constituted concepts. Theoretical presuppositions shape perception and determine what will be taken as a fact; they confer meaning on experience and control the demarcation of significant from trivial events; they afford criteria of relevance according to which facts can be organized, tests envisioned, and the acceptability of scientific conclusions assessed; they accredit particular models of explanation and strategies of understanding; and they sustain specific methodological techniques for gathering, classifying, and analyzing data. Theoretical presuppositions set the terms of scientific debate and organize the elements of scientific activity. Moreover, they typically do so at a tacit or preconscious level, and it is for this reason that they appear to hold such unquestionable authority.

On this view, the pervasive role of theoretical assumptions upon the practice of science has profound implications for the correspondence theory of truth and for the notion of empirical "reality" upon which it depends. The correspondence theory of truth is premised upon a belief in the autonomy of facts, a belief which rests upon the assumption that facts are given, that experience is ontologically distinct from the theoretical constructs which are advanced to explain it. The conception of a fact as a theoretically constituted entity calls into question this basic assumption. It suggests that "the noun, 'experience', the verb, 'to experience' and the adjective, 'empirical' are not univocal terms that can be transferred from one system to another without change of meaning. . . . Experience does not come labeled as 'empirical', nor does it come self-certified as such. What we call experience depends upon assumptions hidden beyond scrutiny which define it and which in turn it supports."[29] Recognition that 'facts' can be so designated only in terms of prior theoretical presuppositions implies that any quest for an unmediated reality is necessarily futile. Any attempt to identify an unmediated fact must either mistake the conventional for the natural, as in cases which define brute facts as "social facts which are largely the product of well-understood, reliable tools, facts that are not likely to be vitiated by pitfalls . . . in part [because of] the ease and certainty with which [they] can be determined and in part [because of] the incontestability of [their] conceptual base."[30] Or the attempt to conceive a fact which exists prior to any description of it, prior to any theoretical or conceptual mediation, must generate an empty notion of something completely unspecified and unspecifiable, a notion which will be of little use to science.[31]

Recognizing the manifold ways in which perceptions of reality are theoretically mediated raises a serious challenge not only to notions of 'brute data' and the 'giveness' of experience, but also to the possibility of falsification as a strategy for testing theories against an independent reality. If falsification is to provide an adequate test of a scientific theory, there must be a clear distinction between theoretical postulates and independent correspondence rules which link theoretical principles to particular observations. Embodying the idea of theory-independent evidence, neutral correspondence rules are essential to the very possibility of refutation, to the possibility that the world could prove a theory to be wrong. If however, there is no tenable distinction between theoretical assumptions and correspondence rules, if what is taken to be the 'world,' what is understood as 'brute data' is itself theoretically constituted (indeed, constituted by the same theory which is undergoing the test), then no conclusive disproof of a theory is likely. For the independent evidence upon which falsification depends does not exist, the available evidence is pre-constituted by the same theoretical presuppositions as the scientific theory under scrutiny.[32]

Contrary to Popper's conviction that empirical reality could provide an ultimate court of appeal for the judgment of scientific theories and that the critical, undogmatic attitude of scientists would ensure that their theories were constantly being put to the test, presupposition theorists emphasize that it is always possible to save a theory from refutation. The existence of one disconfirming instance is not sufficient to falsify a theory because it is always possible to evade falsification on the grounds that future research will demonstrate that a counter-instance is really only an apparent counter-instance.[33] Moreover, the theory-laden character of observation and the theory constituted character of evidence provide ample grounds on which to dispute the validity of the evidence and to challenge the design or the findings of specific experiments which claim to falsify respected theories. Further, post-positivist examinations of the history of scientific practice suggest that, contrary to Popper's claim that scientists are quick to discard discredited theories, there is a great deal of evidence that neither the existence of counter-instances nor the persistence of anomalies necessarily lead to the abandonment of scientific theories. Indeed, the overwhelming evidence of scientific practice suggests that scientists cling to long-established views tenaciously, in spite of the existence of telling criticisms, persistent anomalies, and unresolved problems. Thus it has been suggested that the theory that scientists themselves are always skeptical, undogmatic, critical of received views, and quick to repudiate questionable notions has itself been falsified and should be abandoned.[34]

The problem of falsification is exacerbated by the conflation of explanation and prediction in positivist accounts of science. For the belief that a corroborated prediction constitutes proof of the validity of a scientific explanation fails to recognize that an erroneous theory can generate correct predictions.[35] The logical distinction between prediction and explanation thus provides further support for the view that no theory can ever be conclusively falsified. The problem of induction also raises doubts about the possibility of definitive refutations. In calling attention to the possibility that the future could be different from the past and present in unforeseeable ways, the problem of induction arouses the suspicion that a theory falsified today might not *stay* falsified. The assumption of regularity which sustains Popper's belief that a falsified theory will remain falsified permanently is itself as inductionist presupposition which suggests that the falsifiability principle does not constitute the escape from induction which

Popper had hoped.[36] Thus despite the logical asymmetry between verification and falsification, no falsification can be any stronger or more final than any corroboration.[37]

Presupposition theorists acknowledge that "ideally, scientists would like to examine the structure of the world which exists independent of our knowledge—but the nature of perception and the role of presuppositions preclude direct access to it: the only access available is through theory-directed research."[38] Recognition that theoretical presuppositions organize and structure research by determining the meanings of observed events, identifying relevant data and significant problems for investigation and indicating both strategies for solving problems and methods by which to test the validity of proposed solutions, requires the abandonment of the correspondence theory of truth as incompatible with ineliminable conditions of human cognition. It requires the realization that science is no more capable of achieving the Archimedean point or of escaping human fallibility than is any other human endeavor. Indeed, it demands acknowledgement of science as a human convention rooted in the practical judgments of a community of fallible scientists struggling to resolve theory-generated problems under specific historical conditions. It sustains an image of science which is far less heroic and far more human.

As an alternative to the correspondence theory of truth, presupposition theorists suggest a coherence theory of truth premised on the recognition that all human knowledge depends on theoretical presuppositions whose congruence with nature cannot be established conclusively by reason or experience. Theoretical presuppositions, rooted in living traditions, provide the conceptual frameworks through which the world is viewed; they exude a 'natural attitude' which demarcates what is taken as normal, natural, real, reasonable, or sane, from what is understood as deviant, unnatural, utopian, impossible, irrational, or insane. In contrast to Popper's conception of theories as conscious conjectures which can be systematically elaborated and deductively elucidated, the notion of theoretical presuppositions suggests that theories operate at the tacit level. They structure 'preunderstandings' and 'prejudgments' in such a way that it is difficult to isolate and illuminate the full range of presuppositions which affect cognition at any given time.[39] Moreover, any attempt to elucidate presuppositions must operate within a hermeneutic circle. Any attempt to examine or to challenge certain assumptions or expectations must occur within the frame of reference established by other presuppositions. Certain presuppositions must remain fixed if others are to be subjected to systematic critique. This does not imply that individuals are prisoners trapped within in the framework of theories, expectations, past experiences, and language in such a way that critical reflection becomes impossible.[40] Critical reflection upon and abandonment of certain theoretical presuppositions is possible within the hermeneutic cricle; but the goal of transparency, of the unmediated grasp of things as they are, is not. For no reflective investigation, no matter how critical, can escape the fundamental conditions of human cognition.

A coherence theory of truth accepts that the world is richer than theories devised to grasp it; it accepts that theories are underdetermined by facts and consequently, that there can always be alternative and competing theoretical explanations of particular events. It does not however, imply the relativist conclusion that all theoretical interpretations are equal. That there can be no appeal to neutral, theory-independent facts to adjudicate between competing theoretical interpretations does not mean that there is no rational way to make and warrant critical evaluative judgments concerning alternative views. Indeed, presupposition theorists have shown that the belief that the absence of independent evidence necessarily entails relativism depends itself on a positivist commitment to the verification criterion of meaning. Only if one starts from the assumption that the sole test for the validity of a proposition lies in its measurement against the empirically 'given,' does it follow that in the absence of the 'given,' no rational judgments can be made concerning the validity of particular claims.[41]

Once the 'myth of the given'[42] has been abandoned and once the belief that the absence of one invariant empirical test for the truth of a theory implies the absence of all criteria for evaluative judgment has been repudiated, then it is possible to recognize that there are rational grounds for assessing the merits of alternative theoretical interpretations. To comprehend the nature of such assessments it is necessary to acknowledge that although theoretical presuppositions structure the perception of events, they do not create perceptions out of nothing. Theoretical interpretations are *world-guided*.[43] They involve both the preunderstanding brought to an event by an individual perceiver, and the stimuli in the external (or internal) world which instigate the process of cognition. Because of this dual source of theoretical interpretations, objects can be characterized in many different ways, "but it does not follow that a given object can be seen in any way at all or that all descriptions are equal."[44] The stimuli which trigger interpretation limit the class of plausible characterizations without dictating one absolute description.

Assessment of alternative theoretical interpretations involves *deliberation*, a rational activity which requires that imagination and judgment be used to consider the range of evidence and arguments which can be advanced to support various positions. The reasons offered in support of alternative views marshall evidence, organize data, apply various criteria of explanation, address multiple levels of analysis with varying degrees of abstraction, and employ divergent strategies of argumentation. This range of reasons offers a rich field for deliberation and assessment. It provides an opportunity to exercise judgment and it ensures that when scientists reject a theory, they do so because they believe they can demonstrate that the reasons offered in support of that theory are deficient. That the reasons advanced to sustain the rejection of one theory do not constitute absolute proof of the validity of an alternative theory is simply a testament to human fallibility. Admission that the cumulative weight of current evidence and compelling argument cannot protect scientific judgments against future discoveries which may warrant the repudiation of those theories currently accepted is altogether consonant with the recognition of the finitude of human rationality and the contingency of empirical relations.

Presupposition theorists suggest that any account of science which fails to accredit the rationality of the considered judgments which inform the choice between alternative scientific theories must be committed to a defective conception of reason. Although the standards of evidence and the criteria for assessment brought to bear upon theoretical questions cannot be encapsulated in a simple rule or summarized in rigid methodological principles, deliberation involves the exercise of a range of intellectual skills. Conceptions of science which define rationality in terms of one technique, be it logical deduction or empirical verification, are simply too narrow to encompass the multiple forms of rationality manifested in scientific research. The interpretive judgments which are characteristic of every phase of scientific investigations and which culminate in the rational choice of particular scientific theories on the basis of the cumulative weight of evidence and argument are too rich and various to be captured by the rules governing inductive or deductive logic. For this reason, *phronesis*, practical reason, manifested in the processes of interpretation and judgment characteristic of all understanding, is advanced by presupposition theorists as an alternative to logic as the paradigmatic form of scientific rationality.[45]

Presupposition theorists suggest that a conception of practical reason more accurately depicts the forms of rationality exhibited in scientific research. In contrast to the restrictive view advanced by positivism, which reduces the arsenal of reason to the techniques of logic and thereby rejects creativity, deliberative judgment, and evaluative assessments as varying forms of irrationality, *phronesis* constitutes a more expansive conception of the powers of the human intellect. Presupposition theorists suggest that a consideration of the various processes of contemplation, conceptualization, representation, remembrance, reflection, speculation, rationalization, inference, deduction, and deliberation (to name but a few manifestations of human cognition) reveals that the dimensions of reason are diverse. And they argue that an adequate conception of reason must encompass these diverse cognitive practices. Because the instrumental conception of rationality advanced by positivists is clearly incapable of accounting for these various forms of reason, it must be rejected as defective. Thus presupposition theorists suggest that science must be freed from the parochial beliefs which obscure reason's diverse manifestations and restrict its operation to a narrow set of rules. The equation of scientific rationality with an infallible formal logic must be abandoned not only because there is no reason to suppose that there must be some indubitable foundation or some ahistorical, invariant method for scientific inquiry in order to establish the rationality of scientific practices; but also because the belief that science can provide final truths cannot be sustained by the principles of formal logic, the methods of empirical inquiry, or the characteristics of fallible human cognition. *Phronesis* constitutes a conception of rationality which can encompass the diverse uses of reason in scientific practices, identify the manifold sources of potential error in theoretical interpretations, and illuminate the criteria of assessment and the standards of evidence and argument operative in the choice between alternative theoretical explanations of events. As a conception of scientific rationality, then, *phronesis* is more comprehensive and has greater explanatory power than the discredited positivist alternative.

Presupposition theorists offer a revised conception of science which emphasizes the conventional nature of scientific practices and the fallible character of scientific explanations and predictions. Confronted with a world richer than any partial perception of it, scientists draw on the resources of tradition and imagination in an effort to comprehend the world before them. The theories they devise to explain objects and events are structured by a host of presuppositions concerning meaning, relevance, experience, explanation, and evaluation. Operating within the limits imposed by fallibility and contingency, scientists employ creative insights, practical reason, formal logic, and an arsenal of conventional techniques and methods in their effort to approximate the truth about the world. But their approximations always operate within the parameters set by theoretical presuppositions; their approximations always address an empirical realm which is itself theoretically constituted. The undetermination of theory by data ensures that multiple interpretations of the same phenomena are possible.

When alternative theoretical explanations conflict, the judgment of the scientific community is brought to bear upon the competing interpretations. Exercising practical reason, the scientific community deliberates upon the evidence and arguments sustaining the alternative views. The practical judgment of the practioners in particular fields of science is exercised in weighing the evidence, replicating experiments, examining computations, investigating the applicability of innovative methods, assessing the potential of new concepts, and considering the validity of particular conclusions. Through a process of deliberation and debate, a consensus emerges among researchers within a discipline concerning what will be taken as the valid theory. The choice is sustained by reasons that can be articulated and advanced as proof of the inadequacy of alternative interpretations. The method of scientific deliberation is eminently rational: it provides mechanisms for the identification of charlatans and incompetents, as well as for the recognition of more subtle errors and more sophisticated approximations of truth. But the rationality of the process cannot guarantee the eternal verity of particular conclusions. The exercise of scientific reason is fallible; the judgments of the scientific community are corrigible.

The revised conception of science advanced by presupposition theorists suggests that attempts to divide the world into ontologically distinct categories of facts and values, or into dichotomous realms of the empirical and the normative are fundamentally flawed. Such attempts fail to grasp the implications of the theoretical constitution of all knowledge and the theoretical mediation of the empirical realm. They fail to recognize the valuative character of all presuppositions and the consequent valuative component of all empirical propositions. The theoretically mediated world is one in which description, explanation, and evaluation are inextricably linked. Any attempt to impose a dichotomous relation upon such inseparable processes constitutes a fallacy of false alternatives which is as distorting as it is logically untenable. The suggestion that pure facts can be isolated and analyzed free of all valuation masks the theoretical constitution of facticity and denies the cognitive processes through which knowledge of the empirical realm is generated. Moreover, the dichotomous schism of the world into facts and values endorses an erroneous and excessively limiting conception of human reason, a conception which fails to comprehend the role of practical rationality in scientific deliberation, and which fails to recognize that science is simply one manifestation of the use of practical reason in human life. Informed by flawed assumptions, the instrumental conception of reason fails to understand that *phronesis* is operative in philosophical analysis, ethical deliberation, normative argument, political decisions, and the practical choices of daily life, as well as in scientific analysis. In stipulating that reason can operate only in a naively simple, 'value-free' empirical realm, the theoretical presuppositions which inform the fact/value dichotomy render reason impotent and thereby preclude the possibility that rational solutions might exist for the most pressing problems of the contemporary age.

Post-Behavioral Policy Analysis: Post-Positivist or Neo-Positivist?

The critique of positivism developed by philosophers of science has not gone altogether without notice in policy studies. During the past two decades, the positivist presuppositions that inform most policy analysis have come under consistent attack. Arguments have been advanced to suggest that the demand for value-neutrality is both impossible and undesirable. It has been repeatedly asserted that the "idea of theory-free, immediate experiential access to reality or 'brute facts' has been thoroughly discredited. Whether experience is interior or exterior, of the senses or of meanings, it is inadequate to understand it as a passive incorporation of the 'given'".[46] Hundreds of articles have been written to demonstrate the tacit normative bias incorporated into allegedly value-neutral policy studies.[47] And with increasing regularity, texts in policy analysis have noted that a rigid distinction between facts and values is difficult to maintain in policy research.[48] Reluctantly, policy researchers have admitted that "social science contributions to the understanding of an issue must be partial both in the sense of being incomplete and in the sense of being non-neutral as between policy options."[49] Indeed it has been suggested that in the 1980s a "basic shift in the logical foundations undergirding policy inquiry has taken place," a shift which recognizes that "values are intimately and properly involved in social science research and policy inquiry."[50]

Not only has the possibility of preserving the fact/value dichotomy in policy research been challenged, but a number of policy researchers have argued that even if it were possible to pursue value-free inquiry, it would be undesirable to do so. It has been suggested that the responsibility of the policy analyst to provide professional advice concerning the best course of action for a political decision-maker is incompatible with the "straitjacket" of value-neutrality.[51] For this reason, a good deal of energy has been devoted to efforts to deploy the techniques of behavioral research for purposes of strategic policy advocacy. As Randall Ripley has noted:

> A moderately sizable group of political scientists in the 1970s and 1980s emphasize policy analysis and evaluation. They are concerned with reaching normatively based conclusions and making prescriptions as well as doing solid empirical work based upon longitudinal data, appropriate quantification and methodological rigor. They seek to stress the systematic, rigorous aspects of political science to analyze policy but they deny that a concern with prescription is prohibited by concern with rigor or 'science'. They find the two enterprises compatible although they understand the difference between them.[52]

Increasing recognition that value-free policy science may be impossible or undesirable has generated a variety of strategies for dealing with values in post-behavioral studies. Prominent among these are proposals for value identification, for normative policy analysis, and for developing an applied ethics uniquely suited to policy assessments.[53] Are these post-behavioral approaches to policy analysis truly post-positivist, incorporating the systematic insights of presupposition theories of science, or are they neo-positivist, retaining and subtly reintroducing the bifurcated view of the world institutionalized in the fact/value dichotomy? This issue will be explored in the remaining sections of this chapter.

Value Identification

It is now fairly well-established that the desire to eliminate all value bias from policy inquiry results more often in the denial of the valuative dimension of policy prescriptions than in the elimination of tacit bias. As Douglas Amy has noted, "The attempt to engage in 'value-free' analysis cannot eliminate the normative dimensions but can only obscure them. The result is that normative assumptions are surreptitiously and arbitrarily introduced into studies (embedded in the definitions of the problem being studied, in the models used in analysis, in the choice of alternatives to be investigated, etc.) and are beyond the range of public scrutiny."[54] Recognition that policy analysis cannot be value-free, however, does not imply that the values sustaining research must remain hidden, arbitrary, or obscure. On the contrary, acknowledgement that policy "analysts are not machines, that they have philosophical and disciplinary views" which may infiltrate their substantive recommendations suggests that they also have an obligation to make those commitments known.[55]

Adopting a stance reminiscent of "truth in labelling" legislation, several policy researchers have therefore recommended that the best means for dealing with the problem of covert value-infiltration is to require policy analysts to make their values explicit. The great virtue of requiring analysts "to come up front with values" is that it would allow others (decision-makers, the public) to "pass personal judgments on the desirability of the ends a particular policy analyst advocates and evaluate how effective or efficient the means proposed are to attain the policy objectives."[56] Like the principle of *caveat emptor*, the requirement that policy analysts identify their value commitments would enable decision-makers to make more informed choices with respect to conflicting policy recommendations.

Accounts of the precise mechanics of value identification vary, ranging from the suggestion that value identification proceed by sincere introspection and confessional statement,[57] to the recommendation that analysts engage in a far more exacting process, identifying methodological assumptions influencing data collection (reliability of sample, nature of questionnaire, response rates, etc.), specifying criteria employed in adjustments to data (explicit assumption, inputation of missing values, non-duplication of counts, etc.), and describing assumptions used in the applications of data (choices of data sets, rejection of similar data from alternative sources, organization and categorization of data, choices of statistical techniques, etc.).[58] Indeed, numerous policy researchers have attempted to develop quantitative techniques to facilitate value identification. Sensitivity analysis,[59] the Delphi technique,[60] strategic assumption surfacing,[61] value weighting schemes,[62] and analytic policy grids[63] have all been advanced as mechanisms to illuminate the influence of values upon the frames of reference, research design, data collection and measurement, sampling techniques, statistical tests, and research conclusions of policy studies.

Using statistical techniques to identify values places responsibility for indicating those values operative in policy analysis with the professional policy analyst, who works in accordance with the methodological canons of scientific research. Alternative strategies, however, impose the responsibility on the scientific community. Suggesting that the good intentions of the individual analyst might not be sufficient to ensure that all the values influencing a particular study are identified, several scholars have recommended the institutionalization of an 'adversarial process,' pitting policy analysts against one another as a better means of value identification.[64] The examination of policy studies by multiple analysts, generating competing assessments of problem formulations, choices of research methods, and substantive findings is designed to provide a more rigorous method for discovering implicit value bias. Open criticism by a variety of professionals with diverse methodological and value preferences is characterized as "the best technique available for generating a comprehensive list of plausible alternative interpretations of a piece of research," precisely because it capitalizes on psychological propensities of competitive academics.[65] On this view, it is "only because of the personal hostilities between scholars, the passions engendered by ideological and personal intellectual commitments and ambitious young scholars and outsiders who want to overthrow the conventional widsom that science and critical reason can flourish."[66] Thus, the incorporation of an adversarial process into the standard operating procedures of policy research could facilitate the identification of values while simultaneously promoting the objectivity of science understood in terms of rigorous intersubjective testing.

Any examination of the literature which endorses value identification, whether through introspection, statistical technique, or adversarial process, quickly reveals that it is premised upon a dichotomy between facts and values. Acknowledging that values may infiltrate policy research, proponents of value identification nonetheless believe that facts and values are altogether distinct, that facts are empirically verifiable, testable, or falsifiable propositions, and that values are individual preferences devoid of any ultimate justification.[67] Value noncognitivism is asserted as the only conceivable theory of values, although it is occasionally noted that recognition of the irrationality of personal value preferences should not be allowed to immunize individual values from critical examination.[68]

The point of value identification is precisely to eliminate the troublesome traces of nonempirical factors from policy research in order to get on with the empirical studies.[69] The presence of normative presuppositions is not taken as a major challenge to the possibility of scientific policy analysis, rather it is treated as a minor inconvenience which requires passing attention. Thus the recognition of value infiltration coexists with clear affirmations that the empirical validity of policy studies turns upon factual matters such as the representativeness of the sample, the accuracy of measurement of variables, and the rigorous analysis of data.[70] Failure to differentiate clearly between facts and values in the origin, design, intent, and execution of a policy study continues to be identified as a form of flawed analysis which can be rectified by stricter adherence to the methodological canons of the discipline.[71]

Although many proponents of these various techniques describe their stance as post-positivist, value identification is more aptly characterized as a neo-positivist strategy of recuperation, for it accepts the validity of the anti-positivist charge that policy studies are value-laden even as it undercuts the force of that charge. Rather than reconsider the question of the facticity of empirical relations or the nature of scientific investigations, post-behavioral proponents of value identification admit the presence of value infiltration as a demonstration of their own methodological sophistication, and insist that it poses no real threat to the discipline. Granting the anti-positivist point thus serves as a means of diffusing and dismissing it, for the methodologically sophisticated policy analysts assert that the spectre of values requires no major methodological reform, no systematic revision of standard operating procedures. Positivist assumptions continue to structure their understanding of the empirical realm and of the methodology devised to investigate that realm.

Normative Policy Analysis

Arguments that the positivist premises of most policy research are inadequate have been advanced by a small group of scholars working within the policy studies disciplines.[72] Through detailed examinations of the applied social science and applied pluralist models of policy analysis, and through exacting analyses of the dominant methods advocated within these competing paradigms, it has been demonstrated that the belief that values play an inconsequential role in quantitative studies is illusory.[73] Moreover, it has been argued that rigid adherence to the postulates of behavioral policy studies results in marginalization of policy analysis both because efforts to refrain from the examination of value questions place the most important policy questions beyond empirical policy inquiry, and because the principal logical tenet of the fact/value dichotomy, the insistence upon the existence of a 'gulf' between the '*is*' and the '*ought*,' ensures that even if purely factual policy analyses could be produced, they could not stimulate policy action. To treat value questions both in the policy process and in policy research adequately, a normative approach to policy analysis is advocated.

Normative policy analysis is conceived as an enterprise which integrates normative and empirical judgments in the study of public policy. Accepting that facts and values are thoroughly intertwined in policy questions and in the methods of social science, normative policy inquiry seeks to bring reason to bear on both empirical and valuative claims. Using the norms of clarity, logical consistency, and generality, normative policy analysis seeks to identify 'good reasons' for adopting particular policies. Committed to a model of practical reason, normative policy analysts advocate the use of rational argument to illuminate the value implications related to the implementation of particular policy options, to assess the compatibility of the values incorporated within specific policy proposals with those value commitments dominant in a political system, and to raise questions concerning the validity of the range of value commitments characteristic of a particular polity.[74]

Proponents of normative policy analysis have argued forcefully that the emotivist conception of values characteristic of positivism is defective. Indeed, they have suggested that the notion that values are arbitrary sentiments or irrational choices of individuals fails to grasp the distinctive character of morality. As assertions concerning what is right, what is good, or what ought to be done, value statements represent far more than individual preferences. Based on reasoned judgments concerning appropriate forms of behavior and desirable states of affairs, individual value commitments are far from arbitrary choices. Contrary to the emotivist assumption that it is impossible to debate value preferences, normative policy analysts have pointed out that deliberation is integral to valuative discourse. Critical reflection upon the reasons sustaining alternative value positions and upon consequences likely to follow from the adoption of various normative principles is central to moral reasoning and ethical decision-making.

Drawing models of normative reasoning from forensics, jurisprudence, ideology critique, and informal logic, proponents of normative policy analysis have offered rich examples of the manifold ways in which rationality functions in valuative discourse. They have demonstrated that systematic examination of normative premises of alternative policy proposals and of the valuative presuppositions of quantitative policy studies can explain the persistence of intractable policy disputes and the failure of a variety of policy initiatives. Moreover, they have shown that normative policy inquiry can identify probable consequences of adopting particular policy options which quantitative studies miss as a result of their tendency to allow 'hard values' (those which are tangible and susceptible to fairly precise measurement) to drive out 'soft values' (those which are intangible, non-instrumental and incommensurable). They have introduced a variety of defensible normative principles (e.g., justice, fairness, equity, legitimacy) which can supplement efficiency as decision criteria for policy analysis. And they have argued persuasively that grounds for rational justification of public policies constitute important determinants of the choice between policy options as well as useful tools for the *post hoc* rationalization of decisions by politicians.

Despite their compelling critiques of the myth of value-neutrality, their trenchant rebuttals of emotivism, their cogent defense of the possibility of rational analysis of normative issues, and their forceful demonstrations of the potential utility of normative policy analysis, the proponents of normative policy analysis have not fully escaped the consequences of positivist presuppositions. Positivist precepts concerning the nature of science and prescriptivist versions of noncognitivism continue to haunt their work with the unfortunate result that normative policy analysis is conceived as a complement to rather than a comprehensive challenge to empirical policy analysis.

As an alternative to emotivism, prescriptivism is a noncognitivist meta-ethical theory which posits that the distinctive feature of moral language is that it is *action-guiding*. Functioning as a regulator of conduct, moral language is prescriptive. On this view, ethical precepts constitute commands or recommendations for particular courses of action; hence, the form of moral discourse is imperative. Central to the prescriptive force of ethical language are the reasons which can be offered to support every moral prescription. Thus, in contrast to emotivism, prescriptivism suggests that a distinguishing characteristic of normative discourse is that reasons can always be advanced to support specific recommendations. However, as a form of value noncognitivism, prescriptivism accepts that value statements do not convey information about matters of fact, and therefore cannot be properly said to be true or false; they are not amenable to ultimate rational justification.[75]

Prescriptivism has a number of virtues for proponents of normative policy analysis. Its emphasis on the action-guiding nature of valuative discourse provides ready arguments for the position that normative policy analysis can generate effective policy prescriptions which elude purely factual policy studies. Its insistence upon the existence of reasons to sustain any normative recommendation provides ample grounds for repudiating emotivist conceptions of value, and provides strong arguments in support of claims that normative policy analysis can be a thoroughly rational enterprise. Its focus on generating good reasons for a particular course of action is premised upon a conception of people as rational agents capable of autonomous decision-making, a premise which provides a model for the deployment of normative arguments consonant with commitments to democratic decision-making, thereby rescuing policy analysis from the manipulative implications of emotivism. Moreover, prescriptivism's consequentialist approach to normative decision-making, its commitment to an examination of the consequences likely to follow from adopting various moral principles in particular situations, is well-suited to the demands for prescient policy analysis capable of contributing to rational political decision-making.

But prescriptivism also bears a number of liabilities. As a form of noncognitivism, it leaves the fact/value dichotomy intact. Thus, rather than pose a systematic challenge to mistaken notions of value-free policy analysis, prescriptivism subtly reinforces those notions. Within the works of proponents of normative policy analysis, prescriptivist commitments produce the noncognitivist avowal that values are ultimately indefensible, that in the final analysis, they rest upon irrational elements.[76] But if this is so, how can normative policy analysis be a legitimate enterprise? If ultimately, the valuative arguments advanced by policy analysts are indefensible, why should anyone bother to heed them?

This problem is exacerbated by normative policy analysts' tendency to accept the positivist account of facts. Within the works of normative policy analysts, it is common to find assertions that empirical science, functioning in accordance with the hypothetico-deductive model (just as behavioralists and positivists describe it) provides a source of empirical knowledge upon which normative policy analysts may draw.[77] Thus, it is suggested that a tidy division of labor in policy inquiry between those who would focus on scientific empirical analysis and those who would devote their energies to the complementary task of normative policy analysis is both legitimate and useful. Rather than provide an argument concerning the impossibility of value-free policy analysis, proponents of normative policy inquiry tend to fall into a rhetoric of complementarity, which defends and legitimates a division of labor along the axis of the fact/value dichotomy. Depicting positivist approaches as incomplete rather than erroneous, this rhetoric suggests that empirical policy analysis and normative policy inquiry may co-exist peacefully, each providing a useful complement to the other.

The problem with this division of labor is that it endorses a demarcation between facts and values which accredits the scientific status of facts while it leaves values on an ultimately irrational ground. Despite detailed arguments concerning the scope of reason in normative policy analysis, the persistence of noncognitivist commitments narrowly circumscribes the sphere of normative inquiry and undercuts the force of practical reason. In leaving the giveness of empirical relations largely intact and concentrating on efforts to resuscitate rational discourse on values within the parameters set by value noncognitivism, proponents of normative policy analysis face an awkward question: If there is ground to believe that empirical analysis can generate authoritative generalizations concerning factual matters, why should any self-respecting policy analyst dally with the less authoritative and ultimately irrational defense of normative propositions? Operating within the bounds of noncognitivism, the rhetoric of complementarity undermines the legitimacy of normative analysis and renders the enterprise marginal, if not altogether mistaken.

The dimensions of this problem can be illuminated by considering discussions of ideology within the normative policy literature. Identification of the tacit normative assumptions incorporated in allegedly value-free policy studies, coupled with a demonstration that the recommendations of such studies promote the interests of a specific individual or group, provide a foundation for the charge that such studies are ideologically biased. In the context of specific studies, the validity of the charge of ideological distortion depends on the demonstration of how the covert values unmasked in the ideology critique advance the interests of a determinate group. Thus, the validity of the charge cannot be assessed without carefully considering the evidence in particular cases. Within certain strains of the normative policy literature, however, there has been a tendency to combine acknowledgement that certain specific policy prescriptions are ideologically biased with arguments concerning the valuative dimension of all description and explanation in order to arrive at the conclusion that all policy inquiry is ideological.

Operating within the parameters set by prescriptivism, the claim that all policy inquiry is ideological receives a new twist. On the grounds that reasons can always be offered to support valuative recommendations, and that some reasons are better than others, it is suggested that a distinction can be made between 'rational' ideologies and 'irrational' ideologies.[78] On this view, rational ideologies are those which have been subjected to systematic examination and which, having withstood rational scrutiny, provide a system of values which are clear, consistent, coherent, congruent with the external world, and pragmatically useful.[79] By contrast, irrational ideologies are unexamined, dogmatic, and insulated from refutation or alteration by experience.[80] The task of normative policy inquiry, then, is "to develop the normative component of rational ideology, broad in its compass, specified in some detail and as defensible as normative theory can be. This ideology can then be applied to elucidate the normative aspects of policy problems and guide their resolution."[81]

Although advanced as part of an effort to demonstrate the importance of normative policy analysis, arguments concerning the possibility of rational ideology are unpersuasive and ultimately self-defeating. Effective ideology critique turns upon a distinction between truth and error.[82] The force of the charge of ideological distortion lies in the demonstration that certain beliefs mask the truth, mystify existing relations, or interfere with an accurate perception of events. When all belief systems are labelled ideologies, the grounds for differentiating between error and truth become suspect. As arguments in the sociology of knowledge have so clearly demonstrated, claims that all belief systems are ideological support unending rounds of ideological unmasking, but they afford little room for the rational assessment of the merits of arguments. Thus, in the absence of a meaningful criterion of demarcation between truthful and distorted belief systems, the claim that it is possible to distinguish between rational and irrational ideologies on procedural grounds rings hollow. Moreover, the noncognitivist avowal that ultimately all valuative beliefs lie beyond rational defense reinforces the shallowness of this distinction. In addition, when advanced in the context of the fact/value dichotomy and in the absence of any clear distinction between truth and error, the claim that all policy inquiry is ideological only undermines the force of the specific charge that behavioral policy analysis generates ideological policy prescriptions in particular cases.[83] Rather than prove the importance of normative policy analysis, arguments concerning ubiquitous ideologies, rational or not, facilitate the dismissal of the charge of ideological bias. Thus they are unlikely to persuade empirical policy analysts of either the need for or the merits of normative analysis. Confronted by a choice between an unchallenged belief in 'hard data' and manifold varieties of ideology, it is unlikely that quantitative policy analysts would choose to reorient their endeavors toward normative inquiry which promises such an elusive and limited rationality.

The positivist heritage of noncognitivism which sustains a division of the world into verifiable facts and unverifiable values works to ensure that valuative discourse is severely disadvantaged in any debate with empirical science. Thus the proponents of normative policy analysis strive against impossible odds when they attempt to provide a rational foundation for normative inquiry structured in accordance with the precepts of value noncognitivism. Despite their heroic efforts to rescue policy analysis from the defects of emotivism, their turn to prescriptivism leaves them captives of the terms of debate established by positivism.

Ethics and Policy Analysis

A number of philosophers working in the field of applied ethics have also turned their attention to policy analysis in an effort to identify ethical principles uniquely suited to political decision-making. Like proponents of normative policy analysis, they have devoted a good deal of energy to the demonstration that empirical policy analysis, whether conceived in terms of applied social science or applied pluralism, cannot be either theory-free or value-neutral.[84] Once the normative component of policy analysis has been recognized, it becomes apparent that ethics and ethicists have a great deal to contribute to policy research. They can provide guidance for resolving the ethical dilemmas which confront decision-makers and policy analysts. They can help clarify the ethical implications of the various courses of action open to politicians and to policy scientists. They can identify value-laden assumptions embedded in various models of decision-making and policy analysis. They can suggest ethical principles adequate for the thorough evaluation of public programs and alternative policy responses. By raising moral questions, stimulating consideration of forgotten factors, and revealing previously unperceived angles for approaching policy issues, applied ethics can help to "unparalyze the mind at the moment of action."[85]

Within the literature on ethics and public policy, there has been extensive debate concerning the particular ethical theory and specific moral principles most appropriate for policy-making situations and for policy research. The options considered in this debate range from eclectic strategies, which suggest that a variety of moral theories should be employed at varying stages in the decision-making process and that specific forms of ethical analysis are applicable to specific problems confronted by decision-makers, to the systematic endorsement of a unitary ethical theory for all policy-making issues.

On the side of eclecticism, it has been suggested that the history of ethics is rich in useful insights, providing theories, principles, and models applicable to a variety of policy-making contexts.[86] Utilitarian principles, consequentialist in focus and designed to calculate the net benefits associated with competing proposals, can facilitate the comparative assessment of policy alternatives in light of the forseeable consequences of various policy options. Casuistry, the art of applying authoritative rules and precedents to particular cases, can provide a model of reasoning appropriate for administrative decision-making and the formulation and implementation of bureaucratic regulations. Deployment of a form of dialectical reasoning suggested by Plato can aid the development of internally consistent policy agendas and illuminate appropriate criteria to guide choices between conflicting policy alternatives. The Kantian principle of universalizability can be employed as a test of policy proposals capable of eliminating any options which fail to ensure that all citizens are treated consistently in accordance with the requirements of fairness and respect for human dignity. Stoic principles can be used to distinguish between problems which are amenable to political solution and problems which remain beyond human power, providing a model for resignation to the unalterable constraints upon policy and enduring lessons concerning the adjustment of desires to available resources. Aristotle's discussion of the *golden mean* can provide useful criteria for personnel decisions, indicating the characteristics most desirable in professional staff. Consideration of the psychological profiles of political actors advanced by Hobbes and Butler can help decision-makers to design their policies in light of worst case scenarios, thereby avoiding utopian expectations. The historical logic of Hegel and Marx can afford useful insights into the dynamics of collective action in politics while dispelling myths about the permanence of existing political institutions and conditions. Dewey's model of instrumental thinking can direct attention to the institutional background of policy-making, illuminating group interests, organizational processes, and idiosyncratic personality factors which may have an enormous influence upon the choice of policy options and the implementation of political decisions. On this view, policy analysts and decision-makers who are adept in the utilization of these various frames of reference in particular problem contexts will produce policy recommendations and political decisions which are sophisticated, well-conceived, politically astute, and ethical.

In contrast to the extrapolation of insights from a wide range of ethical theories which is characteristic of the eclectic approach to ethics and public policy, however, most of the ethicists who address policy issues endorse one particular ethical theory as a comprehensive guide for moral questions which arise in relation to policy analysis and policy-making. Utilitarianism, with its consequentialist focus and its commitment to maximizing the greatest good of the greatest number, or to minimizing harm, is frequently invoked as the ethical theory most appropriate for policy analysis and for public decision-making.[87] But utilitarianism is not without its detractors.[88] Emphasizing utilitarianism's tendency to sacrifice the individual for the sake of the greater good, its ability to justify unreasonable actions, and its inability to justify reasonable proposals, as well as the difficulties related to interpersonal utility comparisons and to efforts to treat commensurably incommensurable values, some ethicists have recommended deontological or contractarian ethics as an alternative guide to policy issues.[89] Placing the concepts of rights and duties at the center of their ethical system, deontological and contractarian ethical theorists suggest that they can provide moral principles for policy-making which can foster and protect the development of individual autonomy, preserve individual liberty, institutionalize individual rights, and promote fundamental fairness. In addition to utilitarianism and deontological moral theories, a phenomenological ethics grounded in lived experience,[90] an egalitarian ethics derived from historical materialism,[91] an intuitionist ethics founded on the plurality of incommensurable moral principles,[92] and an ethics of virtue which substitutes concern with moral character for reliance upon the identification and application of moral rules,[93] have been advanced as models which can provide useful guidance for policy analysts and public decision-makers.

Beyond the dispute concerning the ethical theory most appropriate for public policy, ethicists have also devoted much discussion to ethical dilemmas confronting policy analysts and to evaluation of a wide range of policy questions. The nature of the policy expert's 'mandate,' conflicting obligations to government (contracting agencies and the Congress), to the profession and to the public, issues pertaining to advocacy and to representation of and consultation with affected stakeholders, the requirements of full disclosure and informed consent in the context of experimentation on human subjects, permissible secrecy and its limits, paternalism in policy prescriptions, and justifiable whistle-blowing have all been considered in detail.[94] Moreover, the applied ethics literature is rich in case studies of particular policy questions. Whether considering the ethical issues related to nuclear power or nuclear war, to abortion, affirmative action, reverse discrimination, poverty and welfare policy, educational opportunity, housing, health care, energy policies, environmental issues, public transportation, race relations, employment policies, technology assessment, prison reform, defense expenditures, or foreign policy ventures, ethical theorists have demonstrated the vast potential for rational analysis of the normative dimensions of public policy.[95] And they have helped to shape public debate on these policy questions.

As in the case of normative policy analysis, attempts to bring applied ethics to bear on policy questions help to move policy inquiry beyond the positivist notion that valuative discourse is arbitrary and irrational. They help to dispel the myth that normative analysis can offer nothing to political decision-makers or to policy analysts. They generate a wide array of ethical criteria which can be used to examine particular policy debates. But despite these considerable virtues, ethicists' efforts to inject normative issues into policy debates have not systematically challenged the 'separate spheres' doctrine, the notion that empirical and normative policy analysis are relatively autonomous enterprises which can be conducted either in isolation or with some degree of consultation.

Among the factors contributing to the failure of applied ethics to challenge the separate spheres doctrine are the insularity of the disciplines involved in ethics and in policy analysis, and the implications of the complementarity arguments which are advanced to overcome this insularity. With few exceptions, the philosophers who work in the area of ethics and public policy publish in philosophical journals quite remote from those frequently consulted or subscribed to by the practitioners of policy analysis.[96] In order to make articles dealing with ethics and public policy relevant to the concerns of a wider philosophical audience, specific policy studies are often situated in the context of larger philosophical debates concerning meta-ethics, the history of ethics, or the validity of particular forms of ethical reasoning. The level of sophistication in these articles, as well as their reliance upon hypothetical, counterfactual, and "crazy" cases[97] to illustrate particular points, tends to curtail their usefulness for policy analysts trained in social science. Policy analysts often find the approach quite foreign, the technical vocabulary impenetrable, the philosophical issues undecipherable, and the insights marginal to immediate policy problems.

In order to overcome this insularity, a number of ethicists have tried to develop arguments more accessible and more relevant to the needs of policy analysts.[98] Yet in order to demonstrate the relevance and utility of applied ethics without insulting or threatening the pol-

icy analysts who constitute the target audience for these works, a recurrent resort to the rhetoric of complementarity arises in these
texts. Thus it is common to find encomiums to the autonomy and authority of social science inquiry as prolegomena to arguments for the
complementarity of the two approaches. Social scientists are acknowledged to have total authority for the choice of models, methods, and
techniques most appropriate to empirical policy analysis; while
applied ethicists are assigned responsibility for the ethical principles
and arguments necessary for the normative evaluation of alternative
policy options.[99] It is suggested that in combination, empirical
analysis and applied ethics can provide a comprehensive treatment of
policy issues: "systematic connections between empirical and evaluative propositions on all levels of analysis [can] help the policy sciences realize their early evaluative promise."[100]

Whether considered as a strategic rhetoric or as a confident conviction of the analytic power of the empirical policy sciences,[101] discussions of the joint practice of the social and moral sciences, of the
complementary interaction between social science and ethics, of the
merger of horizons of the empirical and the ethical, only reinforce the
separate spheres doctrine. For the implication of the suggestion that
the two endeavors could be fruitfully joined is that they are distinct
and disparate. The suggestion that empirical and normative policy
analysis are distinct but complementary endeavors fuels the notion
that questions of value *may* be brought into the policy process *post
hoc* to help analysts, decision-makers, or citizens appraise the moral
merits of their policies, but they need not be. For empirical policy
analysis can be systematic and complete, independent of and insulated from normative considerations.

Thus applied ethicists confront the same problem encountered
by normative policy analysts. The rhetoric of complementarity allows proponents of the fact/value dichotomy to reject applied ethics as
peripheral; it provides nourishment for the belief in the autonomy of
facts. Many ethicists who address policy issues may reject value noncognitivism as a defective conception of morality, but the substantive
ethical arguments which have been advanced in particular policy contexts have not systematically challenged the beliefs which sustain the
entrenchment of the fact/value dichotomy in the policy sciences.

The Institutionalization of the Fact/Value Dichotomy

Examination of the major texts in policy analysis and the substantive research of policy analysts reveals that their fundamental pre-

suppositions are positivist. Although there is on-going debate concerning the comparative merits of verificationism versus falsificationism, of early positivist precepts versus the Popperian emendation, the fact/value dichotomy is thoroughly institutionalized within the policy studies discipline. Indeed, it is precisely the institutionalization of this dichotomy which gives force to the demarcation between empirical and normative approaches to policy studies. Within the boundaries of the empirical realm established by the fact/value dichotomy, the model of scientific theory, the methods advocated for the generation of scientific and political knowledge, the tests identified to vindicate knowledge claims, the strategies of explanation certified as valid, the emphasis on prediction as a scientific objective, and the criteria for the utility of various conceptions of policy analysis, gain their meaning.

The attempts of scholars to move policy research beyond positivist presuppositions, either by advocating normative policy analysis or by introducing applied ethics to policy issues, fail to challenge the fact/value dichotomy precisely because they operate within the terms of debate constituted by that dichotomy. They reinforce the separate spheres doctrine with its corollary assumptions concerning the autonomy and complementarity of the disparate endeavors. Focusing their energies on demonstrations that reason can operate in the realm of values, both normative policy analysts and applied ethicists wage a battle that makes sense only within positivist conceptions of the world, conceptions that curtail the scope of rationality so radically that normative discourse is dismissed as irrational or meaningless. Despite their important contributions to an expansion of the understanding of the power of the human intellect, to the reconceptualization of valuative discourse, to the repudiation of emotivism, and to the illustration of the potential uses for normative inquiry in policy studies, normative policy analysts and applied ethical theorists have not successfully challenged the prevailing belief in the unproblematic facticity of the empirical realm. To date, the meaning and importance of the full range of insights of presupposition theories of science have not penetrated the policy studies discipline. Positivism has not been eclipsed; the fact/value dichotomy remains entrenched.

4

The Fallacy of
False Alternatives

THE fact/value dichotomy which underlies the positivist conception of science and which has been incorporated as a fundamental principle within policy analysis is intimately related to the quest for truth. The bifurcation of the world into distinct realms of facts and values is part of a strategy to achieve objective knowledge, to establish canons of science free from distortion, bias, and prejudice, to construct a system of scientific principles which transcend the fallibility of human knowers. According to positivist precepts, differentiating between factual claims and evaluative judgments is the first step in the scientific process, which culminates in the vindication of empirical propositions as objective representations of the world. Categorizing claims as empirical and separating them from those which are normative constitutes a crucial precondition for the acquisition of valid knowledge, for it demarcates the range of propositions amenable to scientific investigation. Once claims have been identified as assertions about the empirical world, scientists can proceed with their investigations, using sophisticated techniques to assess the merits of those claims. Thus, one argument supporting the fact/value dichotomy is grounded in claims concerning its utility. On this view, the dichotomous classification of phenomena is justified because it

73

facilitates the achievement of objective knowledge by providing a clear demarcation of that which can be known from that which lies beyond the scope of human reason. The utility of the dichotomy is inextricably linked to epistemological claims concerning the limits of rationality.

In addition to arguments which justify the fact/value dichotomy in terms of its utility for scientific investigations, an ontological legitimation of the dichotomy has also been advanced. Thus it has been suggested that categorizing claims as 'factual' or 'valuative' reflects an ontological distinction between 'facts' and 'values' which exists in the world. On this view, the validity of the distinction between facts and values is rooted not in its utility, but rather in its ability to capture the truth about the world.

Whether the arguments advanced in support of the fact/value dichotomy emphasize utilitarian, epistemological, or ontological claims, they are premised on the belief that it is possible to distinguish straightforwardly between description, explanation, and evaluation. They are committed to the belief that the identification of the empirical realm is unproblematic, and that the differences between facts and values are sufficiently obvious that the dichotomous classification of statements is a fairly easy matter.

The task of this chapter is to scrutinize critically the arguments supporting the fact/value dichotomy, to explore in detail the merits of claims concerning the utility, as well as the epistemological and the ontological validity, of the fact/value dichotomy, and to identify the defects of these justificatory claims. The chapter will suggest that if policy analysis is to take advantage of the insights of presupposition theories of science, it must move beyond the fact/value dichotomy in all its various manifestations. The final sections of the chapter will consider the implications of such a move for the practice of policy inquiry.

The Validity of the Fact/Value Dichotomy

To assess the utility of the fact/value dichotomy within policy studies, it is important to consider the effect of its regular deployment within the discipline, to consider the results of uniform application of its precepts in relation to the achievement of objective knowledge concerning policy questions. Although the positivist conception of facts and values is just one of many competing accounts of these phenomena,[1] it is widely accepted by policy analysts to be unproblematic, or indeed to represent the truth of the matter. As a result of this conviction, issues pertaining to policy questions are routinely categorized as 'empirical' or 'valuative.' Those questions labeled 'normative' are excluded from the legitimate sphere of scientific policy inquiry; while those questions considered to be 'factual' are designated the appropriate target for detailed analysis. Does this preliminary classification facilitate the achievement of objective knowledge?

There is good reason to believe that the widespread acceptance of the validity of the positivist distinction between facts and values creates a situation in which the quest for truth is impaired rather than advanced. This difficulty arises in part because normative questions are removed from direct consideration, and in part because the classification of a claim as 'factual' (i.e., empirical) frequently is confused in the minds of many with a demonstration that a particular factual claim is 'true.'[2] This confusion is related to the equivocal meaning of 'factual,' for the ordinary meaning and the positivist meaning of factual are not identical. Within ordinary usage, a fact is used as a synonym for 'true,'[3] as an expression of something which is the case and which stands in opposition to falsehoods, errors, or mistaken beliefs. However, in the technical language of positivist science, a fact refers to a proposition which is in principle empirically verifiable. Understood in opposition to the speculative and the valuative, the classification of a claim as empirical does not in itself resolve the question of its truth; it simply designates the proposition as a legitimate target for scientific investigation.

Within the policy literature, there is a good deal of equivocation concerning the meaning the factual in particular analyses. The positivist conception of a factual statement as one which in principle could be verified is often subtly displaced by the assumption that claims classified as factual have been verified. The initial process of classification is conflated with vindication, the outcome of the arduous process of testing and assessment. And by this means, preliminary categorizations are rhetorically transformed into assertions that the truth is known, that the facts speak for themselves. But whether this confusion is the result of honest error or of an intentional rhetorical ploy, it produces unwarranted conclusions about the validity of particular claims. To assert that a statement such as "The C.I.A. has attempted during the past forty years to influence the outcome of elections in every nation except Britain," is empirical, is one thing: to assert that the statement is true is another. To conflate the two assertions is to equivocate upon the meaning of the term 'factual.'[4]

This kind of equivocation is manifested in several ways in the policy literature. It is apparent in rhetorical strategies which suggest that the facts (in the classificatory sense) pertaining to particular policy options are relatively easy to establish and hence should be introduced prior to any consideration of the messy evaluative issues which surround the policy decision. Yet once the facts (in the sense of 'truth') have been adduced, it appears that one and only one policy option is feasible or efficient or optimal. By this ploy, the evaluative judgments which structure empirical policy analysts' identification of the best policy proposal are masked under the neutral rubric of 'facts', the need for specific consideration of normative issues is effectively negated, and the ground for the acceptance of a value-laden policy prescription is laid by trading upon the authority of unquestionably true, 'facts.'[5]

The equivocation may also involve a covert appeal to the authority of science, more generally.[6] This form of equivocation begins with straightforward classificatory claims which couple propositions such as, "There are some important factual matters at the heart of the debate on nuclear energy," with assertions that there are "experts" in that field. Such an expert (a nuclear physicist, for example) is then introduced to produce the facts of the matter with the intended result that people accept the expert's assertions as conclusive proof of what is the case. The expert's credentials as a scientist are used to validate specific empirical claims without any systematic examination of the evidence supporting those claims. A similar strategy is often used in policy analysis when the authority invoked is not a particular scientist or group of researchers, but rather statistical computations or probabilities which trade upon the popular myth that the numbers can not be wrong. But whether the shift from the identification of a claim as factual to the suggestion that the claim is true turns upon an appeal to the authority of science, a particular expert, or to statistics, the shift involves a faulty inference; for logically, it is impossible to derive epistemological appraisals of the truth of a claim from the mere classification of a claim as empirical.

The import of this kind of equivocation lies in its power to lull people into assuming precisely what needs to be proven. Whether in the context of policy analysis or in the realm of 'empirical' science more generally, the use of the fact/value dichotomy suspends doubt concerning the truth of hypotheses labeled 'empirical,' precludes detailed analysis of particular propositions, and undermines the critical investigation of specific claims. Rather than promote the quest for truth, rather than stimulate efforts to examine the evidence in support of particular empirical claims, the classification of a statement as empirical serves as a form of self-certification, an accreditation which truncates further inquiry.

If the employment of the fact/value dichotomy regularly obstructs rather than facilitates the quest for truth, then that constitutes one reason for questioning its utility and for reconsidering its preservation within policy studies. One might object, however, that the abuse of a distinction, no matter how pervasive, does not challenge the validity of the distinction itself. Critics might suggest that however flawed the use of the dichotomy might be in particular cases, facts and values are ontologically disparate phenomena. On this view, the opposition between empirical and evaluative statements is grounded in the nature of the world; the demarcation of facts from values simply reflects differences which exist in reality. Thus, the dichotomy between facts and values must be preserved because it embodies an objective truth about the world.

Arguments introduced in support of the claim that the fact/value dichotomy reflects an ontological distinction often draw upon a notion of objective truth conceived as intersubjective agreement. Thus it is suggested that facts are different from values in that (1) people agree about factual statements but they do not agree about evaluative judgments;[7] and (2) in cases where people disagree about factual claims, the cause of the disagreement can be traced to errors of observation upon the part of certain individuals, and hence the disagreement could in principle be eliminated as soon as the error is identified, whereas when people disagree about values, arbitrary choices or subjective feelings are at issue, hence there is no rational way to locate the cause of the disagreement, much less to resolve the dispute among them.[8]

Neither of these claims provides sufficient ground to support an ontological distinction between facts and values. For, as even the most cursory examination of the history of science or of the history of criminal proceedings will attest, there are many instances in which no agreement exists concerning the 'facts' of a particular case, nor does any method exist which could locate the cause of such disagreement in observation error. Moreover, there are numerous evaluative judgments (e.g., that it is better to be alive than dead, that it is better to have a happy life than a wretched life, that it is better to be free to pursue one's self-determined objectives than to be manipulated and victimized by others) on which it is possible to find virtually universal agreement. Further, a range of analytic techniques is available to identify the reasons for lingering disagreement on such evaluative questions, and in some instances, to eliminate that disagreement. But even if agreement were more readily secured in questions of fact than in questions of value, the assumption that intersubjective agreement alone constitutes a demonstration of the truth of a particular claim will not withstand scrutiny. For although a consensus may help to eliminate obvious distortions and errors, it is not sufficient to prove a claim to be true: the majority might be wrong.

Because intersubjective agreement cannot guarantee the truth of any proposition, those who support the claim that facts and values are ontologically distinct frequently invoke certain precepts of positivism to reinforce their case. But there are important defects in such a strategy; chief among them is the problem of circularity. For example, one might appeal to the verification criterion of meaning to support the ontological distinction between facts and values. The verification criterion of meaning gives the fact/value dichotomy its force by defining factual statements as empirically verifiable propositions, and by defining evaluative claims as irrational sentiments or arbitrary preferences that cannot be validated by reference to empirical events. But for this very reason, it is viciously circular to reintroduce the verification criterion as proof that facts and values are ontologically distinct. At best, the positivist criterion of verification can reinforce claims about facts and values only as a matter of stipulative definition and as in the case of all stipulative definitions, this leaves the ontological question unresolved. However, since the verification criterion of meaning is self-referentially destructive, it hardly provides a firm foundation for the ontological distinction between facts and values.[9]

Recourse to the correspondence theory of truth does not fare any better. The correspondence theory of truth itself is marked by serious deficiencies, most notably that it presupposes that human knowers can grasp an independent reality without the mediation of the human mind, that there can be knowledge without human cognition. But even if it were possible to overcome the difficulties with the conceptions of perception, cognition, verification, and falsification, which have raised such serious doubts about the adequacy of the correspondence theory of truth, the appeal to the correspondence theory of truth as support for the ontological distinction between facts and values is also circular. The correspondence theory of truth depends on and gains its force in relation to an account of the world and of scientific knowledge which accepts that the world is 'naturally' bifurcated into objective phenomena amenable to sense perception and other phenomena about which the senses can provide no evidence. This tenet constitutes a fundamental presupposition which gives meaning and relevance to the entire project of empirical science. But precisely because this empiricist premise is assumed to be true in order for the correspondence theory of truth to make sense, it cannot provide independent evidence of the validity of the fact/value dichotomy. Any evidence advanced by the correspondence theory of truth in support of the ontological distinction between facts and values will be contaminated by the fundamental empiricist presupposition upon which the theory rests.

If no independent evidence can be adduced to support the claim that the fact/value dichotomy reflects a fundamental ontological distinction, if the opposition between empirical and valuative assertions gains its force only within a constellation of empiricist presuppositions devised to promote particular scientific strategies as mechanisms for the production of truth, then the usefulness of the dichotomy within that context is of paramount importance. And if, as has been suggested, equivocation surfaces with sufficient regularity in the deployment of the fact/value dichotomy to render it an obstacle to, rather than an enhancement of, efforts to discern the merits of particular claims about the world, this becomes a compelling reason to abandon attempts to classify every claim about the world as either 'factual' or 'valuative.'

Additional arguments for abandoning the fact/value dichotomy can be drawn from the central insights of post-positivist presupposition theories of science. As noted in the last chapter, presupposition theories of science have challenged the belief that it is possible to make 'purely factual' assertions. Recognition of the pervasive role of theoretical presuppositions in perception and cognition suggests that elements of description, explanation, and evaluation are thoroughly intertwined in every observation of and every assertion about the world. Attempts to force theoretically constituted and value permeated claims about objects and events into a dichotomous classification of facts or values can only succeed in suppressing awareness of the valuative components of theoretical presuppositions. The valuative dimension of theory-laden facts is not eliminated by adding a label 'purely empirical,' it is merely masked and thereby exempted from critical scrutiny. Thus a commitment to systematic inquiry, to the exhaustive examination of all dimensions of theoretically constituted claims about the world, also warrants the abandonment of the fact/value dichotomy.

And yet, it might be objected that however compelling the arguments based upon the problem of equivocation and the theory-laden nature of all empirical claims might be, it is crucial to preserve the fact/value dichotomy, to attempt to distinguish the normative from the empirical elements of any claim, because reason operates reliably only at the empirical level. Indeed, it might be suggested that in the absence of the fact/value distinction, there can be no hope for scientific knowledge about the world. For the abandonment of the fact/value dichotomy entails resignation to relativism. This objection not only fails to take seriously the implications of the theoretical constitution of facticity by suggesting that it *is* possible to eliminate the valuative component of human cognition from factual claims, but it also is informed by a discredited and overly restrictive conception of rationality, a conception which has been shown to be founded upon unwarranted optimism concerning the powers of inductive and deductive logic, to be drawn from an erroneous conception of science, and to misrepresent the diverse manifestations of reason in scientific practices as well as in daily life.[10]

Once mutually reinforcing positivist premises concerning the nature of meaning, truth, and reason have been rejected, this objection loses is force. Relativism is not the inevitable consequence of abandoning the fact/value dichotomy, nor is it the chief threat to the acquisition of knowledge within the natural science and social science disciplines.[11] A far greater threat to the development of sophistication in the understanding of the natural and social sciences is posed by adherence to the flawed fact/value dichotomy with its corollary insistence upon conceiving the world in terms of false alternatives and denying the multiple powers of reason manifested in a variety of cognitive practices. If progress is to be made in science, if more sophisticated techniques for the identification of distortion, error, and bias are to be developed, then faulty dichotomies and mystifying myths must be dispelled. Whether it be the mythical bifurcation of the world into facts and values, the myth of an unmediated reality accessible to human knowers, or the myth that reason functions only in a fictive value-free sphere, the repudiation of such notions is necessary if postpositivist policy inquiry is to overcome rather than succumb to the defects of positivism.

Beyond the Myths: Implications of the Theoretical Constitution of Human Cognition

The resilience of the fact/value dichotomy is undoubtedly related to the prevalent belief that it is a relatively easy matter to identify a 'fact', that a criterion of the empirical is readily available, that the truth conditions for empirical analysis are unproblematic, and hence the truth of empirical claims can be easily demonstrated. Unfortunately, none of these assumptions can withstand scrutiny. As Alex Michalos has pointed out, since the publication of Hempel's "Problems and Changes in the Empiricist Criterion of Meaning" in 1950, "it has been known that there is not and there is not likely to be any generally acceptable criterion of empirical meaningfulness which would allow decisive categorization of sentences as 'empirical' or 'factual.'"[12] Although verifiability, confirmability, testability, and falsifiability have all been suggested as reliable criteria for empirical meaningfulness, systematic analyses by philosophers of science have demonstrated that none of these is adequate. Moreover, "philosophy in the mid-part of the twentieth century concerned itself almost exclusively with the search for truth condition analyses . . . in the realms of perception, other minds, necessary truth, but all failed . . . virtually none was ever found."[13]

If neither a criterion of empirical meaningfulness nor the truth conditions for empirical analysis can be identified, then empirical research, whether it be in the natural or the social sciences, cannot be as unproblematic as is commonly thought. Indeed, recent work in the philosophy of science suggests that contrary to the popular belief that empirical analysis is relatively simple and straightforward, at least compared with philosophical or 'normative' analysis, the difficulties involved in the quest for truth are markedly similar in all areas of thought.[14] Attempts to grasp the 'way things are', to capture the truth about the world, whether in the physical sciences, the social sciences, or the moral sciences, encounter comparable problems and deploy parallel techniques to surmount those problems. The commonality in these various forms of inquiry is rooted in the theoretical constitution of human cognition and the theoretical mediation of all claims advanced about the world. To understand fully the implications of the theoretical constitution of knowledge, it is necessary to reconsider the nature of theory, the relation of the theoretical to the empirical, and the role of a variety of cognitive practices in structuring knowledge about the world.

Theory

The insights of the presupposition theories of science suggest that traditional accounts of theory are inadequate.[15] Although discussions and characterizations of theory are legion, the conceptions of theory most frequently encountered in the policy literature invoke distinctions between scientific theories, speculative or philosophical theories, and theories conceived in terms of ideology. Scientific theories have been variously described as interrelated sets of inductive generalizations, as systems of empirically derived scientific laws and as systems of hypotheses with predictive and explanatory power. Philosophical theories are typically depicted as systematic speculations concerning the nature and purpose of the world or of some phenomena in the world, as systematizations of experience. Theories conceived in terms of ideology are characterized as systems of belief which promote the interests of a particular group or class.[16]

Despite marked differences in the sphere of application, the authority accorded to, and the utility of these conceptions of theory, they share certain features. Each of these models conceives theory in reconstructive and instrumental terms. Theories are depicted as instruments or tools that help humans to understand their world and function in it. Within the terms set by these conceptions, theories are identified as "something to be built and applied to a prior and independently specifiable and determinate datum."[17] On this view, things exist, events occur, and then they are reflected upon. Through the process of retrospective reflection, whether aided by the experiments of science, the "arm-chair" of philosophy, or the self-interest of particular classes, a theory is created and advanced. Although retrospective and reconstructive in origin, the mark of a good theory is that it not only makes sense of the past, but it illuminates the present and provides guidance for the future. Those theories which are not good, which lack explanatory and predictive power, can be cast off. Like defective tools, they can be thrown out and replaced by better models. Thus, whether the theory under discussion is scientific, philosophical, or ideological, it is conceived as a *post hoc* creation, consciously constructed, of variable utility and subject to willed repudiation.

The alternative conception of theory suggested by presupposition theories of science conceives theory as a constellation of presuppositions that provide a context in which perception and cognition occur. Rather than being consciously created after retrospective reflection, the theoretical assumptions which organize perception and confer meaning on experience operate at a tacit or preconscious level, having been acquired through a process of indirect learning inseparable from immersion in and socialization to a particular culture.[18] For the thinking subject, theoretical presuppositions are always 'already there,' structuring perception and shaping experience.[19]

Moored in the sedimentation of meanings of specific linguistic and cultural communities, theoretical presuppositions sustain a substantive understanding of reality with innumerable pragmatic implications.[20] As a sedimentation of conventional attempts to comprehend the world correctly, theoretical presuppositions afford the individual a natural attitude, an attitude of suspended doubt with respect to a wide range of issues based on the conviction that one understands how the world works.[21] Conceptions of human nature, of human possibility, of the natural environment, of interpersonal and social relations, of the normal course of events, of the expected and the exceptional, of worthy ambitions and respectable conduct commingle in the theoretically constituted preconscious realm, providing the frames of reference within which the individual experiences the world. Providing a conception of how things are and how things work, theoretical presuppositions generate clear guidelines for individuals behavior.[22] For in providing a constellation of beliefs which explain the most fundamental nature of reality, theories circumscribe a particular range of actions as sensible, rational, and desirable; they endorse a repertoire of responses to specific events; thus, they provide reasons for action and standards for assessing the appropriateness of the actions undertaken.[23]

The conception of theory as a preconscious constellation of presuppositions coincides with traditional accounts of theory in suggesting that theories do help individuals to make sense of the past, to comprehend the present, and to expect certain future events. But the presupposition conception of theory disagrees with the traditional scientific, philosophical, and ideological accounts of theory about the stage at which theory enters the process of cognition. The reconstructive image of theory characteristic of traditional accounts suggests a possibility of an unmediated knowledge of the world: for in the reconstructive model the world comes first, then it is contemplated by the individual and then, the results of the individual's contemplation are systematized and put forth as a theory about that world, to be tested against the world. In contrast, the presupposition conception of theory insists that it is not possible to have the world first: all perceptions of the world and all contemplation about those perceptions are already theoretically mediated. The theoretical presuppositions acquired with language and enculturation structure even the first experience of the world.

A second major point of disagreement between traditional and presupposition conceptions of theory involves the precise relation between individuals and theories. The traditional conceptions suggest that theories are consciously created, consciously held, and that they can be consciously repudiated. Invoking metaphors of tools, instruments, or models to convey this conception, the traditional views imply that the individual's relation to theories is one of convenience. A theory is invented to help people comprehend or gain mastery over the world. If a particular theory is inadequate to that task, it can be easily discarded. Again the notion of an unmediated reality surfaces in these metaphors, suggesting that if all existing theories are defective, then the individual can repudiate them all and deal with the world directly, in a theory-free fashion. Yet, as John Gunnell has shown, those who advance instrumental conceptions of theory confront a dilemma concerning the necessity of any theory, if the world itself is accessible. It seems very odd to claim that facts can be explained only in terms of a theory, if the facts themselves are at once the source of the theory and the grounds for its dismissal. Proponents of instrumental conceptions of theory are caught in the paradox of claiming that "the world is unknowable without models, yet their validity is a matter of correspondence with a world that is necessarily distorted by their application."[24]

Presupposition conceptions of theory, on the other hand, suggest that theoretical presuppositions have their most profound influence at a preconscious level. In establishing what will be taken as normal, natural, and expected, theoretical presuppositions camouflage themselves, blurring their contributions to cognition and masking their influence on understanding. For this reason, it is very difficult to articulate the most fundamental presuppositions that structure one's thought. Efforts to crystallize these internalized commitments often produce caricatures that can be dismissed easily, having failed to capture, much less to challenge, their authentic counterparts.[25] It is for this reason as well that presupposition theorists are suspicious of traditional claims that theories are merely heuristic devices, instruments of the understanding, which can be consciously and definitively rejected.

Although it is possible to subject theoretical presuppositions to critical scrutiny, this can occur only within the context of other mutually reinforcing presuppositions. There is no process by which all theoretical presuppositions can be questioned at once: particular assumptions and beliefs can be challenged, justified, or adjusted only while others are kept constant.[26] But the tacit nature of theoretical presuppositions, as well as the mutually reinforcing relations among constellations of theoretical assumptions, makes the process of critical reflection far more complex and difficult than instrumental conceptions of theory suggest. The tacit and mutually reinforcing character of theoretical presuppositions creates a situation in which serious objections to a particular presupposition may be defused or rebutted by reference to the tenets of the theory which remain fixed at the moment of critique. Such a rebuttal of a specific objection can thus reinforce rather than challenge the system of assumptions as a whole.[27] The refutation of an objection through the introduction of evidence and arguments grounded upon mutually reinforcing presuppositions contributes to the stability of theories despite the existence of anomalies, counter-evidence, counter-arguments, and unresolved problems. The mutually reinforcing character of theoretical assumptions also helps to explain why debate among proponents of alternative theories is so often at cross-purposes.

In contrast to the notion that theories are merely heuristic models which can be easily identified, repudiated at will, or done without, presupposition theorists suggest that theoretical presuppositions constitute the ineliminable condition of human cognition. They cannot be done without because it is impossible to acquire human knowledge without them. Thus presupposition theorists attempt to replace the instrumental metaphors typical in traditional discourses on theory with alternative images which capture the centrality of theory to human understanding. Michael Polanyi's image of "indwelling" is advanced precisely to suggest this difference: theories are not mere tools or instruments which individuals use; rather they are the medium in which individuals live; they are constitutive of what individuals are and may become.[28]

Recognition of the pervasive influence of tacit theoretical presuppositions upon the perception and comprehension of objects and events does not entail solipsism, irrationalism, or relativism. Theoretical presuppositions are created socially through an extended historical process. They are acquired through a process of socialization or enculturation. Constellations of theoretical assumptions are, therefore, neither irrational nor arbitrary. On the contrary, they embody the collective wisdom of determinate traditions; they comprise the sedimented and thoroughly rational judgments of generations of people who have struggled to capture the truth about reality. Moreover, the plurality of competing theories does not prove that all constellations of theoretical presuppositions are equal, that the particular theory held by specific individuals is necessarily right for them or that there are no rational grounds on which to criticize divergent theories.[29] Despite their attempt to capture the truth about the world, constellations of theoretical presuppositions may be flawed in fundamental ways and these flaws may be demonstrable through a process of rational argumentation.

Theories conceived as constellations of interrelated presuppositions which exude substantive beliefs about reality are world-guided. Rooted in the sedimented meanings of particular linguistic and cultural communities, they afford alternative conceptions of the conditions of and possibilities for human existence. Yet in drawing on the collected wisdom of determinate traditions and reaching out to grasp the truth about the world, theories still involve simplifications which are necessarily selective. Both constellations of theoretical presuppositions and the claims about the world which they sustain are partial and incomplete. For this reason, alternative theoretical formulations are always possible.[30] Moreover, because the world is richer than any particular theory, because theories are underdetermined by evidence, constellations of theoretical presuppositions are contentious. That theories aspire to provide the truth about the world does not constitute a guarantee of success nor does it imply that all attempts to get the world right are equally successful.[31]

Presupposition theorists have suggested that an acknowledgment of the tacit and mutually reinforcing nature of theoretical presuppositions, a recognition of their relation to specific historical traditions, and a comprehension of the partiality and incompleteness which comprise their perennial character are essential for an adequate understanding of the rational criteria available for the examination and critique of competing theories. The judgments involved in the critical examination of theoretical presuppositions are complex and the standards of assessment multiple.[32] Consideration of the internal consistency and coherence of basic theoretical assumptions must be supplemented by assessments of the depth of their explanatory power and the richness of their insights. Attention must be given to the range of issues illuminated by one theory that remain mysterious or unexplained by other accounts. A theory's ability to explain actions and events which are neglected by alternative formulations must be assessed in relation to its predictions. Specific claims concerning universal laws or predictions of invariant relations must be considered in relation to phenomena which appear to deviate from these specifications. Moreover, the scope of a theory's explanatory power and its predictive force must be assessed in light of its own significant omissions, of that which is neglected, of that which cannot be articulated, explained or understood within the frames set by its presuppositions. In addition, theoretical presuppositions must be judged in terms of the world they envision and the life they make possible, in terms of their implications for a way of being in the world, for self-understanding, and for forms of physical, interpersonal, and social life. They must be judged on the basis of the world they would

produce if significant numbers of people acted according to their precepts.

The choice of the most adequate theory available at a particular
point in history results from rational deliberation concerning the
manifold considerations stemming from the comparative assessment
of competing alternatives in light of these multiple criteria. The precise weight given to particular factors and the cumulative force of evidence and argument sustaining alternative theoretical formulations
provide space for intensive debate and disagreement. The underdeter-
mination of all theories ensures that however systematic the deliberation, however exhaustive the arguments advanced in support of one
position, considered judgments concerning the best theory will remain contentious and tentative, and will remain open to subsequent
revision on the basis of new evidence or additional arguments. The
"essentially contestable"[33] character of any such judgment does not
prove that the choice among competing theoretical accounts is not rational; nor does persistent disagreement prove that the choice is
wrong.[34] The contentious character of rational judgments is the unav-
oidable consequence of the theoretical constitution of cognition. The
reason that contestability must remain a defining characteristic of
theoretical discourse may become more apparent when the relation
between the theoretical and the empirical is considered in greater detail.

The Theoretical Constitution of the Empirical Realm

The conception of theory as a constellation of presuppositions which
structure perception and cognition challenges the possibility of unmediated knowledge of the world, as well as such concepts as 'brute
facts,' the 'immediately given,' the 'innocent eye,' 'neutral observation language,' 'theory-free research,' and 'self-evident truths' which
suggest that possibility. Because cognition is always theoretically
mediated, the world captured in human knowledge and designated
'empirical' is itself theoretically constituted. Divergent cognitive
practices rooted in conventions such as comon sense, religion, science, philosophy, and the arts, construe the empirical realm differently, identifying and emphasizing various dimensions, accrediting
different forms of evidence, different criteria of meaning, different
standards of explanation, different tokens of truthfulness. An understanding of the theoretical constitution of the empirical realm in the
context of specific cognitive practices requires a reformulation of the
notion of facts. A fact is a theoretically constituted proposition, sup-

ported by theoretically mediated evidence and put forward as part of a theoretical formulation of reality. A fact is a contestable component of a theoretically constituted order of things.[35]

To suggest that all knowledge of the empirical realm and all claims about the empirical realm are theoretically constituted, indeed to say that what is called the 'empirical realm' is structured by theoretical presuppositions, is not to say that the external world is a mental fiction.[36] It is simply to assert that it is impossible for humans to grasp external reality without the mediation of the human mind. Nor is it the case that to accept that human cognition occurs in the context of conventionally generated theoretical presuppositions acquired in the course of learning a language and a culture is to suggest that an individual's understanding of reality is permanently confined to the system of theoretical presuppositions internalized during infancy and early childhood.[37] Through participation in divergent social and cultural practices and through encounters with different cognitive traditions, it is possible to gain critical distance from the natural attitude, to begin to recognize how the domain of facticity is constituted within particular conventional contexts.[38]

But increasing awareness of the theoretical constitution of the empirical realm, of the presuppositions which circumscribe what is believed to exist and the mechanisms by which facticity is accredited and rendered unproblematic is not the same thing as escaping theoretical presuppositions altogether.[39] The presupposition conception of theory suggests that the notions of unmediated reality, the belief in the immediate grasp of reality without the mediation of cognitive presuppositions, or of pure self-transparency, the belief in the possibility of perfect comprehension of all mediating assumptions, are fictions which serve only to obfuscate the fundamental conditions of human cognition and to promote uncritical arrogance with respect to specific knowledge claims.

Critical perspective may be gained by comparing and contrasting the observations, concepts, standards, and problems sustained by divergent theoretical formulations in particular contexts. The interrelated issues of theoretically mediated evidence, arguments, and implications can be rationally adjudicated by examining them in light of questions raised in a determinate situation. Using analytic and methodological techniques drawn from a variety of conventional cognitive traditions when considering particular issues can heighten the sophistication of critical assessments. Cultivation of a capacity to move between different frames of reference, to see things differently from divergent theoretical angles, to hold certain assumptions constant while exploring the effects of alternative theoretical formulations, and to exercise judgment on the basis of the cumulative weight of theoretically constituted evidence, cultivated insight, and detailed argumentation constitute the best possible strategy for rational deliberation. Yet because finite human knowers cannot escape the fallibility of their condition, because they cannot eliminate the finitude of their perspective, and because they cannot eradicate the contingency which circumscribes their existence, the substantive claims about the world generated by even the most rational process of deliberation and analysis remain incomplete and open to debate and subsequent revision.

Science and philosophy, the cognitive traditions typically taken to provide a paradigm of human rationality, also operate within the constraints imposed by fallibility, finitude, and contingency. These disciplines are respected not because they can produce theory-free descriptions, neutral explanations, or error-free analyses, but rather because of the sophistication with which they assess evidence, the exhaustiveness with which they examine available alternatives, and the systematicity of the arguments which they offer to support their conclusions. Science and philosophy are admired because of the arsenal of conventional techniques which they have generated to probe the adequacy of theoretical suppositions. Their demarcations of the empirical realm carry force precisely because they provide detailed justifications for viewing the world in a particular way. But the justifications they advance depend on contentious presuppositions which can be challenged, subjected to scrutiny, and overturned. Neither science nor philosophy "provides an ultimate description of the world, nor a description of the world in itself."[40]

Science and philosophy are conventional cognitive practices which have achieved paradigmatic status, in part because they have endorsed standards which demand critical examination of all empirical (and ontological) claims and intensive debate and deliberation upon all theoretically generated substantive propositions. The reasons that these cognitive practices have flourished are also the reasons that their tasks will never be completed. That contentious theoretical presuppositions have been identified, discredited, and replaced with alternatives by scientists and philosophers does not imply that transtheoretical or atheoretical truth has been attained. The contours of the empirical world accredited by science and by philosophy are established by the critical judgments of practitioners

working within these traditions in specific historical contexts. Even
the most sophisticated of these formulations remains open to challenge and revision by other practitioners in these fields.

Cognitive Practices

To take the implications of the theoretical constitution of human cognition seriously is to realize that there are far greater commonalities
among disciplines conventionally organized in terms of the humanities, the natural sciences, and the social sciences than is commonly
thought.[41] All are conventional practices with determinate historical
traditions.[42] All offer theoretically constituted conceptions of the
world, supported by theoretically mediated evidence and validated by
theoretically generated testing procedures. All organize perception
according to theoretically structured criteria of meaning, conceptions
of experience, and standards of evidence. All engage in a variety of discursive activities designed to disseminate their accredited conception of the world and to legitimate their cognitive practices. All generate a hierarchy of practitioners, ranked in relation to degrees of expertise and technical mastery of disciplinary concepts and techniques, in
accordance with standards of excellence internal to and parasitic
upon disciplinary practices. All attempt to recruit new practitioners
and to train them through a process of immersion in the tradition, involving explicit mastery of disciplinary principles and techniques,
and tacit internalization of the standards of judgment and criteria of
assessment deemed appropriate to the discipline. All disciplines endeavor to safeguard their practices from abuse by charlatans and im-
postors. All strive to increase the sophistication of their knowledge by
purging misinterpretations, misrepresentations, and misunderstand-
ings through a continuing process of critical examination, debate, and
deliberation among practitioners in the field.

The cognitive practices developed within the humanities, the
natural sciences, and the social sciences are eminently rational.
In construing the world in accordance with their disciplinary presuppositions, they marshal evidence, they deploy various forms of
explanation, they use a wide range of critical techniques to assess alternative views, they exercise deliberative judgment, and they devise discursive strategies to identify error and dispel distortion.
Whether one considers the humanities, the natural sciences, or the
social sciences, the variety of methodologies, the range of analytic
techniques, and the repertoire of investigative strategies developed
within these disciplines testify to the commitment to comprehend

the world correctly, to grasp the truth of existence.

Recognition of the commonalities of these diverse cognitive practices renders many of the grounds typically advanced for distinguishing among them suspect. Attempts to establish a dichotomous opposition between science and all the other disciplines whether on the ground that science deals with facts and the others deal with values, or because science grasps the world in itself while the others deal only in interpretations of the world, or because science operates in the realm of truth and the others are mired in the realm of opinion, or because the language of science is exact, formalizable, and empirically testable whereas the languages of the others are irreducibly equivocal, metaphorical and ambiguous, or because science is a thoroughly rational enterprise and the others are not, will not withstand scrutiny.[43] Awareness of the structuring role of theoretical presuppositions in all scientific endeavors and the resulting contestability of all scientific claims causes these dichotomous criteria of demarcation to break down. The diverse cognitive practices conventionally classified as humanities, social sciences, and natural sciences operate under the same constraints. The absence of absolute and infallible standards is as characteristic of mathematics and the natural sciences as it is of philosophy and the humanities.[44] The persistence of partiality, contestability, and incompleteness (the legacy of human cognition) is as pervasive in the sphere of the sciences as it is in all other spheres of human cognition.

There are of course many differences among these diverse disciplines, differences which cannot be reduced to any binary opposition.[45] Differences among the sciences are as pronounced as the differences between the sciences and the humanities. Differences within a particular science, between the most gifted practitioners and those who are less competent, can be far more marked than the differences across disciplinary boundaries. Recognition of the theoretical constitution of human cognition suggests that the differences among these many practices must be grasped in their complexity and must be conceived in terms of pluralities rather than dichotomies. For the differences which are central to these diverse cognitive practices and which provide the criteria for distinguishing among them are related inextricably to the questions which they have raised, the angle of vision which they have cultivated, the kinds of knowledge which they have sought, the concepts, methods, and techniques which they have generated to advance that knowledge, and the characterizations of the world which they have developed.

The exalted status of science in the contemporary world tends to mask both the commonalities among cognitive practices and the enormous range of differences among and within discrete disciplines. Calls for greater attention to these underlying commonalities and for heightened sensitivity to this plurality of differences have been a recurrent motif in the works of presupposition theories of science that seek to revive a conception of science as a more human and more fallible practice. In stressing the similarities between scientific practices and other forms of human cognition, in identifying the commonalities between scientific rationality and the practical reason manifested in manifold disciplines and in the pragmatic judgments of every day life, in emphasizing the fallibility of the scientific constitution of the empirical realm, presupposition theories of science restore an understanding of the contentious and tentative nature of scientific claims. Presupposition theorists caution against excessive optimism toward the powers of science, suggesting that the heroic image of science is founded upon the mistaken belief that truth is already possessed by the scientific community. And they warn against the equally flawed notion that once science speaks, no further issues remain to be resolved, no other questions need be asked.

Implications for Policy Analysis

An understanding of the theoretical constitution of human cognition and of the manifold ways in which theory structures all claims about the empirical realm has important implications for the conduct of policy analysis. Most of the current work in the policy disciplines rests on epistemological and methodological assumptions which have been discredited by post-positivist presupposition theories of science. Failure to recognize the grave deficiences of positivist conceptions of science poses several dangers for policy inquiry. Unquestioned allegiance to verificationism and falsificationism sustains unwarranted confidence in the conclusiveness of findings generated by quantitative analysis. Uncritical acceptance of a conception of objectivity rooted in a mistaken notion of value-neutrality blinds analysts to the tacit theoretical assumptions which structure their work. Rigid adherence to the misguided fact/value dichotomy masks the valuative component of all policy research, while simultaneously eliminating crucial issues from the legitimate sphere of policy inquiry. An excessively restrictive conception of rationality renders policy analysts impotent when confronted with the most pressing political problems, even as it fosters a false sense of certainty about putative scientific laws.

If policy analysis is to transcend the problematic presuppositions of positivism, it must be prepared to reassess some of its most
prized principles. The fact/value dichotomy, the conception of empirical theory, the assumption that the demarcation of the empirical
realm is unproblematic, the many manifestations of the myth of the
given, the instrumental conception of reason, and the emotivist and
prescriptivist conceptions of value must all be reconsidered. In addition, the belief that confessional statements of value preferences and
a division of labor between empirical policy analysis and normative
policy analysis (or applied ethics) can sufficiently deal with theoretically constituted and value-permeated facticity must be rejected.

If the theoretical constitution of the empirical realm is to be
taken seriously, then the techniques of policy analysis must be recon-
structed in order to probe the presuppositions which structure perceptions, organize facticity, and accredit events as normal, natural, and
expected. Much greater sophistication must be cultivated in the
analysis of contentious definitions, controversial evidence, contestable explanations, and disputable arguments. Much greater attention
must be paid to the theoretical assumptions which structure political
discourse, subtly shaping the perception of policy alternatives, unob-
trusively altering available options, narrowly circumscribing the
range of choice, and imperceptibly delimiting decisions.

A policy analysis attuned to the theoretical constitution of facticity must direct its critical investigations toward dimensions of the
policy process which are overlooked or even rendered invisible by the
myth of the given. In seeking to answer questions which remain un-
asked by the prevailing models of policy analysis, theoretically
sophisticated policy analysis must aspire to illuminate the complex
interactions between theoretical commitments and political possibilities. In pursuing a more comprehensive range of questions, a
theoretically informed policy analysis must strive to identify the extensive grounds for contention which arise from the theoretical presuppositions, the conceptual commitments, the methodological assumptions, the disciplinary practices, and the rhetorical strategies intimately intertwined in policy debates.

In taking the insights of presupposition theories of science to
heart, a post-positivist policy analysis must be acutely aware of the
political dimensions of scientific investigation. It must draw upon an
understanding of the essential contestability of scientific formulations in order to consider the political character of allegedly neutral
scientific policy prescriptions.[46] In seeking to illuminate the range of
contestable issues which surround policy questions, post-positivist

policy science must reconceive the nature of its task. For once the contestable and, hence, political dimensions of cognitive practices are comprehended, the task of scientific policy analysis can no longer be understood as the identification of scientifically validated policy options sufficient to eliminate the burden of choice from political decision-makers. Recognition of the theoretically constituted and essentially contestable character of empirical claims requires policy analysis to understand its task in terms of identifying the diverse dimensions of debate pertinent to particular policy questions. Identifying the areas of contention related to theoretical assumptions and methodological commitments, as well as to popular political principles, will enable policy analysis to facilitate rather than to supplant informed political choice.

In the context of particular policy issues, each of the next four chapters will demonstrate the kinds of questions, the forms of investigation, and the range of issues pertinent to, as well as the potential utility of, policy analysis attuned to the theoretical constitution of cognition and to the theoretical mediation of empirical claims.

5

Identifying and Assessing Theoretical Presuppositions: The Case of Affirmative Action

IT HAS been suggested that recognition of the theoretical constitution of facticity requires the reorientation of policy analysis. Rather than accept the facts as given, policy analysts must investigate the means by which theoretical presuppositions shape what is perceived as a fact, what combinations of facts are perceived as a political problem, and what alternative courses of action are identified as possible political remedies. This chapter examines the influence of theoretical presuppositions on the perception of racial and sexual discrimination in the contemporary United States. It examines the manner in which a constellation of tacit presuppositions concerning the nature of individuality has a profound affect not only on the arguments advanced concerning appropriate remedies for discrimination, but also on the most fundamental perception of the facts of the case; that is, upon the perception of the existence of discrimination as a political problem in the late twentieth-century United States.[1] The operation of these theoretical assumptions can be documented by examining the arguments concerning affirmative action advanced by politicians, scholars, and jurists, for it is in these debates that divergent understandings of individuality are articulated in detail.

The debate over the legitimacy of affirmative action[2] and the related issues of preferential treatment[3] and reverse discrimination[4] has steadily intensified during the two decades since the program's inception. Arguments supporting and denouncing the government policy have been aired in scholarly journals, in court cases, and in the chambers of the U.S. Congress. Proponents have attempted to justify this governmental program as a mechanism of compensatory justice affording benefits to individuals as a counterbalance to burdens and injuries previously imposed, as an instrument of distributive justice intended to eliminate inequities in the distribution of income, power, education, and other social benefits, and as a way to maximize social utility by reducing poverty and its attendant evils, using human resources and talents more efficiently, and providing needed services for the economically disadvantaged. Opponents have castigated the program for being overinclusive (providing compensation to individuals who have suffered no personal injury), underinclusive (failing to compensate victims of discrimination who are not members of targeted minority groups), and for sacrificing individual rights to an ill-conceived notion of social justice. These various political and moral arguments have in turn been related to constitutional issues in an effort to establish either the constitutional permissibility of affirmative action in terms of the state's compelling interest in social justice, or the impermissibility of the program as a violation of the individual's right to the equal protection of the law.

The intensity of this debate among politicians, scholars, and jurists committed to constitutionalism, justice, and the protection of individual rights may be illuminated by considering divergent assumptions about the fundamental nature of individuality, which underlie opposing views. Two different conceptions of individuality, replete with presuppositions about the nature of individual identity and individual freedom, and about the relationship of the individual to other people, to social groups, and to impersonal forces, surface in the arguments surrounding affirmative action. Opponents of affirmative action posit a model of *atomistic individuality*, which is characterized by the belief that identity is a matter of individual choice and will, unconstrained by racial, sexual, or cultural experiences, and that freedom consists in the absence of external coercion. Proponents of affirmative action tacitly adopt a conception of *socialized individu-*

ality which emphasizes the impact of cultural norms and group practices on the development of individual identity, and the pervasive influence of internal and external obstacles on the possibility of individual freedom.

The tacit acceptance of these divergent conceptions of individuality structures the very capacity to perceive the existence of discrimination in the contemporary United States and hence affects the assessment of the need for a remedy and of the propriety of affirmative action as such a remedy. This chapter will begin with a demonstration of the means by which these competing conceptions of individuality mediate the perception of discrimination and shape the moral and constitutional arguments concerning affirmative action as a remedy for discrimination. It will then examine the theoretical adequacy of these divergent conceptions of individuality in order to assess the merits of several arguments central to the affirmative action debate.

Conflicting Conceptions of Individuality

Individualism, as a social doctrine, asserts the moral primacy of the individual in society and recognizes the right of the individual to freedom and self-realization. Yet, what it means to be an individual, the processes by which individual identity is constituted, the nature of the individual's relation to other people and to social institutions, and the scope and depth of self-realization, may be topics of debate among those equally committed to the protection of individualism.[5] Those who understand individuality in terms of atomistic individualism and those who conceive individuality in terms of socialized individualism are equally committed to the protection and enhancement of individual freedom. They differ, however, in their understandings of the constitution of individual identity and the elements of individual liberty.

The Conception of Atomistic Individuality

The atomistic conception envisions the individual as radically independent, in the sense that the individual exists as a self-determining entity, motivated solely by desires and aversions which are subjectively determined and relatively fixed.[6] Individuals differ from one another both in the objects they desire and in the amount of effort which they expend to satisfy their desires. Indeed, it is precisely the subjective determination of desire and the particular degree of success with which the individual satisfies desires which comprise the individual's uniqueness.

According to the atomistic conception, a scarce supply of most goods dictates that competition will characterize the relations among individuals as they strive to satisfy their desires, and that the outcome of such competition will be largely zero-sum. But the atomistic conception of individuality posits that all individuals are endowed with fairly equal capacities and, therefore, have an equal opportunity to emerge victorious from the throes of competition. Given the assumption of fairly equal natural assets, differences in outcome can be attributed solely to variations in individual effort. But because intensity of effort is a matter of individual choice, and because an individual who chooses to work hard can scarcely be faulted for achieving a great deal, the unequal outcome of the competitive process is morally justifiable. Success is a function of individual initiative and effort, and is, consequently, deserved.[7]

The atomistic conception of the individual understands self-realization in terms of the satisfaction of subjectively determined desires. To attain full self-actualization, individuals must devote their energies toward the achievement of success through competition. Precisely because scarcity and competition are accepted as given within this frame of reference, obstacles to self-realization are defined in terms of external constraints intentionally imposed by other human beings to thwart the individual's success. Thus, the individual is free in the absence of the willful coercion of other persons.

According to the tenets of atomistic individualism, human freedom is not incompatible with subjection to objective external forces, as long as these objective forces are 'impersonal,' such as the products of the market's Invisible Hand. Although the market is acknowledged as a stern task master, its functioning is deemed essential to the distribution of economic rewards on the basis of individual effort. On this view, individuals may freely reap the rewards of their hard work, if and only if, the market distribution is safeguarded. For the only alternative to the market is the arbitrary command of some self-serving individual whose decisions would undermine the very possibility of freedom.

Man in a complex society can have no choice between adjusting himself to what seem to be the blind forces of the social process and obeying the orders of a superior. So long as he knows only the hard discipline of the market, he may well think the direction by some other human brain preferable; but when he tries it, he soon discovers that the former still leaves him at least some choice, while the latter leaves him none and that it is better to have a choice between several unpleasant alternatives than being coerced into one.[8]

When the options available to individuals are construed this narrowly, either subordination to the command of a fallible decision-maker or open competition with the prospect of unlimited success, it is clear that only the latter sustains a conception of meaningful freedom. Thus it is not surprising that the market is depicted as a precondition of freedom, "so essential that it must not be sacrificed to the gratification of our sense of justice or of envy."[9]

Within the parameters of the atomistic conception then, the individual is 'self-made.' Individual identity reflects choices determined by subjective desires and manifested in acts of will and degrees of effort. Freedom consists in the power to do or forbear according to one's subjectively determined desires and aversions, unconstrained by other human beings. And self-realization is nothing more than success in the competition for necessarily scarce goods. The individual alone is responsible for choices made, for effort invested, and for the outcomes achieved, be they successes or failures. Impersonal forces mediate the competition among individuals, but because they cannot be controlled by humans and because they affect all individuals in the same neutral way, these forces cannot be considered constraints on individual freedom. Impersonal forces may establish the rules of the game, but individual effort determines specific outcomes.

The Conception of Socialized Individuality

The conception of socialized individuality is premised upon an image of society and culture as a "complex web of values, norms, roles, relationships and customs which do not merely confront the individual as external barriers or constraints, but which are internalized by individuals,"[10] shaping their self-understanding, their interests, and their desires. The individual's identity, expectations, and aspirations are formed within the context of a host of intersubjective understandings incorporated in a language, a culture, and a particular history. Whether described as a process of socialization or enculturation, individuals are taught determinate ways of being human. Although individuals are not merely passive recipients of cultural norms, their options for response to existing patterns of interaction are circumscribed by the range of possibility incorporated in the existing cultural universe. Any individual may perpetuate or repudiate dominant cultural values, but no individual can escape altogether the legacy of membership in a particular community within a specific nation at a determinate point in history.

The conception of socialized individualism suggests that freedom involves a great deal more than absence of coercion. For the individual's capacity to act freely, to choose certain options, to undertake particular risks, may be undermined by the internalization of images, insults and stigmas associated with group membership. The inculcation of cultural, ethnic, racial, or sexual norms may constitute formidable internal obstacles to individual freedom. The very meaning of self-realization may be unduly constricted by the tacit incorporation of derogatory stereotypes within the individual's self-understanding.

In addition to recognizing that certain cultural values may limit the scope of individual freedom, the conception of socialized individuality suggests that impersonal or objective forces may also be an enormous impediment to personal liberty. Rather than accept that impersonal forces, such as market mechanisms, are a necessary evil which people must accept if they desire any freedom whatsoever, the conception of socialized individualism admits the possibility that human agency may underlie objective forces. The Invisible Hand can be conceived as a cultural creation which serves the interests of some to the detriment of others. Once conceived as cultural constructs, market mechanisms too can be considered targets for political action. If particular human actions responsible for the 'blind forces of the social process' could be identified, then it is possible that the intended and unintended consequences of such behavior could be isolated and altered. Modifying individual action in order to eliminate deleterious social consequences could thereby enhance the prospects for individual freedom.

The perspective of socialized individualism acknowledges individual identity, as well as the conceptions of personal liberty and objective forces, to be social products, shaped by the beliefs and values of the prevailing culture. While such cultural constructs circumscribe the possibilities for individual choice and action, they are not invariable; they can themselves become the target for systematic criticism and reform. Existing beliefs and values may narrow the range of choice available to individuals, but they cannot foreclose choice or change altogether.

Atomistic Individuality and the Rejection
of Affirmative Action

A recurrent theme among opponents of affirmative action is the denial that discrimination in hiring, wage scales, promotion, and admissions currently exists in the United States.[11] While they acknowledge that "Blacks as a group earned less than Whites as a group and women as a group earned less than men as a group and both minorities and women were a smaller percentage of the academic and other professions than of the general population,"[12] they deny that the explanation of these facts lies in employers' or admissions officers' deliberate discrimination. They suggest that a combination of personal choices made by individuals of their own free will, and objective forces over which discrete individuals have no control, provide a more adequate explanation of these phenomena.

Opponents of affirmative action typically begin their arguments with a caution concerning the limits of statistical data. They point out that "superficial, raw and uninterpreted statistical data concerning the relative distribution of members of minorities and women,"[13] in particular jobs are not sufficient to prove that intentional discrimination has occurred. Statistics cannot prove discrimination, because proof of discrimination requires a demonstration of intentional exclusion of particular individuals by particular individuals. As a descriptive indicator which operates at the aggregate level, statistics can provide no information at all about individual intentions. Thus, any conclusion about the existence of discrimination in admissions, hiring, or promotions drawn from statistical data involves an invalid inference.

Opponents of affirmative action suggest that the problem of underrepresentation does not reflect discrimination against qualified applicants, but rather reflects the fact that women and minorities lack the requisite qualifications for certain positions, therefore, they either fail to apply, or are rightly rejected upon application. The problem is primarily one of inadequate supply of qualified women and minority applicants, not one of demand hampered by willful discrimination.[14] In its most extreme form, this view claims that not only are there too few qualified women and minority applicants in general, but also that women and minority applicants who are hired in academia, for example, are less qualified than their white male colleagues. "Blacks or female academics have a Ph.D. less than half as often as the rest of the profession, publish less than half as many articles per person and specialize in the lowest paying fields—notably education, the social sciences and the humanities, with very few being trained in the natural sciences, medicine, law or other highly paid specialities. Thus even if no employer had a speck of prejudice, black and female academics would still have lower pay and promotion prospects."[15] A lack of qualifications impairs the employment potential of women and minorities, not discrimination.

Two factors are emphasized in explanations of the lack of qualifications among women and minorities: individual choices and objective forces. Empirical evidence is said to indicate that women and minority individuals freely choose career patterns which differ from those of white males, and "this crucial element of individual choice is routinely ignored in syllogistic arguments that go directly from statistical 'underrepresentation' to 'exclusion' or 'discrimination'."[16] A second approach to the explanation of lack of qualifications emphasizes the operation of certain objective forces typically described as the "lack of equitable social, economic and educational stimuli or opportunities, for which the entire community must accept blame,"[17] or the pervasive effect of social attitudes concerning the proper role of women and minorities. But whether social attitudes or the absence of social, economic, and educational opportunities is responsible for the dearth of qualified female and minority applicants, affirmative action is clearly a misguided and inappropriate remedy.

Affirmative action is designed as a social policy to end intentional discrimination in admission, employment, pay, promotion, etc. Since any underrepresentation which currently exists can at best be described as the unintended consequence of social attitudes and is not related to any deliberate policies of discrimination, the disease and the cure are mismatched. The basic lack of correspondence between problem and solution stems from the failure to draw an important distinction between problems caused by deliberate individual actions, which are susceptible to solutions aimed at specific individuals, and problems caused by impersonal and objective social forces, for which no individual can justly be held accountable.

Imbued with the perspective of atomistic individualism, critics of affirmative action argue that since the lack of requisite qualifications is the unfortunate consequence of pervasive social attitudes, it falls under the category of objective forces which lie beyond the scope of political remedies. Solutions to problems rooted in impersonal social processes are extraordinarily complex and elusive, and, unfortunately, political efforts to implement them frequently degenerate into hapless social engineering which strips individuals of their freedom and autonomy. If individual freedom is not to be sacrificed, the most acceptable remedies for problems caused by objective forces must be recognized as time and education: with time and increasing education, social attitudes can be expected to change. Education affords a comprehensive remedy which can influence the values and choices of the entire community contributing to the elimination of all prejudice over time. Further, as the level of education of all community members is raised, the education level and qualifications of women and minority group members will be raised simultaneously, thereby eliminating the inadequate supply of qualified female and minority applicants.

Affirmative action, on the other hand, is a thoroughly inappropriate remedy for a problem caused by impersonal social forces, for it arbitrarily imposes responsibility for a collective problem on specific individuals. It requires preferential treatment for 'unqualified' women and minority group applicants, and consequently, it discriminates in reverse against the 'best qualified' candidates who just happen to be nonminority men. Such reverse discrimination is all the more intolerable because it is not the result of the market's Invisible Hand, but the clear manifestation of government bureaucrats' attempts to impose their subjective vision of the good upon society at large. The bureaucracy's usurpation of the "power of judge, jury, accuser and patron combined"[18] places universities and employers in the position of having to placate federal officials under penalty of loss of federal contracts vital to their very survival. Thus, bureaucratic whim becomes a tyrannical task master, stripping would-be federal contractors of their autonomy and their fidelity to standards of pure meritocratic excellence.

Having diagnosed the cause of underrepresentation as an insufficient supply of qualified women and minority applicants, opponents of affirmative action insist that affirmative action is synonymous with reverse discrimination: government policies necessitate the use of quotas, the hiring of less qualified candidates, the obliteration of merit as a criteria of desert, and consequently, the sacrifice of creative, hard-working individuals. Since qualified women and minority applicants are not available according to this analysis of the facts, it follows that school administrators and employers must engage in all these abuses in order to increase the number of women and blacks in their institutions as a demonstration to the government of their good faith. Giving less qualified women and minority group members preference in admissions, hiring, and promotion can only result in new forms of discrimination which will entail "the erosion of the principles of merit, scholarly quality, and integrity . . . which is not only unconstitutional, but immoral, for it makes mockery of the principle of desert which was the basis of denunciation of past discriminatory practices."[19]

Opponents of affirmative action also argue that it is naive to believe that reverse discrimination can remedy the current effects of past discrimination. On the contrary, they assert that it can only create further injustices:

> The belief that discrimination can be administered to the body politic in judicious doses in order to create non-discrimination is akin to the medical wisdom of curing an alcoholic with whiskey. Discrimination is addictive. Its use cannot be precisely controlled . . . [It is wrong] to imagine that one discrimination can compensate for another. Discrimination causes individuals to suffer. If they can be individually compensated, well and good. But compensating their grandchildren at the cost of discriminating against someone else does not compensate them in the slightest. It does replace private discrimination (or at least supplement it) with public discrimination, sanctioned by the laws. It also sets up another imaginary debt for the social engineer, whose successors will one day have to compensate the grandchild of the one victimized today, at the expense of the one benefitted today.[20]

These objections to reverse discrimination express the belief of many opponents of affirmative action: that in the absence of deliberate discriminatory policies in the contemporary United States, the only possible moral justification for the government's policies is compensatory justice for groups. They suggest that "the entire early federal affirmative action drive was motivated and stimulated by the history of three hundred years of injustice against blacks. Only after the argument for reparation to blacks had prevailed as the single determining factor of overriding importance in justifying a temporary preferential treatment for aggrieved groups were the programs for minorities implemented. Women were added later."[21] Yet this concept of compensatory justice to groups for past injustices suffered by them as groups is completely foreign to the notions of morality associated with atomistic individualism. Not surprisingly then, opponents of reverse discrimination have little difficulty identifying sufficient deficiencies in the arguments for compensatory justice to sustain its rejection.

The assault on compensatory justice for groups frequently begins with a brief reference to Aristotle, who orginally formulated the concept of compensatory justice as a rectifying or reparatory transaction between one person and another. The goal of corrective justice was to impose a penalty upon the party who inflicted the injury, and to confer a corresponding benefit upon the injured individual in order to restore the kind of equality which existed prior to the injury. Aristotle envisioned a close correspondence or proportionality between the harm suffered and the compensation received. Those who advocate affirmative action as a mechanism of compensatory justice stray markedly from Aristotle's ideals. They insist upon blanket preferential treatment for certain persons on the basis of race, sex, or minority group membership, even if those persons did not personally suffer past injustices. Thus, preferential treatment for groups as a social policy is notoriously overinclusive. But it is simultaneously underinclusive: while providing compensation only for specific groups, it ignores the claims of other individuals who have personally suffered injustice yet are not members of the groups targeted for compensation. Further, reverse discrimination imposes the cost of compensation upon individuals who did not perpetrate the injustice and who cannot fairly be dubbed beneficiaries of the injustice, since they neither sought the benefit nor had the opportunity to reject it; in other words, reverse discrimination imposes the cost of compensation upon innocent parties. Thus, reverse discrimination can be faulted as arbitrary both in the distribution of benefits to the disadvantaged, and in the assignment of the costs of compensation.[22] And such rampant arbitrariness seriously impairs any moral justification for affirmative action.

According to opponents, reverse discrimination's most heinous crime is that is substitutes concern with "abstract groups and their purported rights," for concern with the atomistic individual. It violates the "essence of liberalism which has always been concerned with the welfare, rights, and responsibilities of individuals *qua* individuals, not the masses or classes or other such linguistic abstractions."[23] Those who accept the atomistic conception of the individual cannot make sense out of claims that certain groups have inflicted and continue to inflict sufferings upon other groups, much less that individuals experience injury as members of distinctive groups and therefore deserve to receive compensation as members of the group. Focusing solely upon individuals who 'make themselves,' they reject any notion of a legacy of group injury, just as they reject any notion of collective guilt on the part of the group which historically imposed the suffering. They argue instead that preferential treatment for specific groups violates the "spirit of the laws, the Constitution and the Declaration of Independence which assert that governments are created to assure individuals (not groups) the retention of their inalienable natural rights, one of which is the pursuit of happiness."[24]

On this view, to endorse a policy of preferential treatment for groups would be to subordinate individuals' rights to equal treatment to the broader social aim of making amends for a past injustice which contemporary individuals did not perpetrate, a policy which is clearly unconstitutional. According to the opponents of affirmative action, justice can require nothing more than the use of neutral principles, such as nondiscrimination, in admissions and employment. Since deliberate discrimination is not a contemporary problem, the use of neutral principles will promote meritocratic decisions and simultaneously accord justice to individuals, regardless of the group to which they happen to belong. For it will allow each individual to "make it" independently.

Under the Equal Protection clause of the Fourteenth Amendment, the constitutional permissibility of differential treatment for different groups hinges upon the demonstration of relevant grounds for the difference in treatment. Moreover, in cases which involve a suspect classification, such as race, the state must show not only that there are relevant grounds to sustain the use of the classification, but that the state has a *compelling interest* in achieving the ends which the classification is devised to facilitate, and that no alternative and less harmful means are available to achieve the same end.

For those who accept a conception of atomistic individualism, compelling state interest constitutes an exceptionally stringent standard which can legitimize overriding individual rights only in the most desperate circumstances, such as a war-time emergency.[25] Indeed, Chief Justice Burger argued in his dissent in *Dunn v. Blumstein* that no state law has ever "satisfied this seemingly insurmountable standard."[26] It is not surprising then that numerous Constitutional scholars, as well as Justice Powell speaking for the Supreme Court majority in *Regents of the University of California v. Bakke,*[27] have argued that preferential treatment also fails to satisfy this insurmountable standard.

Justice Powell acknowledged that, in the past, the Court had ordered extreme remedies involving preferential treatment and the use of quotas in cases in which there had been a judicial or administrative finding of intentional discrimination on the part of employers, unions, or school authorities. However, in the case of the University of California Davis Medical School, he argued, "there has been no determination by the legislature or a responsible administrative agency that the University engaged in a discriminatory practice requiring remedial efforts."[28] Moreover, underrepresentation could not be accepted as a demonstration of a policy of discrimination. The fact that in the two years prior to the establishment of a special admissions program for minorities and the economically disadvantaged, only two Blacks and one Mexican-American had been admitted to the medical school, while in the four years of program operation twenty-six Blacks, thirty-three Mexican-Americans and one American Indian had been admitted, did not prove that exclusion of minorities had been based upon racial grounds. On the contrary, Justice Powell cited a study published in the *New England Journal of Medicine* which attributed the underrepresentation of blacks in medical schools to "the small size of the national pool of qualified black applicants," and which endorsed pre-college remedial programs for blacks as an appropriate remedy.[29]

Given the Court's conviction that no intentional discrimination had occurred, Justice Powell examined the claim that it was "societal discrimination" that warranted a voluntary special admissions program for minority applicants. Rejecting societal discrimination as "an amorphous concept of injury that may be ageless in its reach into the past,"[30] Justice Powell asserted that there is "nothing in the Constitution [which] supports the notion that individuals may be asked to suffer otherwise impermissible burdens in order to enhance the societal standing of ethnic groups."[31] In the absence of proof of intentional discrimination, "it cannot be said that the government has any greater interest in helping one individual than in refraining from harming another."[32] Thus, Justice Powell concluded that "the purpose of helping certain groups whom the faculty of the Davis Medical School *perceived* as victims of 'societal discrimination' does not justify a classification that imposes disadvantages upon persons like the respondent [Bakke] who bear no responsibility for whatever harm the beneficiaries of the special admissions program are *thought* to have suffered."[33]

Echoing the assumptions of atomistic individualism, Justice Powell's decision insisted that discrimination is not the problem, that the Davis preferential treatment policy is an inappropriate and unconstitutional remedy, and that discussions of societal discrimination conjure images wholly at odds with the atomistic assessment of what it takes to succeed: individual will and initiative. Thus, Justice Powell concluded his decision with a reaffirmation of the atomistic principle that applicants should be treated as individuals in the admissions process. While race or sex might be important factors in considering a par-

ticular individual's merits, they must not be given undue weight. In a
"nation of minorities" where the "white 'majority' itself is composed
of various minority groups, most of which can lay claim to a history of
prior discrimination at the hands of the state and private individuals,"[34] it is the individual and not the group who should be carefully
considered. Race, ethnic background, or sex should be considered on
the same footing as other qualities, such as "exceptional personal talents, unique work or service experience, leadership potential, maturity, demonstrated compassion, a history of overcoming disadvantage,
ability to communicate with the poor or other qualifications deemed
important"[35] in any selection process. Open competition among
talented and ambitious individuals ought not to be corrupted with
arbitrary standards imposed by misguided administrators. No
bureaucratic obstacles should interfere with the free rein of individual will and initiative.[36]

In a number of subsequent decisions involving the limits of permissible affirmative action programs, assumptions concerning atomistic individualism have also been manifested in the Court's rulings.
Central to the determination of these cases has been the question of
the existence of discrimination. The Court has repeatedly maintained that only after a judicial or administrative finding that intentional and systematic exclusion of minorities or women has occurred
does the state have a sufficiently weighty interest to warrant the remedial use of an affirmative action plan.

In *Wygant v. Jackson Board of Education*, the Court again af-
firmed that in the absence of a specific finding of prior discrimination,
voluntary affirmative action programs which detrimentally affected
the employment of white individuals were unconstitutional.[37] Speaking for the majority, Justice Powell again asserted that claims concerning societal discrimination were insufficient to justify a policy which
used a racial classification. Rejecting the arguments advanced by the
Jackson County school board that the state had a compelling interest
in eliminating societal discrimination, and that the maintenance of a
presence of black teachers in the schools to serve as role models served
that interest, Justice Powell noted that "societal discrimination,
without more, is too amorphous a basis for finding race conscious
state action and for imposing a racially classified remedy."[38]

Less than a year after the ruling in *Wygant*, the Court handed
down a decision in *Johnson v. Transportation Agency of Santa Clara
County* that involved the charge of reverse discrimination on the
basis of sex rather than race.[39] Because sex is not a suspect classification requiring the same standard of scrutiny as race, and because

Johnson was argued solely on the grounds afforded by Title VII of the Civil Rights Act, rather than raising issues concerning the Equal Protection Clause, the Court ruled it permissible to consider the sex of a job applicant as one qualification among others in promotion cases pertaining to traditionally segregated job classifications. The majority ruling in this case provoked trenchant dissents by Justices White, Rehnquist, and Scalia, dissents which reiterated some of the central tenets of atomistic individualism.

Labeling the majority's decision a "perversion of Title VII," Justice White castigated the majority for altering the meaning of "traditionally segregated jobs." For rather than link the notion of traditionally segregated jobs to a judicial finding of intentional and systematic exclusion by employers or unions, the majority "interprets it now to mean nothing more than a manifest imbalance between one identifiable group and another in an employer's labor force."[40] On Justice White's view, the Court had fallen into the marked error of assuming that statistical underrepresentation could afford proof of discrimination.

The dissent of Justice Scalia (concurred in by Chief Justice Rehnquist and Justice White) was more detailed. Arguing that the Transportation Agency's affirmative action plan "was assuredly not to remedy prior sex discrimination in the Agency . . . because there was no prior discrimination to remedy,"[41] Justice Scalia insisted that the absence of any women working in skilled craft positions could not be taken as evidence of discrimination. Indeed, he suggested that "it is absurd to think that the nationwide failure of road maintenance crews, for example, to achieve the Agency's ambition of 36.4% female representation is attributable primarily, if even substantially, to systematic exclusion of women eager to shoulder the pick and shovel."[42] On the contrary, he argued that the absence of women was simply a function of individual choice linked to prevailing social attitudes: "It is a 'traditionally segregated job category' not in the Weber sense, but in the sense that because of long standing social attitudes, it has not been regarded by women themselves as desirable work."[43]

Given the absence of discrimination, the Agency's affirmative action plan did not seek to redress injuries borne by particular individuals; rather, it constituted an "engine of discrimination" created by the Agency in order to realize its "Platonic Ideal of a work force."[44] For in Justice Scalia's opinion: "In a discrimination-free world, it would obviously be a statistical oddity for every job category to match the racial and sexual composition of even that portion of the county work force qualified for that job; it would be miraculous for each of them to match, as the plan expected, the composition of the entire work force. Quite obviously the plan did not seek to replicate what a lack of discrimination would produce but rather imposed racial and sexual tailoring that would, in defiance of normal expectations and laws of probability, give each protected racial and sexual group a governmentally determined 'proper' proportion of each job category."[45]

Like other adherents of atomistic individualism, Justice Scalia argued that the use of affirmative action for "the alteration of social attitudes rather than the elimination of discrimination" constitutes nothing less than a justification for state-enforced discrimination, a discrimination which not only violates the rights of the best qualified candidates, who just happen to be white men, but a discrimination which also ensures that legitimate standards of merit and excellence will be eroded.[46] Thus, Justice Scalia noted that the "requirement that the employer take 'distinctions in qualifications into account' turns out to be an assurance, not that candidates comparative merits will always be considered, but that none of the successful candidates selected over the others solely on the basis of their sex or race will be utterly unqualified."[47] Lamenting the implications for individual rights and the future productivity of the American work force, Justice Scalia concluded his dissent by reiterating that the majority's decision mandated reverse discrimination: "A statute designed to establish a color blind and gender blind work place has thus been converted into a powerful engine of racism and sexism, not merely permitting intentional race- and sex-based discrimination, but often making it, through the operation of the legal system, practically compelled."[48]

Socialized Individuality and the Justification of Affirmative Action

Proponents of affirmative action often introduce their arguments with the assertion that "racial, sexual and no doubt other forms of discrimination are not antique relics but are living patterns which continue to warp selection and ranking procedures."[49] Rather than assume that the United States represents a just and primarily non-discriminatory society, they suggest that empirical evidence supports the belief that discrimination is currently widespread and that present discrimination differs from past discrimination only in the degree of subtlety and visibility. While this very subtlety makes present discrimination far more difficult "to prove statistically," it renders the effects of discrimination no less pernicious.

Acknowledging that statistics cannot provide definitive indicators of discrimination, proponents of affirmative action still insist that the pervasiveness of statistical underrepresentation of women and minorities in higher education, in higher paying employment, and in positions of prestige and power is sufficient to establish a *prima facie* case of discrimination.[50] But proponents of affirmative action do not rest their arguments concerning the persistence of discrimination on a demonstration of underrepresentation alone, for as their opponents have argued, any number of variables can be introduced to explain such underrepresentation. Instead, they emphasize 'underutilization' in an effort to explode the myth that the principle cause of underrepresentation is the inadequate supply of qualified women and minority applicants. "Underutilization is defined as having fewer members of the group in the category actually employed than would reasonably be expected from their availability (e.g., in universities, from the percentage of available Ph.D.s in a given field)."[51] The phenomena to be explained then, is not the dearth of minority or female professionals, *per se,* but the dearth of such professionals given the availability of a certain percentage of qualified minority and female candidates.[52] The pervasive underutilization of qualified women and minorities in the United States renders suspicious any explanation of the phenomenon that emphasizes personal choice. For it seems unlikely that individuals who have invested great effort to become qualified to apply for certain careers should suddenly choose not to pursue those professions.[53]

Having challenged the adequacy of 'personal choice' and 'lack of qualified applicant' explanations of underrepresentation, proponents of affirmative action also challenge the assumption that all individuals have an equal opportunity to compete for economic and educational benefits in the contemporary United States, and that differential rewards simply reflect differences in effort. Proponents of affirmative action argue that "background conditions, such as unequal treatment relating to occupational preparation and expectations in the course of childhood, upbringing and education, ego development, psychological counseling, technical and higher education, etc., which would make it more difficult for women and non-whites as a group than for white men as a group to succeed occupationally, are factors contributing to the denial of equal opportunity for occupational attainment."[54] In short, they argue that racist and sexist biases pervading American culture establish a system of differential rewards that benefit certain individuals, but not on the basis of neutral criteria of talent and effort.

On this view, one great benefit of affirmative action's insistence that group results be considered stems from its demand "that whites recognize that their own advantages are, in significant measure, group benefits, rather than individual achievements and that their own success has been, in part, a matter of their own superior group opportunities, purchased at the expense of opportunities for non-whites."[55] Opportunities accrue not to atomistic individuals, but to individuals as members of particular families, particular communities, particular ethnic, racial, and sexual groups.

Articulating the premises of socialized individualism, proponents of affirmative action emphasize that individual identity as well as preparation for educational and economic opportunities ordinarily develop within the confines of family life. "The self-concept, lifestyle and careers of parents have a tremendous impact upon their children. Such factors greatly influence the home environment and in turn play a significant role in shaping a child's interests and motivations. The financial, intellectual and social resources accumulated by parents play a large role in determining the opportunities their children get."[56] To the extent that diet, housing, medical care, intellectual stimulation, cultural enrichment, and family connections can enhance the individual's chances for success, mobility within the meritocracy is and will continue to be a function of luck in the birth lottery. Success will come more readily to the sons and daughters of the successful and disadvantage will remain a legacy to those born of the disadvantaged.[57]

Proponents of affirmative action argue that racism and sexism may handicap minority and female applicants in a number of ways. Racist and sexist stereotypes may curb the expectations and aspirations of women and minorities. Disadvantaged backgrounds and inadequate education may make it more difficult for women and minorities to achieve particular goals than it is for a middle-class white male to achieve those same goals. But more importantly, when women, minorities, and white males do achieve the same goals, racism and sexism may preclude recognition of the accomplishments as identical. The tendency to view women and minorities as less capable, less creative, less willing to work, and less deserving of serious consideration and respect culminates in a refusal to acknowledge the merit of members of oppressed groups. Given identical qualifications or performance, psychologists have documented that "there is a general tendency to give men more favorable evaluations than women"[58] and to give whites more favorable evaluations than minorities. Moreover, "there is psychological evidence to indicate that women and minority group members are systematically down-graded by school teachers (and graded higher when race or sex is unknown to the grader) . . . and that a woman's name on an assigned paper leads students to rate it lower than the same paper with a man's name on it."[59] Thus, women and minorities experience a form of discrimination which exists over and above the problems of underrepresentation and pay differentials.[60] They are treated as beings less worthy of respect than the average white male, not because of any individual foible, but simply because they are members of a particular group.

The disrespect shown to women and minorities on the basis of their sex, race, or ethnicity highlights the fact that the competition for educational and economic opportunities is neither neutral nor fair, for women and minorities are judged by standards irrelevant to the competition.[61] A tacit pro-white, pro-male bias in admissions, hiring, and evaluation procedures constitutes a form of discrimination which continues to harm women and minorities, not because of their individual characteristics, but because of their membership in particular groups. Thus, proponents of affirmative action insist that:

> It is absurd to suppose that young blacks and women now of an age to apply for jobs have not been wronged . . . It is only within the last 25 years (perhaps the last 10 years in the case of women) that it has become at all widely agreed in this country that blacks and women must be recognized as having, not merely this or that particular right normally recognized as belonging to white males, but all of the rights and respect which go with full membership in the community. Even young blacks and women have lived through down-grading for being black or female; they have not merely not been given that very equal chance at the benefits generated by what the community owns which is so firmly insisted on for white males, they have not until lately even been felt to have a right to it.[62]

Discussions of continuing racist and sexist bias illuminate one other factor central to admissions, hiring, and promotion procedures: neither the criteria employed nor the individuals employing them are neutral or impersonal. Objective forces do not determine individual applicants' merit and prospects for success—the decisions of fallible administrators do. "In the modern meritocracy, the process of selection is not made by nature or by Adam Smith's Invisible Hand, but by admissions and personnel officers who apply cultural standards to applicants for admissions, appointment and promotion."[63] Thus, it is not blind social processes which affirmative action must remedy, but rather the particular decisions of specific individuals who serve as gate-keepers to the positions of power and privilege in contemporary society.

Given their diagnosis of the problem as continuing discrimination in the form of anti-minority and anti-female bias, those who accept the socialized conception of individuality suggest that affirmative action is a fair and appropriate remedy. As a mechanism for cultivating a "mature recognition of the talent of all persons in society,"[64] affirmative action does not jeopardize principles of merit or standards of excellence. It simply prohibits situations in which "the only ones allowed to demonstrate their 'merit' are white males."[65] By establishing fair hiring practices and opening competition to public inspection, affirmative action ensures "that men . . . compete fairly on the basis of merit, not fraternity, on demonstrated capability, not assumed superiority."[66] By focusing attention on admitting, hiring, and promoting members of particular target groups, affirmative action draws attention to both the consequences of historic racism and sexism, and to the extent, the gravity, and the immediacy of the injuries still sustained by minorities and women in the United States.[67]

Recognition of the tenacity of the presumption of racial and sexual superiority, and of the pervasive discrimination in the contemporary United States, causes believers in the socialized individualism to reject the claim that compensatory justice is the only moral ground for the justification of social policies designed to ameliorate the conditions of women and minorities. They reject compensatory justice in part because it perpetuates the myth that discrimination is a social atavism. Instead they insist that the appropriate moral justification for contemporary programs to eliminate current discrimination lies in arguments for distributive justice. Both affirmative action and the more stringent policy of preferential treatment can promote the redistribution of income, power, and prestige, reduce the distributive inequities which plague the present racist and sexist society, and thereby enhance the freedom and the possibility for self-realization of women and minority group members.

Concern with distributive justice focuses attention on the crucial role which higher education performs in certifying individuals for positions of power and prestige. Ending the exclusion of women and minorities from higher education can contribute to the creation of a society in which "the power of the white middle-class male is broken . . . where those who are now the victims of the social order have their fair share of power."[68] Affirmative action and preferential treatment in admissions to higher education, then, is cast as one means by which to improve the employment prospects, income, status, security, and chance for self-determination of women and minorities. Awareness of underutilization, of the truncated life prospects of women and minority group members who are qualified for, but not employed in, positions of power and prestige, cautions against too great a reliance on affirmative action in educational opportunities as a remedy to racial and sexual discrimination.

This awareness has culminated in the rejection of excessive reliance on neutral or 'color-blind' principles, such as nondiscrimination, as inadequate to accomplish the goals of distributive justice. For nondiscrimination alone can make no assault upon the standards of excellence devised by white middle-class males as admission criteria, which have not been proven to have any direct relation to an individual's performance in a professional capacity, but which have effectively screened out women and minority candidates.[69] Proponents of affirmative action point out that implementation of the nondiscrimination principle since 1964 has had virtually no impact upon the problem of underrepresentation. For that reason, many who hold the socialized conception of individuality have concluded that "when society has committed past injustices or when historically disadvantaged groups exist side by side with more advantaged groups, it simply is not possible to achieve equality and fairness by applying neutral principles."[70]

Arguments on the grounds of distributive justice, therefore, justify not only affirmative action, but also preferential treatment, emphasizing that without such stringent measures little progress will be made toward the elimination of racial and sexual inequality. The conception of socialized individuality allows a construction of the case for the legitimacy of preferential treatment, which simultaneously recognizes that such a policy will cause white males to lose certain advantages, yet denies that the loss violates individual rights. Socialized individualism suggests that the white men currently occupying favored positions in organizations have themselves been the beneficiaries of some preferential treatment: "they are members of a group of persons who have been privileged in hiring and promotion in accordance with normal pratices of long-standing, persons who have been offered better educational preparation than others of the same basic talents, persons whose egos have been strengthened more than members of other groups."[71] Because these white males did not deserve such preferential treatment, because they had no right to the advantages afforded by a racist and sexist society, no rights are being violated by removing those advantages. Policies to promote justice for the victims of injustice may require that white men lose their unwarranted privilege in society but they do not strip these individuals of legitimate rights.

Constitutional arguments concerning the permissibility of both affirmative action and preferential treatment have also articulated the assumptions incorporated in the socialized conception of individuality. In their separate opinion in the *Bakke* case, dissenting from the Court's decision to rule the Davis Special Admissions Program unconstitutional, Justices Brennan, White, Marshall, and Blackmun insisted that "a glance at our docket and at those of the lower courts will show that even today officially sanctioned discrimination is not a thing of the past."[72] Indeed, they argued that "the generation of minority students applying to Davis Medical School since it opened in 1968—most of whom were born before or about the time Brown I was decided—clearly have been the victims of discrimination,"[73] a discrimination based solely on membership in particular racial and ethnic groups. Justice Marshall added that, "It is unnecessary in twentieth century America to have individual Negroes demonstrate that they have been victims of racial discrimination, the racism of our society has been so pervasive that none, regardless of wealth or position, has managed to escape its impact."[74] The justices also argued that there was good reason to believe that "the failure of certain racial minorities to satisfy entrance requirements is not a measure of their ultimate performance as doctors but a result of the lingering effects of past societal discrimination."[75]

Having argued that discrimination is an ongoing problem in the United States and that the exclusion of minorities from medical school was simply one manifestation of such discrimination, the Justices asserted that it is constitutionally permissible that Federal and State legislatures require and that recipients of federal funds accord "preferential consideration to disadvantaged members of racial minorities as part of a program designed to enable such individuals to surmount obstacles imposed by racial discrimination."[76] Moreover, they insisted that preferential treatment does not violate any fundamental rights, nor does it constitute a form of invidious discrimination against whites.[77] Finally, they urged that the commitment to neutral principles and to the concept of a colorblind constitution not be allowed to "become myopia which masks the reality that many 'created equal' have been treated within our lifetimes as inferior both by the law and by their fellow citizens."[78] Instead, they recommended the implementation of color-conscious remedies, both to prevent the perpetuation of discrimination and to undo the iniquitous effects of social injustice.

One year after the ruling in *Bakke* was handed down, the arguments articulated in the dissenting opinions were adopted by a majority of justices in *Steelworkers v. Weber* to sustain preferential treatment as a constitutionally permissible remedy under certain conditions.[79] In this case, the Court held that race-conscious remedies which involved the use of numerical objectives were constitutionally permissible so long as they were "designed to break down old patterns of racial segregation and hierarchy"; that they did not "unnecessarily trammel the interests of white employees"; that they did not "require the discharge of white workers and their replacement by new black hirees"; that they did not "create an absolute bar to the advancement of white employees"; and that they constituted a temporary measure . . . not intended to maintain racial balance but simply to eliminate manifest racial imbalance in a traditionally segregated job category."[80]

The precedent established in *Weber* was subsequently invoked in the majority's decision in *Johnson v. Transportation Agency, Santa Clara County* in order to sustain voluntary affirmative action programs adopted by public employers in the absence of any prior judicial finding of discrimination. The Court's decision in *Johnson* echoed many of the central tenets of the conception of socialized individuality. Speaking for the Court, Justice Brennan asserted that "to justify the adoption of an affirmative action plan, an employer need not point to its own prior discriminatory practices, but need only point to a conspicuous imbalance in traditionally segregated job categories."[81] Indeed, Justice Brennan accepted that the Agency's "recognition that women were concentrated in traditionally female jobs in the Agency and represented a lower percentage of other job classifications than would be expected if traditional segregation had not occurred" was sufficient to justify the adoption of remedial strategies which took sex into account in hiring and promotion decisions.

Justice Brennan pointed out that allowing race or sex to be considered as one qualification in an overall assessment of candidates did not mandate that an individual be hired solely on the basis of race or sex, nor did it abridge legitimate merit criteria. On the contrary, he argued that such considerations merely allow women or minorities "to compete with other qualified applicants. No persons are automatically excluded from consideration; all are able to have their qualifications weighed against those of other applicants."[82] Justice Brennan also noted that the petitioner, a white male, "had no absolute entitlement to the road dispatcher position,"[83] nor did he possess an indisputable claim to be the "best qualified" candidate. Citing an *amicus curiae* brief submitted by the American Society for Personnel Administration, Justice Brennan indicated that "the Court recognizes that there is rarely a single, 'best qualified' person for a job . . . the selecting official considers several fully qualified candidates who each may possess different attributes which recommend them for selection. The final determinations as to which candidate is 'best qualified' are at best subjective."[84] Thus he suggested that the decision to promote a woman who possessed all the relevant qualifications to the position of road dispatcher did not unsettle any legitimate, firmly rooted expectations on the petitioner's part, nor did it "unnecessarily trammel male employees' rights or create an absolute bar to their advancement."[85] It did, however, constitute a "moderate, flexible, case by case approach to effecting a gradual improvement in the representation of women and minorities in the Agency's work force and is fully consistent with Title VII."[86]

In a concurring opinion, Justice Stevens recommended that the Court accept the implications of the socialized conception of individuality more straightforwardly. Noting that in a series of decisions handed down since 1978, the Court had gradually altered its interpretation of Title VII, Justice Stevens urged the Court to acknowledge fully that although Title VII "does not require employers to grant preferential treatment on the basis of race or sex, the Court has unambiguously interpreted the statute to permit the voluntary adoption of special programs to benefit members of the minority groups for whose protection the statute was enacted."[87] Arguing that the "logic of antidiscrimination legislation requires that judicial constructions of Title VII leave 'breathing room' for employer initiatives to benefit members of minority groups,"[88] Justice Stevens advocated abandoning the requirement that prior discrimination be judicially proven as a precondition for justifying preferential treatment. "The justification of affirmative action need not be tied to a finding of past discrimination,"[89] he suggested, for employers may find it more helpful to focus on the future:

> they might choose to implement affirmative action for many reasons other than to purge their past sins of discrimination. The Jackson School Board, for example, said it had done so in part to improve the quality of education in Jackson whether by improving black students' performance or by dispelling for black and white students alike any idea that white supremacy governs our social institutions. Other employers might advance other forward looking reasons for affirmative action: improving their services to black constituencies, averting racial tension over the allocation of jobs in a communi-

ty, or increasing the diversity of the work force, to name but a few examples. Or they might adopt affirmative action simply to eliminate from their operations all *de facto* embodiment of a system of racial caste. All of these reasons aspire to a racially integrated future, but none reduces to 'racial balancing for its own sake'.[90]

In Justice Stevens's opinion, the Court should openly acknowledge all such efforts to achieve an equitable future to be constitutionally permissible and wholly in keeping with the spirit of Title VII of the Civil Rights Act. Like others who adhere to the precepts of socialized individuality, Justice Stevens's opinion suggests that the persistence of discrimination in the United States is sufficiently pervasive and sufficiently pernicious to warrant diverse endeavors to establish social justice. Moreover, he argues that existing statutes and the constitution provide ample justification for voluntary efforts to achieve that end.

Assessing Competing Theoretical Presuppositions

To this point, the chapter has concentrated on demonstrating that the dispute over the legitimacy of affirmative action involves more than a simple disagreement over the utility of a particular social policy; it reflects fundamental differences in the understanding of the nature of individual identity and freedom. Alternative theoretical presuppositions concerning the nature of individuality not only shape the interpretation of contemporary social life, but structure the very capacity to perceive the existence of discrimination in the contemporary United States. It is important to stress that these conceptions operate at the tacit level, that most people are unaware of the influence of these presuppositions upon their perceptions and analyses of contemporary events, and that this lack of awareness places these fundamental assumptions beyond examination and critical scrutiny. For this reason, there is more at stake in the explication of these divergent conceptions of individuality than a mere plotting of the conceptual terrain. For it is only after the competing constellations of theoretical presuppositions have been identified, that they can be assessed rationally. When tacit assumptions about the nature of individuality are made explicit and subjected to critical assessment, it can be shown that both conceptions are not equally capable of providing an adequate account of the formation and development of individual identity.

The atomistic conception of individuality misconstrues both the developmental nature of individual identity and the role of social and cultural factors in determining the individual's aspirations, expectations, desires, and sense of self. The myth of the 'self-made' individual is at odds with the most rudimentary processes of individual birth, growth, and maturation.[91] Whether one focuses on biological, psychological, intellectual, or moral development, the major determinants of the individual's progress are socially mediated rather than self-determined. Whether one considers the genetic contributions of innumerable ancestors or the educational contributions of parents, relatives, friends, and a fairly extensive number of teachers, the realization of individual potential depends on contributions from and interventions by a large number of people.

In assuming that individual desires are subjectively determined, the atomistic conception overlooks the extent to which the individual's impressions, desires, sensations, and aspirations are socially constructed, founded upon a host of intersubjective understandings incorporated in language, culture and tradition. The atomistic conception of the individual must deny the pervasive impact of socialization, history, and culture upon the formation of individual identity if it is to retain its assumption concerning the radical independence of the individual and the primacy of choice and effort as determinants of individual success. Yet precisely this denial renders the atomistic ideal incapable of accounting for the commonalities in personalities among members of particular ethno-cultural groups, and the diversity in self-understandings among members of disparate historical communities which have been documented in a variety of anthropological and historical studies.[92] The atomistic conception is at a loss to explain the shared values and valuations characteristic of distinct peoples, whether they be tribes, clans, nations, ethnicities, races, religions, or genders.

In addition, in treating individual passions, appetites, and desires as subjectively determined and relatively fixed, the atomistic conception denies the individual's capacity to reflect upon, criticize, and alter both desires and the behavior which is informed by those desires. In short, it denies what many philosophers have considered the essence of moral freedom. While this denial sustains platitudes such as, "You can't change human nature," which serve to challenge the efficacy of any political action designed to achieve social justice, its determinist roots drastically constrict both the meaning of and the possibility for individual freedom.[93] Indeed, the determinist underpinnings of the atomistic account of individual desire might well undermine the claim that choice and effort are the principle determinants of success. For a consistent determinism negates the possibility of choice and nullifies the effect of effort.

The atomistic conception of individuality is marred by its inability to provide an account of individual identity consistent with the biological process of birth and growth, and with findings of anthropologists and historians concerning the influence of society and culture on individual personality and self-understanding. Moreover, its theoretical foundations come perilously close to embracing a logical contradiction. The prospects for future social policy founded upon atomistic assumptions are also problematic. For those who build their political prescriptions upon the atomistic conception of individuality advocate using neutral principles as the sole constitutional remedy for racial and sexual inequality. If underrepresentation, underutilization, pay differentials, and the disrespect for women and minorities linked to racial and sexual prejudice persist, on this view, they must be discounted either as the private preferences of particular individuals or as the consequence of the inexorable workings of impersonal forces. In either case, they are said to lie beyond the scope of a political remedy. The atomistic prescription urges resignation to injustice as an inevitable aspect of the human condition. It renders humanity helpless in the face of grave social evils. It is ironic that the atomistic conception which flaunts a boundless confidence in the capacities of individuals to make anything of themselves as individuals, simultaneously denies their capacity to achieve anything as a community through concerted collective action.

It is time that the atomistic conception of the individual, replete with its empirical and theoretical defects and its overbearing pessimism concerning the possibility of collective choice and action, be subjected to explicit criticism and public scrutiny. The implications that flow from the pervasive acceptance of the atomistic conception of individuality are manifest in the context of the affirmative action debate: the perpetuation of a systematic blindness to the pernicious consequences of racism and sexism, the toleration of racial and sexual inequality with an untroubled conscience, the denial of a wide range of opportunities to members of oppressed groups, and the restriction of the sphere of freedom of the disadvantaged.[94] Such policies challenge the authenticity of any commitment to the principles of liberty, equality, and justice. Until now, such policies have been depicted as the only feasible political possibilities by those who uncritically accept the tenets of atomistic individualism. Yet rigorous examination of the theoretical presuppositions which sustain these policy prescriptions suggests that the very conception of political possibility is itself narrowly circumscribed by implausible assumptions concerning individual identity and freedom. As the alternative conception of socialized individuality suggests, there are other options open to the political community. Resignation to social injustice need not be the inevitable end of those who prize freedom and self-realization.

6

Theoretical Presuppositions and the Problem of Explanation: The Case of Kampuchea

RECENT debates concerning the nature of explanation in policy analysis have mirrored similar debates in the philosophy of social science. Central to the debates in both contexts have been disagreements over the nature of theory (empirical vs. interpretive vs. critical), controversies concerning the appropriate model of explanation (the hypothetico-deductive model vs. the *verstehen* model), and disputes related to the goal of social scientific inquiry (prediction and control vs. understanding and communication vs. emancipation). When one moves from an examination of the canons of the philosophy of social science and the methodology of policy inquiry to an examination of actual attempts to explain socio-political events relevant to policy analysis, one discovers more than a simple failure on the part of analysts to conform to the norms of the scientific method, however that method is defined.

To explore the problem of explanation in detail, this chapter will examine several explanations of the recent political violence in Kampuchea. It will focus on the influence of tacit theoretical presuppositions in structuring the perception of events, the accumulation of evidence, and the construction of arguments advanced to explain nearly two decades of political violence. In particular, the chapter will focus on the manner in which unexamined expectations generated by theoretical assumptions cause analysts to oversimplify events and indeed to caricature participants in those events with the unfortunate consequence that the accounts advanced as explanations tend to obfuscate rather than clarify the situation under examination. Close examination of the alternative explanatory accounts will suggest that in many cases, the explanations advanced reveal more about the theoretical presuppositions of the analysts than they reveal about the phenomena to be explained.

In the final section, the chapter will consider the implications of this problem of explanation for policy analysis. It will suggest that neither the hypothetico-deductive model nor the *verstehen* model of explanation deal adequately with the role of theoretical presuppositions in the generation of explanatory accounts. Finally, it will advance an alternative conception of explanation premised on a recognition of the formative role of theoretical assumptions in all perception and analysis, a conception of explanation rooted in analysis of and extrapolation from multiple, nonpriveleged interpretations of the sociopolitical event to be explained.[1]

Kampuchea Revisited

Kampuchea's recent history has been marked by invasions of foreign armies,[2] systematic aerial bombing for five years,[3] attempted and completed coups d'etat,[4] civil war,[5] revolutionary transformation,[6] purges,[7] summary executions, terrorism,[8] and resumed guerila activity.[9] The presence of so many forms of political violence in one nation in so short a span of time affords an opportunity for a detailed analysis of the dimensions of political strife. Indeed, the sustained tragedy of the Cambodian experience invites attempts to isolate the causal and contributory factors in order to make two decades of devastation comprehensible. In the following sections, competing explanations of recent political events in Kampuchea will be analyzed in terms of the central causal factors which they identify. Explanations which emphasize psychological factors, ideological zeal, defective revolutionary consciousness, rational reconstruction, and imperial malevolence as the primary determinants of the political situation will be considered. In the case of each form of explanation, efforts will be made to trace the oversimplifications and omissions in order to illustrate the deterioration of the explanation into caricature and to identify the major defects of the explanatory account.

Psychological Explanations

It is not uncommon to encounter descriptions of the Khmer Rouge Revolution studded with references to the works of "madmen" and "barbarians,"[10] inspired by "hare-brained theories of decolonization,"[11] implemented by "soldiers addicted to torture,"[12] and comprehensible as nothing less than "monstrous aberrations of human behavior and revolutionary morality."[13] These depictions are typically accompanied by a series of harrowing accounts of atrocities allegedly committed by Khmer Rouge and subsequently related by refugees who have fled the unfathomable madness.[14] Among the abominations attributed to the Revolutionary Organization (Angka Leou)[15] are a determination to "shatter Cambodia to bits," to destroy its culture and its cultural centers (the cities), and to obliterate its history (symbolized by the burning of books, markets, houses). In addition, the desecration of its temples, the abolition of Buddhism as the state religion, the destruction (as opposed to the expropriation) of valuables for the sheer joy of destruction, the ruin of foreign technology, and the extermination of suspect groups, such as prostitutes, former members of Lon Nol's army and civil service, and the intelligentsia, have been noted as the testaments to the Khmer Rouge's remorseless and pitiless will.[16]

How can one account for such a willful destruction of a culture and a people? For some, madness constitutes its own explanation: these are the acts of lunatics who have been locked so long in jungle sanctuaries that they have lost all sense of reality and humanity.[17] By definition, these abominations defy rationality; they can at best be solemnly lamented. Other authors have probed more deeply into the machinations of the demented personality.[18] Indeed, Barron and Paul have suggested that the life and personality of Khieu Samphan, "one of the dominant masters and leading theorists of Angka Leou,"[19] can help explain some of the most inexplicable policies and deeds of the organization.

In an exceptionally brief psychobiography, Barron and Paul recount the tale of a mediocre and quiet student whose most remarkable characteristics were "passivity and a total lack of aggressiveness."[20] Victimized by his schoolmates at an early age, he grew to discover that he was "permanently and incurably" impotent.[21] Retreating to the solace of academic endeavors, Khieu channeled all of his energies into his studies. Upon completing his Ph.D. in economics, he turned to journalism and government service only to suffer a more intense victimization and humiliation at the hands of Prince Sihanouk's police. Moving from this chronicle of Khieu's personal sufferings, Barron and Paul shift to the speculative regions of psychoanalytic theory in order to draw a conclusion so remarkable that it deserves to be quoted at length.

> The origins of some of (Angka's) more extreme policies may lie in the personality of the impotent ideologue, Khieu Samphan. Transient impotence can be the result of many mundane causes, but numerous psychiatrists consider that chronic impotence, unless inflicted by physical factors, is the product of profound hostility. Certainly, Khieu Samphan, the sickly bullied child, the friendless, tormented youth, the meek, persecuted man, had reason to be hostile. Perhaps some of the deathly hostility Angka Leou was to visit upon the Cambodian poeple, such as the savage slaughter of women and children as well as men, the ferocious assault on the Khmer traditions of love, courtship and family, the draconian punishment of extramarital sex, was spawned by the hostility of the unloved and unloving Khieu.[22]

Despite the patent inadequacy of such an explanation for decades of political upheaval, it should not be summarily dismissed. On the contrary, the two instances of psychological explanations, the 'generalized madness' thesis and the 'impotence-hostility' hypothesis deserve systematic refutation precisely because their frequent recurrence suggests some intuitive appeal. It may be that people take some comfort in the belief that sustained political violence can be the handiwork only of those who have renounced reason, but such comfort should not be conflated with a comprehensive explanation.

The most serious shortcoming of any psychological explanation of a political crisis is that it tends to dissociate the political acts of the participants from the social, economic, and political context which generated them. By emphasizing the insanity or irrationality of particular individuals, this mode of explanation tacitly legitimizes existing values and institutions. By suggesting that the world is sane and rational, and therefore what requires investigation is the psychopathology of individuals who attack that world, this form of explanation ignores the possibility that it is the pathology of socio-political processes themselves which have provoked individual acts. In the context of Kampuchea, accounts of the madness of the Khmer Rouge typically neglect to mention that the revolution grew out of a brutal civil war, which had succeeded the systematic bombing of sixty percent of the countryside over a five year period, that the government ousted by revolutionary forces was known chiefly for unparalleled graft, corruption, and incompetence, and that the revolutionary organization had good reason to anticipate counterrevolutionary activity, mass starvation, and disease of epidemic proportions. While none of these factors alone might explain Khmer Rouge behavior, it is reasonable to assume that together they provide crucial background information essential to an interpretation of revolutionary action.

Additional problems surround the impotence-hostility hypothesis. The claim that chronic impotence is caused by hostility presupposes far greater sophistication in psychoanalysis than currently exists. Despite the appeal to authority ("numerous psychiatrists"), this causal claim should be regarded as tenuous at best and specious at worst. But even if such a claim could be proven, the belief that Khieu Samphan's alleged impotence could have such vast social consequences assumes that Samphan held absolute control over the revolutionary organization, that his hostile desires dictated the behavior of some 200,000 soldiers, and that there was perfect congruence between his intentions and their implementation by thousands of poorly trained, war-weary individuals in a country where communication networks were primitive. Such presumptions of Khieu Samphan's monolithic power must be balanced by a consideration of reports that question the centrality of Khieu's role during the revolutionary struggle and that suggest continuous struggle among competing factions within the revolutionary movement, over which no one achieved ascendancy until 1978.[23]

Finally, explanations which turn upon the psychological unmasking of a person's secret or subconscious motives are self referentially destructive, for they invite a refutation of the author's arguments on the grounds that they, too, mask hidden psychological drives. For example, Barron and Paul's claim that Kampuchea's violence could be explained in terms of Khieu Samphan's subconscious hostility manifested in chronic impotence could be debunked as nothing more than a projection of their own sexual inadequacies upon an external object in a truly xenophobic fashion. Such a move brings rational discourse to a halt as it shifts from assessment of the merits of a particular explanatory argument to an *ad hominem* attack consisting of ill-founded psychological allegations.

This focus on hidden psychological causes not only destroys the possibility for rational debate, but also jeopardizes the pertinence of moral and political evaluations of the behavior under examination. The conflation of biological or psychological causes with reasons for action and explanations of events shifts the discussion toward a determined universe in which there is no room for moral judgment or political accountability, for it makes no sense to blame (or praise) a person for behavior over which that person had no control. To posit a world of psychological determinism as the prime explanation of political violence is to move beyond the assignment of personal responsibility and accountability for actions.[24] It is to move from a realm of political argument and assessment to a realm of *pathos* and pathology; it is to substitute medical prognosis for political prescription.

Ideological Zeal

A second explanatory strain in accounts of the Kampuchean revolution links the violence of revolutionary cadres to an excessive commitment to an abstract and inflexible ideology. Thus it has been claimed that the revolutionaries aspired to create a purist and puritanically collectivist utopia.[25] They sought to "invent a radically new kind of man,"[26] by inculcating new values under a discipline unknown to modern Cambodia,[27] with a total disregard for costs in terms of human suffering.[28] While some authors claim that this radical egalitarian ideal follows "in the tradition of Communist movements in other nations,"[29] and adheres to the general rubrics of "Marxist-Leninist Party Organization,"[30] other authors have identified components of the revolutionary ideology which appear to be quite unique.[31]

Francois Ponchaud has suggested that the ideology "reflects a new concept of society in which there is no place even for the idea of a city."[32] The city as a market place, replete with its ties to the colonial heritage, Chinese commerce, and corrupt bureaucratic exchanges, "had to be swept away and an egalitarian rural society put in its place."[33] Agricultural production was to provide the basis for the "independence-sovereignty" of Democratic Kampuchea by creating self-sufficiency through a program of complete self-reliance. Moreover, the purification afforded by intensive agricultural labor could purge the remnants of Western bourgeois and individualistic values from the consciousness of the population. All human relations were to be "completely transformed by the revolution."[34] Family life was to be subordinated to the needs of the work collective; loyalty to the revolutionary organization was to supplant sentimental family attachments. Marriages were to be arranged to suit the needs of the revolution rather than the inclinations of individuals. Children were to be reared collectively to break the hold of familial sentiment and with it the vestiges of class privilege transferred through family ties. Education was to be a pragmatic affair inseparable from peasant work life and the rudimentary tasks of economic reconstruction. "Reactionary religions" were to be prohibited; material goods were to be renounced. Even the language was to be purged of its unequal status designations and thereby simplified. The traditional Khmer costume was to be replaced by unisex black pajamas. Food was to be prepared collectively and allocated on the basis of work contributed to the rebuilding of the nation. Minor infractions were to be punished through evening criticism and self-criticism sessions; major infractions were to be punished by death. To achieve these draconian ends, Khmer society was to be reorganized according to an "army model" under which "nothing seems to happen by chance, everything appears to be planned in advance and executed methodically and with relentless consistency."[35]

Descriptions of this unyielding ideology are indeed formidable, but do they accurately convey the objectives of revolutionary soldiers and the experience of the civilian population at the hands of the revolutionary organization? Several strands of evidence suggest that this explanatory model posits a greater uniformity in the ideological objectives of the revolutionaries than actually existed. Ben Kiernan has provided a detailed account of the existence of at least three factions within the revolutionary leadership distinguishable both by allegiance to different models of revolutionary socialism and by the use of markedly different strategies to win popular support.[36] In addition, he has noted that the intensity of violence accompanying revolutionary action varied in Kampuchea from one region to another and was most intense in areas where the Khmer Rouge had least control.[37]

Other authors have noted that such ideological and regional differences suggest that "it is not absolutely clear whether or not the Khmer Communist Party had a well-defined program of its own—or rather was operating on a pragmatic day by day basis, resorting to violence as a means of asserting authority."[38] It has also been noted by a wide range of commentators that the continuous bombing and shooting in Cambodia from 1969–1975 radicalized the people in rural areas and allied them to the Khmer Rouge resistance, but in no way infused them with ideological zeal.[39] Indeed, it has been suggested that the "worst atrocities may have occurred at the hands of a peasant army driven out of their devastated villages by U.S. bombs, then taking revenge against the urban civilization that they regarded, not without reason, as a collaborator in their destruction and their long history of oppression."[40] In short, the cruelties of revolutionary cadres may have been as much a matter of the vengeance and inexperience of amateurs as of excessive ideologicial zeal.

The emphasis upon abstract ideology also overlooks the significant role played by Khmer nationalism in the Kampuchean revolution. Many atrocities were directed against Chinese and Vietnamese residents of Kampuchea, as well as against Kampuchean ethnic minorities such as the Cham and bear stronger ties to a tradition of racism and nationalism than to any egalitarian socialist ideal. David Chandler has argued that Cambodians have traditionally "associated periods of nationalistic unrest with the killing of Vietnamese."[41] If one combines the force of this tradition with a desire for revenge against the atrocities perpetrated by the South Vietnamese Army acting in accordance with their own anti-Khmer traditions[42] and at the invitation of the Lon Nol government, one has the makings of a plausible explanation of excessive cruelties without reference to ideological fervor. Moreover, Hanoi's expansionist ambitions and its systematic attempts to prevent the consolidation of Pol Pot's regime might be considered a provocation of Khmer nationalist violence, which carries some explanatory power.[43]

Thus, it would seem that claims about an abstract and uniform ideology simply cannot account for ideological differences among the revolutionary elite, variations in revolutionary reconstruction on a regional basis, the absence of ideological commitment on the part of the vast majority of peasant soldiers, the failure to implement ideological reeducation programs during the first two years of revolutionary transformation, the role played by Khmer nationalism, or traditional racist animosities, nor can it account for the pragmatic use of violence in response to foreign provocation or internal subversion. While the systematic exposition of a coherent revolutionary ideology may be intellectually satisfying, it appears to be singularly at odds with the manifold diversity of the Kampuchean revolutionary experience.

Defective Revolutionary Consciousness

Two recent accounts of the Kampuchean tragedy attribute the sustained violence not to excessive ideological zeal, but to deficiencies in the revolutionary consciousness of the 'Pol Pot-Ieng Sary clique'. Ben

Kiernan has argued that Pol Pot's "millenial xenophobia, expansionist militarism based on racism, and chauvinist convictions of Khmer invincibility have corrupted the socialist organization of Kapuchea."[44] Infused with an obsessive concern for moral independence rather than with the objective requirements of socio-economic reconstruction, Pol Pot deliberately isolated Kampuchea from the support of the international socialist community and "fostered that critical level of contempt for the outside world which laid the ideological and psychological bases for even more destruction."[45] Moreover, "the asphyxiating desperation with which Pol Pot bearhugged revolutionary power" inspired systematic purges against the Khmer Rumdos, (Sihanoukists), the Vietnamese-trained Khmer cadres, and the Khmer factions committed to the mass democratic ideology of the Cultural Revolution, while simultaneously promoting anti-Vietnamese racism among the population in order to consolidate support for his government and distract attention from his regime's abuses of the Kampuchean people.[46]

Wilfred Burchett generally concurs with Kiernan's depiction of deficiencies in revolutionary consciousness of the Pol Pot-Ieng Sary clique, but he further suggests that the fanaticism of Khmer chauvinism was fueled by China's obsession with expansion into Southeast Asia.[47] Totally devoid of any notions of proletarian internationalism or revolutionary solidarity, China devised a policy to "divide and rule Indochina" and wantonly manipulated the unwitting Khmer Rouge to advance this end.[48] Thus, the "senseless" Khmer Rouge military adventures against Vietnam and the brutalities committed against the Vietnamese civilian communities in border areas can be understood only in terms of Chinese ambitions to destabilize existing relations and establish hegemony over Indochina. For falling prey to these Chinese machinations to the great detriment of the Khmer people, Burchett claims that Pol Pot should be ejected from the ranks of Cambodian patriots and denounced as a "Chinese robot."[49] According to Burchett, Vietnam, Kampuchea's long term friend and ally, has again demonstrated its commitment to socialist solidarity by rescuing the Khmer population from Pol Pot's butchery, establishing the benign regime of Heng Samrin, and laying the foundation for the first democratic elections ever to be held in Kampuchea in May, 1981.[50]

While a great deal of evidence sustains the depiction of Pol Pot's regime as chauvinist and authoritarian, it is not clear that the vilification of China or the sanctification of either Vietnam in particular or revolutionary socialism in general, helps to explain the regime's policies. It cannot be disputed that two factions of Indochinese communism are currently struggling for control of Kampuchea, but that this dispute can be reduced to a contention over ideological differences is much less obvious.[51] A number of additional factors clearly exacerbate the conflict. The traditional animosity between the Kampuchean and Vietnamese peoples which has smoldered for close to a thousand years and which has been greatly aggravated by atrocities committed by both sides in the past two decades, cannot be discounted. Moreover, perceptions and misperceptions of the opponents' behavior and objectives contribute to a conception of legitimate grievances which fuel the conflict on both sides. For example, many Kampucheans perceive Vietnam to be an expansionist power intent upon engulfing neighboring territory at the first opportunity. Thus, they view Vietnam's continued appeals for a "special relationship" between the two nations as a thinly veiled ploy to annex Khmer soil and ultimately to obliterate the Khmer ethnic identity. Offers of economic assistance are viewed as mechanisms of control that could undermine Khmer independence. In addition, Kampucheans harbor a relentless suspicion that the Vietnamese will use Cambodia to advance Vietnamese ends and will abandon or betray Kampuchea when it is in Vietnam's interest to do so.[52] On the Vietnamese side, there is a strong resentment against the ingratitude of the Khmer Rouge, who appear to have forgotten the importance of the Vietnamese military contribution to the Khmer revolutionary success in the period from 1970 to 1975. Moreover, the Vietnamese consider Pol Pot's divisive tactics and purges of the Viet-trained Khmer cadres as traitorous to the Indochinese revolution. In addition, the Vietnamese consider the Khmer Rouge's prolonged flirtation with China exceedingly dangerous to the stability of the region.[53]

Another critical factor that should not be omitted from any assessment of the protracted conflict between Vietnamese and Khmer Rouge forces is the role played by international alliances and networks. Although the claim that these international actors instigated the fighting remains problematic,[54] the Soviet Union, China, the United States, and the ASEAN nations all have stakes in the outcome of the dispute. The influence of their actions, reactions, and inactions, as well as their economic, military, and humanitarian aid policies, should not be overlooked.[55] Taken in conjunction, factors such as traditional animosities, perceived grievances, and international alliances may have greater explanatory power than claims about the defective revolutionary consciousness of the Khmer Rouge leadership.

Rational Reconstruction

One account of the Kampuchean revolution discounts the charges of revolutionary mania, zeal, and corruption, and argues instead that the Khmer Rouge program constituted a rational and humane response to the dire problems confronting the nation: disease, impending starvation, and economic devastation.[56] Hildebrand and Porter emphasize that the plight of the Kampuchean people was not the result of any natural disaster, but was the consequence of U.S. military intervention, which killed an estimated ten percent of the population and wounded another five percent. The 'secret' bombing initiated by the United States also destroyed the richest farmland, and with it ninety percent of the village housing in the most heavily bombed sections, thereby creating two million refugees who flocked to urban areas. In addition, the sustained bombing destroyed roads, railroads, and communications networks, and prevented the harvesting and replanting of rice, the subsistence crop. Moreover, the United States provided some $748 million to Lon Nol's government to prolong the war; yet with the collapse of Phnom Penh, the United States refused to provide any humanitarian assistance despite its own forecast of probable starvation and disease of epidemic proportions.[57]

Confronted with vast overcrowding in urban areas, the prevalence of serious health hazards due to the collapse of basic public services, widespread malnutrition, and insufficient transportation to transfer food from rural stockpiles to the cities, the Khmer Rouge evacuated the cities to prevent starvation and epidemics. In contrast to claims that the evacuation was conducted callously and brutally, Hildebrand and Porter provide evidence suggesting that great care was taken by the Khmer Rouge to meet the most basic and urgent needs of the population by providing food, water, shelter, and medical care during the relocation process.[58]

Once the population had been resettled in the countryside, the Khmer Rouge mobilized the labor force in order to bring in the dry season harvest in liberated zones and to prepare the rice fields for the primary rainy season crops.[59] During this mobilization effort, the Khmer Rouge built upon traditional Khmer agricultural practices, such as communal sowing and harvesting, while simultaneously abolishing "social institutions which held the peasants in subjection and indebtedness while discouraging innovation and expansion."[60] According to Hildebrand and Porter, the collective agricultural framework institutionalized by the Khmer Rouge released the creative energies of the Khmer population, allocated resources rationally, and succeeded in increasing agricultural production sufficiently to ensure the survival of the nation.[61]

Although Hildebrand's and Porter's detailed descriptions of the reasons for several of the Khmer Rouge revolutionary actions constitute a much needed corrective to the descriptions of lunatics and zealots previously encountered, their own explanation nevertheless fails to account for many dimensions of revolutionary experience. Their idealized treatment of the evacuation and reconstruction underestimates the vast confusion and hardship which would accompany any precipitous effort to relocate 2.5 million people. Moreover, their emphasis on the point that the policies were inspired by benign intentions overlooks the equally important point that these policies were implemented by tough, young peasant soldiers, hardened by the rigors of sustained warfare, trained to obey orders adeptly, and ill-practiced in the art of flexible decision making.[62] The apparent heartlessness of their enforcement of exacting orders cannot be dismissed out of hand. Furthermore, that certain peasant traditions were incorporated into the new agricultural collectives does not imply that the process of collectivization would be pleasant, painless, or appreciated by peasants, much less by recently ruralized urban dwellers. The hardships of agricultural reconstruction, the lack of freedom, privacy, family intimacy, and the rigors of adjusting to a new order of things, exact an enormous toll which should not be ignored in any account of the revolutionary experience.

Like several other modes of explanation, the rational reconstruction model tends to posit far greater harmony within the revolutionary leadership than existed, and therefore it is unable to explain the purges which occurred throughout the early years of the revolution, the continuous fighting between Vietnamese and Khmer Rouge cadres, the ruthless treatment of Vietnamese, Chinese, and ethnic minorities at the hands of the revolutionary forces; nor can it explain the second wave of resettlements orchestrated by the Khmer Rouge after the rice crop had been planted and preliminary villages constructed.

Imperialist Malevolence

A final explanatory theme foreshadowed in Hildebrand's and Porter's discussion and developed in the work of Shawcross and of Chomsky and Herman, attributes profound responsibility for the Cambodian tragedy to the perverted priorities of American imperial power. After providing detailed documentation of the Nixon-Kissinger decisions that culminated in the secret bombing of Cambodia beginning in March 1969, and the subsequent deployment of U.S. and South Vietnamese forces on Cambodian soil, Shawcross suggests that the United States had larger ambitions in Cambodia than its acknowledged desire to cut the supply lines of the Ho Chi Minh trail. United States' objectives went well beyond its explicit goal of mitigating the North Vietnamese assault on the South, thereby facilitating the twin programs of Vietnamization and American troop withdrawal. According to Shawcross, Cambodia's fragile peace was sacrificed in order that U.S. resolve would be demonstrated to the world community.[63] The ferocity and scale of U.S. bombing, as well as the prolonged commitment to Lon Nol's corrupt and incompetent regime, can be attributed only to the fact that in "such a war . . . much more is at stake than the battleground or its inhabitants. The fight is more for myth than reality, more for credibility than for territory, and the prospect of loss is therefore more disconcerting."[64]

Chomsky and Herman suggest that the U.S. did not adjust gracefully to its loss in Southeast Asia. Instead of assisting the reconstruction efforts in war-torn Vietnam, Laos, and Cambodia, "a major thrust of U.S. policy has been to create harsh conditions for its victims struggling to rebuild viable societies."[65] Indeed, Chomsky and Herman reiterate a charge advanced by Michael Vickery that "when it became clear (to U.S. leaders) that they could not win in Cambodia, they preferred to do everything possible to insure that the post-war revolutionary government be extremely brutal, doctrinaire, and frightening to its neighbors, rather than a moderate socialism to which the Thai, for example, might look with envy."[66] Thus, the systematic destruction of rural Cambodia through bombardment is interpreted as an attempt "to impose the harshest possible conditions on the eventual victors" in order to retard social and economic progress and to maximize the brutality of the revolutionary cadres.[67] As a result of these efforts, the U.S. could reap a propaganda victory in the form of the fulfillment of its "Communist bloodbath predictions: A selective version of the facts disseminated systematically, would sustain the belief that atrocities flow from 'Marxism,' and 'atheism' as dire consequences of 'liberation' from the grip of Western benevolence."[68]

In presenting well-documented arguments concerning U.S. culpability in the destruction of the political economy, as well as a significant proportion of the population of prerevolutionary Cambodia, these accounts emphasize a frequently neglected dimension of the

Kampuchean experience. However, these discussions fail to address a number of thorny issues which arise with any attempt to link intention, action, and outcome. Given the secrecy surrounding the decision to bomb and invade Cambodia, Shawcross has good reason to focus on Nixon's and Kissinger's goals in the determination of U.S. policy. Yet these policies had to be implemented by field commanders, immersed in warfare, who may or may not have shared the Nixon-Kissinger concern with U.S. credibility. It is quite possible that competition among divisions of the armed forces for bombing assignments, restlessness among troops, as well as standard operating procedures of unit commanders, bombardiers, and flight crews imbued with their own conceptions of the demands of warfare, had as much to do with the intensity of the bombing of Cambodia as did the ambitions of Nixon and Kissinger.

In considering Chomsky's and Herman's claims that the U.S. specifically intended to heighten the brutality of revolutionary cadres through its bombing effort, several additional questions emerge. Whose intention is implied in this case? Nixon, Kissinger, the State Department, the Pentagon, the C.I.A., as well as U.S. and South Vietnamese fighting units all played some role in the bombing decision and effort. Did all share this intention? Even if all participants shared the desire to intensify Khmer Rouge brutality, is it reasonable to believe that they could have regarded sustained bombing as a reliable means to achieve this end? Given some 200,000 Khmer Rouge troops and the range of possible responses to intensified bombing, it seems improbable that bureaucratic policy makers could have anticipated that heightened brutality would be the uniform reaction. Is it not more plausible to assume that the Khmer Rouge response, brutal or otherwise, was simply an unintended consequence of U.S. bombing? Without an explication of how U.S. policy makers could have arrived at the conclusion that bombing would intensify Khmer cadre brutality, what remains is either a rudimentary conspiracy theory or an *ad hoc* justification of how humane and beneficent Socialist revolutionaries could have developed a capacity to commit atrocities. The hidden assumption about the benign inclinations of revolutionary forces may overestimate the degree of revolutionary consciousness on the part of the Khmer Rouge peasant army, while simultaneously underestimating the amount of violence required to win a revolution and subsequently to consolidate revolutionary power against internal dissension and/or counterrevolution. Even if corrections for these estimates were to be introduced, the authors would still have to confront the almost insuperable task of producing evidence to sustain the belief that commitment to a socialist ideal mitigates an individual's inclination or capacity to do evil.

In summary, a discussion of U.S. intervention should not be omitted from any account of the last two decades of Kampuchean history, but neither should it be isolated as the sole factor responsible for the excessive violence of the past 20 years. To overemphasize the U.S. contribution to the tragedy is to overlook the role played by dissension within the revolutionary leadership, the traditional hostility between the Khmer population and the neighboring Vietnamese, and the desire for revenge by those who had seen their families and friends slaughtered; their communities and their way of life destroyed.

The Problem of Explanation

A close examination of these diverse accounts of Kampuchean politics reveals a great deal about the ideological biases and political commitments of the proponents of each view. An intense anti-communism pervades the psychological explanation advanced by Barron and Paul, while Ponchaud's analysis of excessive ideological zeal denounces the hubris of those who would create a new secular order devoid of the traditional moorings of religion and divine authority. A commitment to socialist internationalism characterizes Kiernan's discussion of Pol Pot's defective revolutionary consciousness, whereas Burchett's analysis reveals an uncompromising loyalty to the regime in Hanoi. Hildebrand and Porter's rational reconstruction model affords a sympathetic and sincere defense of the Khmer Rouge revolution, while the critiques of imperial power provided by Shawcross, Chomsky, and Herman offer an equally sincere condemnation of United States' behavior toward Cambodia.

That ideological and political predilections are discernible in these explanatory works does not imply that the accounts were intentionally constructed for propagandistic purposes.[69] On the contrary, it attests to a fundamental human propensity to assimilate new information into an existing conceptual framework populated with assumptions and presumptions about the way of the world that are seldom, if ever, subjected to critical scrutiny. Whether these presuppositons tend to vilify communists, atheists, capitalists, or primitive peoples, they share a tendency to caricature, to remove the experience of others from the complexities and ambiguities which characterize life in one's own cultural milieu. As a consequence, explanations of political violence in distant places[70] seem far removed from the experiences of human beings who order their lives in accordance with limited objectives and perceived constraints. Instead, violence emerges as a function of madness, fanaticism, excessive intellectualism, racist chauvinism, heroic altruism, or the devious ploys of imperial powers. What is lost in all these explanatory efforts is the diversity, uncertainty, and fallibility of human ventures undertaken in a world of conflicting interests and competing wills where actions may be initiated but outcomes cannot be predicted fully nor controlled completely.[71]

In place of any systematic appreciation of complexity, ambiguity, and fallibility, tacit theoretical presuppositions structure explanations in accordance with simplistic expectations. Although they provide gravely defective accounts of the political world, the caricatured agents and stereotyped behaviors which emerge in such explanations reinforce the presuppositions from which they proceed. Moreover, the interaction between theoretically constituted expectations and the perceptions and explanations informed by them generates a psychological certainty that the account advanced is essentially correct and the intensity of this conviction works against the emergence of doubt concerning the implausibility of specific claims. Psychological certainty concerning the adequacy of explanations which conform to internalized presuppositions receives additional reinforcement from the uncritical acceptance of the belief that perception is neutral and that the facts speak for themselves. Thus, failure to recognize the role of theoretical presuppositions in the constitution of facticity and in the formation of claims about the empirical realm contributes to the production and accreditation of explanations that obfuscate rather than illuminate the political situation under examination.

Now it might be objected that although the accounts of violence in Kampuchea surveyed thus far are indeed unidimensional and defective, these defects could easily be overcome by the addition of specific historical and cultural information that could provide the context for a meaningful interpretation of these events, by the introduction of additional data that could facilitate empirical analysis of the conflict, or by the application of general scientific laws to the particular phenomena observed in Cambodia. The central point of such objections would be that the problem explored in this chapter is related to 'bad' social science, to empirical studies which were erroneously conceived, poorly designed, and methodologically flawed. The clear implication of such criticisms is that the alternative accounts of political violence examined here represent a variety of methodological mistakes for which remedies exist. They do not pose any substantial challenge to the conceptions of explanation which inform social science in general, or policy analysis in particular. For all the defects identified above could have been eliminated by closer adherence to the norms of *verstehen*, rigorous empirical analysis or the sophisticated use of the hypothetico-deductive model of explanation.

Proponents of interpretive theory (*verstehen*) might point out that an explanation of the political situation in Kampuchea could be rescued from the deficiencies of various accounts of monsters, barbarians, or lunatics if greater attention were paid to the specific historical and cultural situation which gave meaning to the actions of fallible human agents. They might suggest that the participants in these events came from varying backgrounds and experiences, possessed divergent hopes and aspirations, acted with differing notions of political possibility, and operated in a context of extreme political vulnerabiltiy. Much greater attention should have been devoted to these cultural contexts and intersubjective meanings in order to generate an adequate interpretation of events. On this view, the lapses of the unidimensional accounts could be overcome by according greater attention to Kampuchean history, a history of recurrent invasions by Thai and Vietnamese forces over several centuries which were brought to an end only through the oppresive intervention of French colonialism. The deficiencies of these models could be rectified by an understanding of the problems created by the post World War II collapse of French power in Indochina, problems related to internal struggles over the future form of Cambodian political life (e.g., monarchy or republic, capitalist or socialist), as well as to struggles with external forces as a legacy of the neighboring war in Vietnam. The specific context of the Khmer Rouge revolution could be illuminated by detailed consideration of the issues for Cambodia created by the Vietnam war: dangers to border areas, the problem of preserving neutrality, the possibility for personal enrichment created by the war trade in scarce commodities, the operation of black markets, the provision of "protection" for war materiel in transit, and the resulting bribery, graft, and corruption which became a way of life for many Cambodian civilian and military officials. A detailed understanding of the heritage of subjugation to neighboring and colonial powers, of the corruption of petty officials, of the commitments of the small contingent of Khmer socialist revolutionaries, of the predominantly peasant population, and of the largely feudal, subsistence economy could provide an explanation of the political violence free of the distortions considered in the previous accounts.

Systematic empiricists might suggest that a more adequate explanation could be developed if a larger number of variables were considered—a wider range of phenomena taken into account. Thus, they might argue that to provide a plausible interpretation of this decade, one would have to learn about the peasant experience of the bombardment. How was this devastation interpreted by its chief victims? Did it radicalize political consciousness or heighten religious devotion? Did it help the peasants choose sides in the ensuing civil war? Or was no choice allowed; were the peasants drafted into opposing armies through coercion alone? If so, what plans did the peasants make to avenge their captivity? During the civil war, what was the nature of the peasants' exposure to North Vietnamese, South Vietnamese and U.S. troops? Were traditional antagonisms aggravated? Were ancient rituals of warfare (such as carving out and eating an enemy's vital organs) practiced? Were practitioners of these ancient rituals punished by their own commanders? How did other soldiers respond to the rituals and/or their punishment? As the fighting dragged on, did the behavior of the peasant soldiers change? What factors contributed to the changes? How did such changes affect the conduct of the war?

In addition to information about the peasants, who were the vast majority of combatants, it could well be suggested that much more information is needed about the leadership of the revolutionary cadres. What were the major differences among revolutionary leaders? How were decisions about policy made? How were such decisions communicated to those who would implement them? How thorough was compliance with orders? What mechanisms were developed to maintain discipline? What efforts were made to inculcate revolutionary consciousness? What roles did ideology, nationalism, and racism play in forming policy? How did the leaders perceive their allies? How accurate were their perceptions of provocations by the Vietnamese? How realistic were their fears of counterrevolution? Did they have alternatives to a policy of self-reliance in the reconstruction of their nation? What alternative remedies were available to the problems of disease and starvation?

At the international level, it might be pointed out that questions remain concerning the role of Vietnam, China, the U.S.S.R., and the United States in exacerbating the conflict in Kampuchea. What objectives were these nations pursuing in their military and humanitarian assistance programs and what goals are they pursuing now? Precisely what was done to aid or interfere with the Kampuchean revolution and who did it? What benefits were perceived to flow from various outcomes in Kampuchea? What costs were considered tolerable to achieve such benefits? Systematic empiricists might suggest that answers to these many questions at these various levels of analysis could afford a compelling explanation of events in Kampuchea, an explanation free of stereotypes and ideological bias.

In addition to objections focusing on the necessity of the appropriate interpretive context and objections which stress the introduction of additional data to overcome the deficiencies of these unidimensional explanations, a third form of objection might emphasize that the problem is not so much one of inadequate information (although that does contribute to the problem), but rather that the central defect of these alternative accounts of political violence in Kampuchea is that they have failed to integrate available information into a scientific theory. They have failed to link the episodes in Kampuchea to a scientific theory of revolution. This failure to apply existing models of political violence, guerilla warfare, and revolutionary reconstruction is responsible for the defective accounts advanced thus far. Once the specific events of Kampuchea's conflict have been subsumed under the general scientific laws pertaining to political violence, an adequate explanation of the experience would be at hand.

The objections raised by proponents of *verstehen*, data-based, and hypothetico-deductive explanations suggest that "good" social science can transcend the problems of distortion and oversimplification introduced by tacit theoretical presuppositions. Strict adherence to the well developed methodological canons of social science could eliminate the deficiencies detailed in this chapter. But there is little reason to be sanguine about such prospects.

Kampuchea undoubtedly represents an extreme case. The Khmer Rouge decision to seal the borders, to cut off contact with other nations, and to prohibit visitation by foreign emissaries, journalists, and scholars unquestionably created atypical problems for data acquisition. Additional information, therefore, would have eased the problem of analysis and explanation. But even if volumes of information had been available, it would never have been in the form of 'brute facts' sufficient to reveal the truth, free of all theoretical mediation. Although the analyses considered in this chapter do represent the atypicality of the extreme case, they have the great virtue of depicting in stark terms the manner in which 'raw data' is assimilated into a pre-existing conceptual framework. The structuring role of theoretical presuppositions is not eliminated in less extreme cases, nor is it obviated in instances where data abounds. Expectations generated by tacit theoretical assumptions continue to order the perception and comprehension of events even in the most familiar contexts;

but in these contexts, familiarity itself masks their operation.

Proponents of *verstehen* are quite correct to stress that interpretation plays a crucial role in perception and understanding, and that sensitivity to historical contexts and cultural conventions can facilitate efforts to decipher the meaning of actions. But it is not clear that a focus upon the cultural context or the meaning which actions hold for the agents who participate in them would suffice to generate an adequate explanation of the political violence in Kampuchea. For attempts to link two decades of violence to previous cultural conventions would have to confront the possibility that neither Kampuchean history nor culture provide any clear precedents to guide an interpretation of the events following 1969, that part of the revolutionary program involved a radical break with cultural traditions. Moreover, efforts to identify the intentions of the participants might encounter the possibility that the intentions were multiple, ill-formed, and ambiguous; that even within a single individual, intentions were characterized by ambivalence and conflict, and that these conflicts and ambiguities increase exponentially when the intentions of thousands of participants are taken into account. To adjudicate among the possible meanings of disparate intentions, analysts will necessarily have to draw upon theoretically constituted criteria of plausibility and relevance. Thus, the problem of theoretical presuppositions does not disappear from endeavors to construct interpretive explanations of events any more than from efforts to produce purely factual accounts. In both cases, tacit theoretical assumptions will mediate perceptions and descriptions of relevant episodes, guide the accumulation of significant evidence, and direct the development of an explanatory account.

Those who urge the application of scientific laws to generate an adequate explanation of the Kampuchean case also encounter severe problems. Chief among these is that no such 'laws' exist. It is widely recognized that "in no area of social inquiry has a body of general laws been established comparable with the outstanding theories in natural science in scope of explanatory power or in capacity to yield precise and reliable predictions."[72] Moreover, those 'law-like generalizations' which have been advanced by social scientists fail to specify precise conditions under which they hold and coexist with counter-examples that are not taken as refutations.[73] Thus, any effort to apply such laws to the case of Kampuchea would necessarily involve a host of theoretically mediated judgments concerning the extent of their applicability. Explanations afforded by such laws would be characterized by a neglect of those factors that were unique to the Cambodian case and hence did not fit the explanatory model. Evidence which did not conform to the parameters established by the model would be discounted. Arguments justifying the exclusion of extraneous evidence would draw upon the tenets of the general law invoked or the explanatory model employed. In short, the explanations developed in accordance with existing social science knowledge about political violence could be expected to manifest the same features of selectivity, one-dimensionality and reductionism as the explanations discussed in this chapter.

The structuring role of theoretical presuppositions is not simply a function of bad social science. On the contrary, it is a feature of all social science and all policy analysis because it is an ineliminable feature of human cognition. Whenever analysts try to treat questions about political life, whether the investigations focus on participants, leaders, or international complexities, upon perceptions or misperceptions, upon intentions and actions, or upon consequences of action, intended or unintended, theoretical assumptions permeate the inquiry, organizing questions, and ordering answers.

The case of Kampuchea is extreme and atypical in many respects, but the role of theoretical presuppositions in structuring explanations is not a part of that atypicality. In the case of Kampuchea, the assimilation of new information into tacit, presupposition-laden conceptual frameworks contributed to an oversimplification of the events to be explained and a caricature of the agents participating in those events. In an effort to make sense of experiences which differ radically from their own, analysts reduced complex situations to manageable proportions by dehumanizing the participants, depicting them as excessively simple, one-dimensional creatures. And this reductionism produced markedly defective explanations.

In contexts less extreme than that of Kampuchea, analysts must still assimilate new information to pre-existing conceptual frameworks. The expectations sustained by theoretical presuppositions will continue to operate on perception, producing descriptions and explanations of events that are simplified and selective. Whether the methodology involved is quantitative or qualitative, informed by behavioral or interpretive presuppositions, the resulting account will often be one dimensional, lacking in complexity and markedly incomplete. If this is a recurrent outcome of social science inquiry, then perhaps it is time to move beyond monistic models of explanation. Perhaps it is time to accept that no single explanation of complex socio-political events is likely to be definitive. Any individual explanation of intricate social phenomena will bear the traces of the tacit theoretical presuppositions which structure its observations and interpretations; consequently, it will have a distinct political cast and it will be contentious.

If the role of theoretical presuppositions in the constitution of human cognition is to be taken seriously, then perhaps a new conception of explanation should be countenanced. Such a conception of explanation might require that multiple interpretations of the same event, representing different theoretical and methodological perspectives, be systematically compared and contrasted. Such an examination of competing explanations might reintroduce the complexity, ambiguity, and multi-dimensionality of human events while it illuminates the influence of theoretical assumptions on the constitution of facticity in particular cases. The comparison of discrepant accounts and the critical assessment of the evidence afforded by each might facilitate the development of a more comprehensive understanding of the dimensions of the socio-political situation.

As the foregoing exploration of five divergent explanations of recent Kampuchean history demonstrates, a great deal more can be learned about the Kampuchean experience from a comparative examination of competing views than can be gleaned from any account taken individually. Information included in one account may illuminate omissions and deficiencies in other accounts. Comparing divergent explanations may reveal the impact of particular methodologies upon the selection of evidence, and stimulate exploration of factors neglected by the methodologies in question. A systematic survey of a wide range of explanatory accounts may highlight the influence of questionable presuppositions and provide grounds for assessing the credibility of particular claims.

If the problems of explanation identified in the Kampuchean case are typical of explanations in the social sciences, then policy analysis has much to gain from the deployment of a conception of explanation which requires the juxtaposition and analysis of and extrapolation from multiple, non-privileged interpretations of the same socio-political phenomenon. The move beyond methodological monism and one-dimensional models of explanation could heighten sensitivity to the influence of theoretical assumptions, stimulate sustained criticism of overly simplistic explanatory accounts, reinforce recognition of intricacy of political events, entrench the expectation of error, and produce more sophisticated policy analyses.

7

Theoretical Presuppositions and Policy Predictions: The Case of Human Rights

Discussions of the possibility of prediction have played a central role in recent debates within the field of policy analysis and within the social sciences at large. The failure of the social sciences to discover any covering laws capable of generating accurate predictions has severely challenged the "dreams of social physics"[1] and has raised important questions concerning the role of the policy expert in the decision-making process. This chapter will explore the possibility that there are grounds other than the illusory laws of social physics upon which policy predictions may be predicated. It will suggest that an understanding of the operation of divergent theoretical presuppositions upon the constitution of political beliefs, and consequently upon the construction of policy options, can facilitate the identification of policy impasses and the prediction of policy failures.

In order to illustrate this possibility, the chapter will examine several issues pertinent to human rights policies. It will suggest that although the language of human rights appears to be univocal, the mediation of key terms by tacit theoretical assumptions insures that the words have radically different meanings for speakers from different traditions. It will consider in detail the manner in which the rhetoric of universal human rights masks markedly different conceptions of the nature of rights and of the fundamental human interests which rights are devised to protect and promote. To demonstrate that human rights do not represent one universal and invariable ideal, the chapter will trace alternative assumptions concerning the relationship between the individual and the political order, which give rise to the divergent conceptions of rights embodied in the Liberal and Marxist traditions.

Since claims concerning the universality of human rights play a crucial role in the justification of international human rights initiatives advanced by particular governments, the identification of divergent notions of rights provides grounds for reassessing the utility of human rights policies in international politics. Indeed, awareness of the discordant assumptions concerning the constitution of rights suggests that appeals to "universal" rights in the international arena will serve little more than propaganda purposes. To illustrate this problem in concrete circumstances, the chapter will conclude by examining the human rights initiative launched by the Carter Administration. It will suggest that the belief that the rhetoric of universal human rights could afford a mechanism by which the United States could alter the practices of the Soviet Union is fundamentally flawed; hence, any foreign policy initiatives premised on such an erroneous conviction would be destined to failure. Thus the chapter will suggest that greater awareness of the role of theoretical presuppositions in structuring policy options would enable analysts not only to predict such policy failures, but to provide advice to policymakers which might help them to avoid such mistakes.[2]

Human Rights: Universal or Particular?

Human rights rhetoric typically emphasizes the "universal," "inalienable," "indefeasible," "imprescriptible," and "absolute" nature of the protections that human rights afford. Indeed, claims about both the universality and absolute character of human rights help to justify the incorporation of human rights concerns into foreign policy objectives. Recently, the appropriateness of a human rights orientation in foreign policy has been challenged on two separate grounds.

Political scientists have suggested that there is an enormous gap between human rights rhetoric and the implementation of human rights policies in the international arena, that the language of universal rights is used for ideological, hegemonial, and propagandistic purposes. Further, moral philosophers have questioned the possibility of providing a universal justification for any set of rights that could sustain foreign policy objectives.

It is helpful to consider these criticisms in tandem, for taken in conjunction, they suggest that the gap between human rights rhetoric and human rights policies is neither coincidental nor attributable solely to the cynical motives of policy makers. On the contrary, they suggest that the discrepancy between the rhetoric of universal rights and particular human rights policies can be traced to fundamental theoretical presuppositions which structure alternative understandings of the nature of rights. They suggest that it is a mistake to conceive rights as primitive notions possessing universal validity: as the practices of different political systems make clear, rights are derivative concepts, parasitic upon more basic assumptions about human nature and human interests, which are culturally specific and historically variable.

The case for the particularity of human rights has been put forcefully by a number of scholars working in the field of international affairs and comparative foreign policy. Hugo Bedau has argued that as a description of empirical practices, human rights rhetoric is woefully inaccurate. In contrast to the bold stipulation of "inalienability," he has noted that "it is doubtful whether any of our most important rights, including life, liberty, and bodily security, are impossible to inalienate."[3] In addition, he has suggested that if "imprescriptible" means "that a right cannot be abrogated, suspended, repudiated or ignored by a government, then it is rhetorical nonsense. [For] any government in fact can (and most of them do even today) abrogate, suspend, repudiate or ignore rights at some time or another."[4] He has also pointed out that rigid adherence to the notion that human rights are absolute in the sense of being unconditional and exceptionless would require that the vast majority of rights currently enshrined in the U.N. Declaration of Human Rights, as well as in the U.S. Bill of Rights, be purged from the ranks of rights. For these protections, privileges, and immunities are subject to careful balancing as a result of legislation, court decisions, and economic exigencies, and as such, cannot comply with the stringent requirements of an absolute right.

The notion that human rights are universal has also been widely contested. Noting that "human rights are but one way that has been devised to realize and protect human dignity,"[5] Jack Donnelly has linked the emergence of human rights rhetoric in the modern world to the breakdown of traditional societies and supportive communities and to the isolation of the individual "who is forced to go it alone against social, economic, and political forces that are far too often aggressive and oppressive."[6] Tracy Strong has suggested a connection between Americans' preoccupations with the dissemination of human rights and their unique experience of founding and legitimizing a Republic which exists in principle to make possible a human life characterized by the protection of particular rights.[7] Pollis and Schwab have argued that "the prevailing conception of human rights is an essentially Western doctrine of little relevance to cultures other than those of the West and to ideologies other than those of Capitalist, pluralist societies."[8] And Eddison Svobgo has noted that the conception of a human being as an autonomous, separate, and self-determining actor which sustains Western conceptions of human rights, "is as non-existent as it is absurd" to Third World people.[9] Further, he has argued that "given the history of colonialism, the exploitation of resources and laborers, racism, forced labor, expropriation and the failure of the West to recognize famine and underdevelopment as serious crises related to the construction of civil liberties,"[10] the Third World must view Western human rights claims with some degree of skepticism.

That skepticism or even cynicism is warranted with respect to Western governments' adoption of international human rights initiatives has been reiterated by a number of social scientists who have provided detailed descriptions of particular instances in which human rights policies have been defined and/or pressed in a biased, self-serving, and chauvinistic manner. Scoble and Wiseberg have demonstrated that 'value neutral', scientific attempts to specify and operationalize the concept of human rights have been essentially political acts which "reflect the power of some persons to define key terms with reference to their own preferred values."[11] Richard Falk has argued that "when the United States explicitly proclaims a human rights diplomcy that it will implement as a general element of its foreign policy, this entails an explicitly hegemonial attitude toward the internal affairs of certain foreign countries."[12] And he has suggested that this hegemonial stance has far more to do with the perpetution of a geopolitical struggle than with the protection of individuals' rights. Paula Newburg's research has indicated that some U.S. government officials perceived the human rights movement to be a "powerful antidote to the ideological force of communism," and promoted the policy expressly for that purpose.[13] David Riesman has described U.S. human rights initiatives as "thinly disguised moral imperialism."[14] Robert Johnson has identified a growing tension between commitments to the protection of universal human rights and to respect for national sovereignty and national self-determination.[15] And Pollis and Schwab have emphasized that the ideological uses of human rights rhetoric undermine the utility of rights-based policies in the international sphere.[16]

While political scientists have focused on the gap between the ideal of universal human rights and the biases and distortions of particular policies that are legitimated by appeals to that ideal, moral philosophers have raised questions about the moral and political obligations flowing from the proclamation of rights. In moral discourse, human rights claims invoke the language of obligation. Thus, to recognize that an individual has a right is to simultaneously assert that other persons have a tripartite obligation with respect to that right: they ought to avoid depriving the individual of the right; they ought to protect the individual from deprivation by others; and they ought to aid the victims of past deprivations.[17] In the context of political discourse, the proclamation of a human right invokes the legitimate use of force to guarantee that right. Thus, to say that an individual has a right recognized by the state is to assert that the state has a responsibility to secure that right against attempted abuses, and to punish individuals when they violate others' rights.

In the international political arena, the proclamation of universal human rights has clear political implications, for any such proclamation suggests that the enforcement of rights cannot be restricted to the internal affairs of particular states. Each state has an obligation to prevent abuses of rights and to punish abusers throughout the world. To invoke the language of universal obligation and universal enforcement implies that human rights have universal validity, that their justification stands outside of the realm of possible dispute. Yet despite numerous efforts, philosophers have failed to locate a foundation for human rights which lies beyond dispute and which is sufficiently sturdy to bear the moral weight which rights language imposes.[18]

When philosophers have considered the various grounds put forward as incontestable justifications for human rights, they have found problems with all the contending arguments. Utilitarian justifications are corrupted by their internal logic; for any right justified on the grounds of social utility can also be overriden on the grounds of social utility. Thus, utilitarian justifications cannot make any human right

secure, much less absolute. Contractarian justifications are stymied
by the absence of agreement concerning the specific rights which all
consenting parties would accept as the basis of their contract. In the
absence of perfect agreement, contractarian justifications deteriorate
into consensual or conventional justifications lacking universal validity. Rationalist justifications, which attempt to derive rights from the
nature of moral agency or personhood *per se,* fail to demonstrate how
it is that individual needs, interests, claims, demands, or actions give
rise to an enforceable right.[19] They fail to bridge the gap between particular facts about people and the special moral considerations which
rights are.[20] For example, theories which link rights to sentience or to
the capacity to feel pain provide an argument not for human rights,
but for rights which would be shared with the whole animal kingdom.
Theories which posit rationality as the essential locus of human
rights are either notoriously vague about the minimal standards of rationality at issue, or identify standards of rationality which exclude
some human beings for all of their lives (e.g., the mentally impaired),
and all human beings for part of their lives (prior to reaching the age of
reason). Theories which rely on intrinsic worth to sustain a system of
rights simply beg the question.[21] Finally, intuitionist arguments,
known for their appeal to the self-evidence of the rights they stipu-
late, are also marred by a radical disagreement over which claims are
to be accorded the status of rights. And in the absence of unanimity,
the grounds for accepting particular intuitions become murky and
the onus of arbitrariness pervades the enterprise.

When critiques of human rights rhetoric that emphasize the discrepancy between the universality of rights language and the par-
ochialism of rights policies are coupled with critiques of alternative
justifications of universal rights claims, serious flaws in the traditional manner of conceptualizing human rights become apparent. Indeed, the very conception of human rights as universal entitlements
possessing transcendent validity, independent of any cultural or historical moorings, becomes suspect. The force of these combined criticisms suggests that the notion of human rights must be reconceived.

To avoid the flaws of universal human rights rhetoric, a reformulated conception of rights must recognize the cultural and historical
particularity of divergent rights claims. "Rights are rules which define the boundaries of what is owed to a specific group of people (rights
holders) by another group (rights respectors)."[22] As such, rights are derivative of and dependent on more fundamental assumptions abut
human nature and human interests, which are not transcendent and
universal, but rather culturally specific and variable. "The institution

of rights is one which protects certain fundamental interests which people have. . . . A conception of rights therefore, already involves a conception of what these fundamental interests are which need to be protected and these interests cannot be specified outside of a social and political context."[23] According to this reformulated conception, human rights claims could not represent one universal and invariant ideal, for they necessarily depend on disparate notions of fundamental human interests.[24]

The extent to which rights are parasitic upon divergent conceptions of human nature and political order can best be illustrated by examining the contrasting assumptions which inform conceptions of human rights within two disparate theoretical contexts. An exposition of the discordant presuppositions concerning individual interests, and the function of the state incorporated in Liberal and Marxist traditions will help to illuminate the markedly different understandings of rights that surface in international human rights debates. Awareness of these discordant notions will also help to explain why discussions of human rights in the international forum tend to be so intractable.

Liberalism: Civil Rights, Civil Liberties, and the Protection of Private Pursuits

Whether traced to efforts to undermine medieval scholasticism, the political power of religious authorities, organic conceptions of social relations, the feudal hierarchy, or absolute monarchy, the atomistic conception of the individual was advanced as part of a strategy to create alternate possibilities for political life.[25] The atomistic presumption of human equality, whether rooted in rational faculties, survival capabilities, a psychology of unlimited desires, or comparable capacities to kill, constituted a marked departure from and a serious challenge to the assumption of natural superiority that sustained classical and medieval political relations.[26] It provided a foundation for arguments that individuals are entitled to liberty and to the right to pursue ends of their own choosing, free of the interference of others. Yet the arguments concerning individual equality and the right to liberty raised two central problems for liberal theorists: a problem of order and a problem of legitimacy.

The problem of order is intimately related to the recognition that the freedom to pursue subjectively determined ends in a world characterized by scarcity would produce intense competition among atomistic individuals who possess roughly equal capacities to satisfy their desires. If such competition is to be prevented from devolving into a "war of all against all," rules must be established to regulate the competition. Yet liberal theorists acknowledged that rules are never neutral: any set of rules would favor the interests of some and impose constraints on the freedom of others. Thus, the introduction of any set of rules created a problem of legitimacy. For if individuals are equal and entitled to equal treatment, then any rules of order which accord disproportionate power to some and impose constraints on others seem arbitrary and unwarranted. The challenge for liberal theorists was to find a solution to the problem of order consistent with their commitment to the equality of individuals, to identify mechanisms which could safeguard the interests of all members of the political community without jeopardizing peace and without legitimizing a permanent political hierarchy.[27]

The notion of civil liberties as rights to be free from governmental intrusion, and of civil rights both as rights to equal treatment before the law and as rights to participate in political decision-making, were advanced as liberal solutions to the dual problems of order and legitimacy. The idea of civil liberties is premised on the assumption that it is the coercion of other human beings which constitutes the fundamental obstacle to, or constraint upon, individual freedom. By ensuring individuals a sphere of action free from intrusion by others, including the state, civil liberties protect the individual's fundamental interest in seeking satisfaction of subjectively determined desires.

The rights devised to protect this fundamental interest, the rights of privacy, of free association, of freedom of movement, of conscience, of speech, of property, are rights which all individuals can enjoy regardless of their particular desires or ends. They presuppose no shared conception of the common good and no collective goals which all individuals are concerned to seek.[28] Indeed, the institution of civil liberties protects individuals from the tyranny of the supposition that shared concerns exist by legitimizing the private pursuit of diverse desires in a sphere beyond government regulation or control.

To afford additional protection to the private sphere as a realm in which diversity, freedom, and the multiplicity of desires could flourish, the liberal tradition devised the status of the citizen. Citizenship accords members of the political community an equal status in terms of the possession of rights and immunities before the law. Citizenship is a guarantee that individuals will be treated equally by the state despite whatever differences characterize their lives in the private realm. The rights to due process of law, to a jury trial, to face one's accusers, to have the assistance of the state in summoning witnesses for one's defense, and most importantly, to vote and to petition the government for the redress of grievances, are designed to ensure that the state will be indifferent to the multiplicity of differences which characterize individuals existence in the private sphere. Wealth, poverty, level of education, religious affiliation, occupation, age, race, sex, ethnicity, and a host of other factors may circumscribe the prospects of individuals in their private endeavors; but in principle, they have no bearing upon the treatment of individuals as citizens in the political forum.

As citizens, all individuals are equal in the eyes of the state. The rights of the citizen are formal rights, concretized in the form of procedual guarantees accorded to all citizens. Precisely because the private sphere is understood as a realm comprising the radical differences produced by the pursuit of subjectively determined ends, procedural guarantees exhaust the possible benefits afforded by the liberal state. The rights to participate in politics, to press claims and promote interests in the public forum, to air perceived grievances and to elect public officials are all neutral with respect to the ends which individuals might pursue. Substantive guarantees on the other hand, whether they are in the form of rights to social benefits or economic benefits, are seen as violations of the liberal commitment to neutrality with respect to individual ends. For they substitute a particular, and on this view arbitrary, conception of the common good for individuals' private determination of their own goods. And they use the power of the state to promote ends which unjustifiably favor certain interests. As such, they constitute an unacceptable infringement of the principle of formal equality which civil rights and civil liberties instantiate.

When liberal conceptions of rights are recast as prescriptions for universal human rights, the legacy of problems and solutions posed by atomistic assumptions is preserved. It is no coincidence then that liberal human rights advocates insist that "political and civil freedoms cannot be compromised,"[29] and that the "content of human rights will always be defined by political and civil rights."[30] This conception of rights is inextricably enmeshed in the liberal tradition and derivative from both the image of individuals as independent agents capable of molding their identities from the raw materials of divergent desires and from the recognition of the fundamental human interest in the pursuit of subjectively determined ends, free from obstruction by other human beings. Within the classical liberal framework, social and economic 'rights' are seen as arbitrary and unwarranted obstructions of individual liberty and as violations of the principle of equality, and are rejected as such.[31]

Marxism: Substantive Rights and the Fulfillment of Needs

The Marxian conception of human nature was developed in response to, and as a critique of, the atomistic assumptions incorporated in liberal theory. Marx argued that the atomistic conception of individuality did not provide a universal characterization of the human condition; rather, it represented a reification of bourgeois social relations, uncritically projected upon all humanity. In contrast to the atomistic conception of individuality, Marx suggested that the individual is a social being,[32] one whose perceptions, ideas, interests, expectations, understandings, and aspirations are shaped by membership in a cultural community at a determinate point in history. On this view, individual identity is not idiosyncratically constituted by personal choices; it is, in an important sense, a social product developed through the incorporation of, the reflection upon, and the response to a host of intersubjective understandings which circumscribe the range of possibility in a particular cultural universe. According to the Marxian conception of individuality, it is not subjectively determined desire but socially mediated needs which constitute the core of individual personality. It is not competition for scarce goods but a determinate form of social cooperation to produce goods to fulfill needs which establishes the context for the development of individual identity and for the determination of need-related objectives.[33]

On the Marxian view, human need is not a static construct; on the contrary, needs continually evolve in response to changing circumstances and through the satisfaction of other needs.[34] Yet Marx suggested that all human beings share the fundamental need to subsist and to develop and express themselves through creative productive activity, a double need which is satisfied in work. The fulfillment of these needs necessarily involve the individual in complex relations with nature and with other human beings, creating determinate social, economic and political relations. For this reason, the standard which Marx devised to measure progress in human history focused primarily on the structural capacities of different societies to fulfill both the subsistence and the expressive-developmental needs of its population.[35]

As a stage in the historical development of social relations, Marx suggested that capitalism's great accomplishment consisted in the creation of a technology of abundance, a technology which made it possible to provide a high standard of living for all individuals. Under capitalism, for the first time in history, productive technology produced goods in abundance, not just enough for all to subsist, but enough for all to develop their capacities fully, to move from the realm of necessity into the realm of freedom.[36] Capitalism's great defect, however, lay in its perpetuation of an irrational distribution system premised upon private ownership of the means of production, which diminished rather than increased the level of subsistence of the working class. Moreover, the structure of the industrial production process developed within capitalism dehumanized the workers by denying their expressive-developmental needs.[37]

Given the Marxian recognition of the fundamental human interest in work, both as a means of subsistence and as a means for the development and expression of the individual's capacities, it is not surprising that the right to work assumes primary importance within Marxist theory. In its original formulation, the right to work implied a great deal more than guaranteed employment with pay. For Marx, all work must be "socially useful,"[38] it must involve the performance of an activity or the production of a good which satisfies a human need and/or is valued by society. Moreover, the work must afford the individual an opportunity to cultivate both physical and intellectual capabilities.[39] It was for this reason that mindless manual labor under the command of a supervisor which substituted "one-sided development" for "all-round development" was so reprehensible to Marx. To fulfill the requirement of intellectual stimulation, workers must participate in management decisions concerning the planning, production, and distribution of socially useful goods.[40] Thus, worker control of the production process was central to Marx's conception of work as free productive activity. In addition, to allow for the expression of the worker's individuality, work must be creative. The expressive opportunities characteristic of the artistic professions and the diversity associated with multiple occupations must be incorporated in the work life of all individuals.[41] Within Marxian theory then, the right to work embodies an expansive promise of freedom: freedom from poverty and from the anxiety associated with unemployment, freedom from control by an employer, freedom to determine, in cooperation with coworkers, both the contours of work life and the contents of the production process, freedom to develop a wide range of skills and talents, and freedom to express one's individuality without fear of reprisal.[42]

To realize these freedoms, Marxist theory specifies certain sub-

sidiary rights, such as the rights to medical care, education, and leisure, all of which satisfy needs and enhance the individual's opportunities to excel in work. But it is clear within the Marxist framework, that neither the fundamental right to work nor the subsidiary
rights to social benefits can be protected until capitalism and its institutionalization in the form of the liberal bourgeois state have been
eliminated.[43] Marx depicted the bourgeois state as an instrument of
capitalist oppression which concretizes and sustains the advantages
of the owners of the means of production through legal mechanisms
such as property rights and laws governing contracts. Despite liberal
rhetoric proclaiming equal rights and equal opportunities, Marxists
have insisted that equal formal rights and civil liberties are hollow in
the context of a capitalist society. For individuals must be in a position to live before they can take advantage of civil rights and liberties,
and it is precisely this right to life in the sense of a right to subsistence
and to meaningful work which capitalism denies to the working
class.

For this reason, Marxists have argued that claims concerning
universal human rights advanced by capitalists are suspect, for the
rhetoric of universality masks the promotion of their own class interests. Indeed, Marxists have suggested that workers must be constantly on guard against abstract and formal declarations of right
which serve only to perpetuate oppression. Thus, Lenin cautioned
that:

> In the guise of equality of persons generally, bourgeois democracy
> proclaims the formal or juridical equality between the property
> owner and the proletarian, between the exploiter and the exploited,
> and thereby greatly deceives the oppressed classes. The bourgeoisie
> transforms the idea of equality which is itself the reflection of com-
> modity production relations into a weapon in the struggle against
> the abolition of classes on the plea of alleged absolute equality be-
> tween individuals.[44]

The belief that liberal rhetoric concerning universal human
rights camouflages the class interests of capitalists has a number of
important implications for political systems committed to Marxist
principles and for the conception of human rights which they endorse. For it introduces a criterion with which to distinguish between
legitimate human rights claims, i.e., those which promote the fundamental interests of workers, and fraudulent human rights claims, i.e.,
those which promote the interests of capitalists. It accords primacy to

the rights to food, clothing, shelter, to work and to rest, and to an education as the fundamental rights which socialism must advance and protect.[45] In addition, suspicions concerning the class-based character of particular human rights claims provide grounds for imposing restrictions upon certain rights, such as freedom of speech, of the press, and of private ownership of the means of production when those rights conflict with the fundamental interests of workers.[46]

Thus, it is no coincidence that states founded upon Marxist principles insist that the substantive commitment to equality, defined in terms of rights to work, to leisure, to medical care, to housing, and to a host of social and economic benefits, must take precedence over procedural guarantees.[47] Nor is it anomalous that the Marxian conception of human rights tolerates the prohibition of certain occupations and activities and the censorship of certain ideas. The prohibition of "capitalist acts between consenting adults,"[48] the censorship of ideas which advocate activities considered exploitative and the punishment of those who violate such prohibitions follows directly from the commitment to the creation of a work life which will enable all individuals to develop fully and from the belief that capitalism is the fundamental obstacle to the realization of that goal.

When Marxian conceptions of fundamental needs and interests are introduced into international debates concerning fundamental human rights, they do not suggest the same agenda for governmental action as do liberal conceptions of rights. On the contrary, they accord the right to work and the rights to substantive social and economic benefits the highest priority on the international agenda. Moreover, they provide grounds for rejecting the liberal insistence on the institutionalization of absolute procedural guarantees relating to civil rights and civil liberties as empty rhetoric, bereft of meaning by the oppressive priorities of the Capitalist system.[49]

Human Rights Policies in International Politics

There is of course a great gulf between the purity of theoretical assumptions in the Liberal and Marxist traditions and the actual practices of particular states. Racial, sexual, and class inequalities in the United States challenge the adequacy of the liberal doctrine of formal equality of rights, and the command economy in the Soviet Union makes a mockery of the Marxian ideal of worker management and control over productive life. But however imperfectly these theoretical presuppositions are instantiated in the practices of particular governments, they help to explain why human rights debates in the international arena are so intractable and why human rights initiatives launched by capitalist and socialist governments will be at cross-purposes.

Despite common appeals to such terms as 'rights', 'justice', 'equality', and 'human dignity', the content of these terms is so laden with divergent theoretical presuppositions, that in an important sense, participants in the human rights debate may not be discussing the same phenomena at all. The operation of discordant theoretical assumptions transforms the rhetoric of human rights into a potent weapon in the political battle between the superpowers, with the unfortunate consequence that irony is the most predictable outcome of international human rights initiatives. The liberal commitment to civil rights and civil liberties, devised to protect the individual's unobstructed pursuit of personal desires, fuels efforts to impose, by force when necessary, particular desires, behaviors, and goals upon foreign populations. And the Marxist commitment to developing the full potential of all individuals legitimizes revolutionary violence, which annihilates not just the expressive capabilities, but the lives of substantial numbers of people. However benign the intentions, human rights initiatives in foreign policy are unlikely to protect the rights or promote the interests of oppressed people.[50]

If human rights initiatives launched by the superpowers are unlikely to protect the rights of individuals in Third World nations, they are surely destined to failure when they target each other for remedial action. An examination of the Carter Administration's human rights initiative toward the Soviet Union can illuminate the futility of any policy advanced by the United States which ignores the divergent presuppositions underlying human rights rhetoric.

The Carter Doctrine

During the first ten months of his administration, President Carter's vague inaugural pledge of concern for human rights was transformed into the highly controversial Carter Doctrine. As articulated by the State Department, this doctrine emphasized three categories of human rights:

(1) The right to be free from governmental violation of the integrity of the person. Such violations include torture; cruel, inhuman or degrading treatment or punishment; arbitrary

arrest or imprisonment, denial of fair public trial; and invasion of the home.

(2) The right to fulfillment of vital needs, such as food, shelter, health care and education.

(3) The right to enjoy civil and political liberties such as freedom of thought, of religion, of assembly, of speech, of the press; freedom of movement both within and outside of one's country; freedom to take part in government.[51]

The explicit goal of the Carter Doctrine was to "promote greater observance by governments of all three groups of the fundamental human rights . . . for it is, after all, these rights which make life worth living."[52]

Because pursuit of this goal could easily be misconstrued as United States' interference in the internal affairs of other nations,[53] the Carter Administration insisted that the legitimacy of the goal was established by international laws which assign the duty to protect human rights to the international community. Noting that the UN charter asserted fundamental obligations for the United Nations and UN member states to protect human rights, President Carter argued that "all signatories of the UN charter have pledged themselves to observe and respect basic human rights. Thus no members of the UN can claim that mistreatment of its citizens is solely its own business. Equally, no member can avoid its responsibility to review and to speak when torture and unwarranted deprivation occurs in any part of the world."[54]

With respect to the Soviet Union, President Carter bolstered his argument with reference to the 1975 Helsinki Accord. Although the Final Act of the Conference on Security and Cooperaton in Europe (CSCE) is only a "declaration of principles on guiding relations between participating states" that is not legally binding, the Carter Administration suggested that the declaration had the following importance:

> The Soviet Union has agreed to include in Basket III humanitarian and human rights issues, thus acknowledging that these rights are of importance to the improvement of relations generally and that they are a legitimate subject of international concern. A participant raising with any other participant any of the issues dealt with in the Final Act can no longer be characterized as "interfering" in domestic affairs. All participating states have promised to implement the results of the Conference and all other participants have the right to make inquiries concerning this commitment.[55]

Having defended the United States' concern for human rights in terms of its duties as a member of the international community, the Carter Administration suggested that the complexities of international affairs necessitate flexibility in the expression or manifestation of this concern. Different countries, different cultures, different priorities and different U.S. national interests require different U.S. responses to human rights violations. Thus, a 'flexible response' repertoire must include a variety of options ranging from quiet diplomacy, public denunciation (e.g., statements to the press, speeches), and requests that an international organization take action, to the application of economic sanctions or arms embargoes, the reduction or termination of economic or military assistance, and action restricting U.S. diplomatic representation.[56]

In his dealings with the Soviet Union, President Carter's manifestation of concern for human rights relied primarily on public denunciation. He also attempted to provide a measure of moral support for Soviet dissidents by personally writing to Sakharov and by receiving the exiled dissident, Bukovsky, at the White House.[57] Carter's reliance on verbal and symbolic strategies suggests that he believed that exposure to the tribunal of world opinion would be sufficient to trigger repentance in governments abusive of human rights and that this burden of guilt coupled with international censure would sufficiently motivate offending governments to reform their policies.[58]

The success of the Carter human rights initiative depended, then, on the willingness of governments accused of human rights violations to redress particular grievances pertaining to their own citizens that had been identified by the United States as human rights abuses. Any such willingness would require that the government in question (1) recognize the validity of the U.S. complaint, that is, acknowledge that a human right had in fact been violated; (2) accept the legitimacy of the role of the United States as accusor, as guardian of human rights; and (3) succumb to U.S. pressure, exhortatory or economic, and desist in the violation.

Awareness of the theoretical presuppositions which sustain the Soviet conception of rights suggests that these conditions could never be met in the Soviet case. The central tenets of Marxist-Leninism preclude the possibility that a socialist state such as the Soviet Union would concur in any capitalist identification of a human rights violation. The theoretical presuppositions which structure Soviet conceptions of rights would immunize the Soviet Union against any verbal or symbolic pressure from the United States. Further, the status of the United States as the foremost defender of capitalism would undermine the legitimacy of any attempt by the United States to assert itself as guardian of human rights. From the Soviet perspective, the capitalist, by definition, is the offender of human rights, and any defense of these rights which the capitalist articulates can be repudiated as deceptive propaganda.

An exploration of the Soviet response to Carter's human rights policy as manifested in statements in the Soviet press reveals the precise contours of the predictable socialist response to any capitalist accusation of a human rights violation.

Perceptions of U.S. Human Rights Policy in the Soviet Press

Statements published in the Soviet press in the aftermath of the Helsinki Accord and in direct response to Carter's human rights initiative indicate a marked similarity between the perceptual categories constructed in Marxist-Leninist theory and those used by Soviet journalists in their analyses of the U.S. human rights policy. The capitalist concern with human rights was portrayed as a highly sophisticated propaganda campaign designed to distract public opinion from the contemporary moral and economic crises of capitalism; to undermine socialism and the government of the Soviet Union, and to mask capitalist violations of human rights and the Helsinki Accord.

Soviet journalists insisted that the furor over human rights could be understood within the context of the ongoing struggle between capitalist and socialist ideologies. "Thousands of threads of cooperation in the areas of economics, science, culture and art bind together countries with differing social structures. But the ideological struggle continues. Day and night the airwaves are filled with the venomous slander of bourgeois propaganda that attempts to discredit socialist society."[59] Further, journalists suggested that the intensity of the capitalists' rhetorical campaign was directly related to the experience of irremedial damages on other fronts. "It is indicative that given the current alignment of forces in conditions in which Capitalism is losing one position after another in the competition with and the struggle with socialism in the economic, socio-political and cultural spheres, increasing emphasis is being placed on ideological means of struggle against real socialism."[60] Thus the human rights rhetoric of the capitalists was interpreted as evidence of capitalists' fear of the "strengthening of the solidarity of socialist countries and the deepening of the fraternal friendship between their Marxist-Leninist parties which are significantly increasing the combined might and influence of socialism on the course of world events."[61] Soviet journalists claimed that the U.S. human rights campaign was neither a manifestation of concern for the rights of individuals nor an indication of capitalism's strength and humaneness. On the contrary, they suggested that it was proof of capitalism's increasing infirmity.

In addition to portraying the capitalist human rights concern as a "last-ditch" propaganda effort premised upon a recognition of capitalism's declining strength, prestige, and appeal, the Soviet press also denounced the hypocrisy of the capitalists' alleged concern with human rights. Emphasizing that the humanist language of the human rights campaign only masked the anti-humanist intentions of its capitalist promoters, Soviet journalists compiled a lengthy list of anti-humanist motives believed to underlie the human rights campaign. Subversive attempts to undermine the Soviet Union in particular, and socialism in general, headed this list.[62] The Soviet press suggested that "ideological myths and social illusions such as 'freedom of the individual,' 'human rights,' and the 'democracy' of Western systems" mask a thinly disguised anti-communism, anti-Sovietism, racism, and chauvinism "while remaining silent about the fact that the Capitalist system gave birth to fascism, racism, unemployment and many other social ills."[63] According to the press, the purpose of such propaganda was obvious: "to evoke on the part of uninformed people in the West and the countries of the Third World a distrust of socialism and to compromise it in the eyes of the world public opinion, particularly among believers, with a view toward weakening the force of attraction of socialism and impeding the development of the process of detente."[64]

In addition to attempting to subvert socialism, the human rights campaign was described as an effort to protect state monopoly capitalism and the interests of the military-industrial complex. Journalists suggested that when carefully examined, the "concern with the fate of mankind turns out to be a defense of the interests of State monopoly Capitalism."[65] Indeed, it was noted that the "noisy campaign about human rights is intended as a cover for aspirations quite different from the defense of those rights. It is no accident that General Haig, Commander-in-Chief of NATO, took satisfaction in informing the *New York Times* that Washington's uproar 'has convinced other members of NATO of the need to improve the West's military defenses.'"[66]

Charges that the human rights campaign was being conducted to promote the anti-humanist designs of imperialism were embellished with a host of other accusations concerning the specific abuses of human rights by imperialist nations. The Soviet press suggested that the entire human rights initiative was undertaken "to distract the attention of the public and of the peoples of capitalist countries from the unsightly picture that bourgeois society presents, especially in the atmosphere of profound economic crises and new social and political upheavals that are now gripping it."[67] It was suggested that this propaganda campaign was orchestrated precisely because it "distracts attention from the systematic and flagrant violations of elementary human rights in capitalist society."[68] The human rights violations in the United States identified by Soviet journalists included the unemployment of millions of people, racial discrimination, the denial of equal rights to women, persecution of dissidents, infringements of personal freedoms, and the growing crime rate which forces the population to live in terror.[69]

Soviet commentators also castigated the United States for its economic, military, and moral support of regimes in other parts of the world which suppress human rights, suggesting that human rights are of concern to capitalists only when their protection does not interfere with the imperialists' investment interests. Characterizing the U.S. as a nation which supports state terrorism, Soviet journalists devoted a good deal of attention to U.S. complicity in the acts of dictatorial regimes in Latin America, South Korea, and South Africa.[70]

The Soviet press also pointed out the irony of the fact that the United States, the self-proclaimed defender of human rights, had ratified only ten of the forty human rights treaties then in effect. Soviet journalists noted that Presidents Ford and Carter seem to "have 'forgotten' that the United States has not yet signed either the International Pact regarding economic, social or cultural rights, or the pact drawn up by the United Nations regarding civil and political rights. Yet these documents have been signed and ratified by the Soviet Union."[71]

Since most of the United States' criticisms of Soviet activity derived their justifications from references to the Helsinki Accord and focused on alleged Soviet violations of "Basket III" provisions of the Final Act, it is not surprising that the Soviet press accumulated its own catalogue of U.S. violations of the Helsinki Agreement. Commentators noted that from the very outset the United States violated one provision of the Final Act which required publication and dissemination of the document by all signatories. Numerous Soviet writers suggested that ordinary American citizens had no access to the information contained in the agreement because it was never published in full in the U.S. press.[72] And they noted that in contrast to the brief abstracts of the document which were published by major American newspapers, two Soviet daily newspapers, *Pravda* and *Izvestia*, published the entire agreement.

Another provision of the Final Act calls for the free exchange of information and ideas and the promotion of cooperation among signatory states. The Soviet press argued that the "anti-Soviet propaganda in the Western media is a clear violation of the Helsinki Accord which states that the information media should work for detente and not against it, and for the expansion and consolidation of cooperation and creation of an atmosphere of trust among peoples and states, and not arouse hostility and alienation among them."[73] According to the Soviet reports, the disseminators of this "mendacious propaganda which alleges infringements of human rights in the U.S.S.R. and which deliberately distorts the policy of the Soviet state,"[74] intended not the free exchange of information and ideas, "but the dissemination of subversive materials."[75]

Additional U.S. infractions of the Final Act reported in the Soviet press included: the retaliatory expulsion from the United States of a Tass correspondent who had violated no American laws; the denial of a U.S. entry visa to the Editor in Chief of the *Literaturnaya Gazeta*; and the repeated denial of tourist visas to Soviet trade union delegates (U.S.S.R. Seamen and River Transport Workers Trade Union) who had been invited to the United States by American trade unions to attend the Congress of West Coast Longshoremen and Warehousemen's Unions.[76]

The Soviets also accused the United States of violating the provision of the Final Act which recognizes the territorial integrity of states. "The Helsinki Agreement declared the boundaries of all European states inviolable. Yet the West continues to provoke incidents that contradict the letter and the spirit of the agreement and can only be regarded as treacherous."[77] And they accused the United States of violating a provision of the Helsinki Accord, which asserts the principle of noninterference in the internal affairs of other states. Indeed, the Soviet press identified the United States' human rights initiative itself as an illicit attempt to interfere in the internal affairs of the U.S.S.R.[78]

No investigation of the Soviet perceptions of the U.S. human rights policy would be complete without a review of the Soviet press's treatment of dissidents. The United States articulated its support for Soviet dissidents, i.e., individuals who have been or are now being persecuted for their beliefs, who are denied the rights of freedom of conscience and freedom of speech. Soviet commentators insisted that no one in the Soviet Union is persecuted or prosecuted for personal beliefs or for constructive criticism of the regime. They repeatedly noted that the Soviet constitution guarantees not only freedom of conscience, freedom of belief, and freedom of speech, but also freedom to criticize the administration. From their perspective, the dissidents are not condemned for either thoughts or words, but for specific subversive actions designed to undermine the socialist system.[79] According to the Soviet press, the "dissidents" are a "handful of characters with anti-Soviet sentiments who are slandering their own homeland and their own people."[80] They are not righteous individuals who are being persecuted for their beliefs, they are "renegades" charged with crimes of anti-Soviet propagandizing and agitation aimed at undermining the social and political system.

The moral character of these "renegades" has been further illuminated in several articles by individuals who are depicted as former dissidents who have grown disillusioned with the "cause" after a long association with the dissident group. According to this testimony, much of their disillusionment arose from recognition of the unsavory characters of their associates and from demands that they join in illegal activities at the behest of foreign governments. Thus denunciations of the corruption of dissidents is common in these essays, a corruption rooted in "self-interested greed and capitalist exchange mentality . . . the dissidents operate in an atmosphere little resembling zeal for 'trampled human rights'; but more like a business atmosphere evincing calculation and trading and the ability to sell rotten goods to the West and extract the utmost money for them."[81] Claims that the dissidents are carrying on illicit activities for the CIA are also frequent: "The dissidents are adventurists and money-grubbers who are disguising themselves as fighters for human rights . . . by staging provocations and giving aid to reactionary forces in the West, their goal is to create publicity for themselves and earn a steady income from abroad. . . . These political and common criminals, the enemies of socialism and the Soviet state are deliberately exploiting the so-called 'human rights' question for the benefit of imperialism and world reaction."[82]

The Soviet press asserted that "bourgeois ideologists have enlisted the services of dissidents—or in plainer terms, renegades, to lend bourgeois propaganda a semblance of 'objectivity' and to create an even more illusory semblance that some kind of 'opposition' to the socialist system exists. In fact, overt opponents of socialism are an insignificant little group of people who do not represent anyone or anything, are remote from the Soviet people and exist only because they are supported, paid and extolled by the West."[83] Yet the fact that some dissidents do exist is taken by Soviet journalists to be troubling, for it indicates that socialism has failed to achieve the total transformation of values at which it aims. Rather than create an atmosphere of tolerance for dissent, Western pressure on behalf of the dissidents illuminates the need for more intensive socialist agitation and reeducation, the need for a crack-down upon, rather than a benign neglect of, dissent. Thus commentators have concluded:

> Needless to say, a handful of renegades presents no danger to the Soviet system. But the very fact of their existence indicates that we have still not completely rid ourselves of the vestiges and the mores and prejudices of the old society, that individual citizens still take the bait of bourgeois propaganda and allow themselves to be dazzled by the tinsel of the bourgeois way of life and to be deceived by cock-and-bull stories about 'human rights' and 'freedoms' in the Capitalist world. Therefore, it is necessary as never before to display a high degree of political vigilance, to give a timely and effective rebuff to bourgeois propaganda, to wage a tireless struggle against the political indifference and lack of ideological principle that still exist in our midst and to instill in the Soviet people a spirit of love for their homeland and of devotion to the cause of the Communist party and lofty communist ideals.[84]

Many of the reports concerning the United States' human rights initiative in the Soviet press juxtaposed the hyprocrisy of the capitalists' alleged concern for human rights against a reaffirmation of the belief that only socialism embodies a true concern with human rights. "The humanist ideal of scientific communism is the welfare of every individual and his/her free and all-round development within a system of intelligently organized social relations based on the unprecedented growth of productive forces, science and culture."[85] In contrast to the plight of the individual in the capitalist system whose life is governed by a philosophy of egoistic individualism, under socialism the individual is a member of a "society in which the law of life is the concern of all for the well-being of each and the concern of each for the well-being of all."[86] This reciprocity between individual and community concern is characterized as the hallmark of socialist society as well as the precondition for the true liberation of the individual. And freedom from the slavery of self-interested egoism is portrayed as more crucial for true human liberation than civil and political rights. It is repeatedly insisted that only the collectivist and communitarian emphasis of socialism can create the conditions in which this kind of freedom is possible.

The argument in the Soviet press is straightforward: the moral quality of life in a socialist democracy is far superior to that which is possible in any capitalist system. No amount of capitalist propaganda can alter that fact. Any attempt by bourgeois ideologists to impugn the Soviet system by reference to "fabrications" concerning human rights violations is destined to refutation by the humane character of socialist life itself.

> Any objective comparison of the situation in the Capitalist world with the socialist countries' real achievements in ensuring human rights is undoubtedly to the advantage of socialism. And the Soviet Union has not the slightest intention of 'pulling up to' or more precisely, sinking down to the American level on the human rights question: it has no intention of introducing the exploitation of man by man, unemployment, social inequality, political gangsterism, discrimination against minorities, etc.[87]

The Soviet position leaves little room for misunderstanding: the forces of social progress operating within the socialist system will never allow a regression to the point of compliance with capitalist demands on the issue of human rights.

Presuppositions and Policy Predictions

A survey of the treatment accorded the U.S. human rights policy in the Soviet press demonstrates clearly that none of the conditions necessary for the success of the human rights initiative were present in the Soviet case. The Soviets do not acknowledge that they have violated or are violating any human rights. Specific acts for which they have been indicted by the West are, on their construal, the legitimate prosecution of individuals for crimes committed against the state. Moreover, from the Soviet perspective, the United States, with its capitalist principles enshrined in the economic structure and protected by the legal system, remains a heinous perpetrator of gross violations of the human rights of working people. Thus, America's rhetorical flourish concerning human rights violations in the Soviet Union must be understood as no more than a thinly disguised propaganda campaign devised to undermine the socialist system. Because the Soviets deny that there have been any legitimate human rights violations, and because they recoil at any attempt by capitalists to impose bourgeois principles on their socialist regime, the Carter Doctrine could never have achieved its desired results. Indeed, rather than protect the rights of the Soviet dissidents, the U.S. human rights initiative, interpreted in terms of the increasing intensity of the ideological struggle, provides the Soviets with a justification for quelling dissent and for intensifying repression in the name of socialist vigilance against the forces of reaction.

The larger claim of this chapter is that the evidence afforded by excerpts from the Soviet press simply confirm the expectation that the Carter Doctrine was destined to fail, an expectation which emerged from the examination of the divergent theoretical assumptions underlying the Liberal and Marxist traditions which give rise to alternative conceptions of human rights. An understanding of the theoretical presuppositions that sustain the Soviet conception of human rights and structure Soviet perceptions of international events generated a firm prediction of the character of the response and the nature of the arguments encountered in the Soviet press. Indeed, recognition of the discordant theoretical assumptions of Liberalism and Marxism provided a fertile ground for producing remarkably accurate predictions concerning the substance, the spirit, and even the details of the Soviet's response to allegations of human rights violations advanced by the United States.

At a time of growing recognition that the social sciences do not possess and are likely never to develop covering laws or law-like generalizations able to provide precise predictions, policy analysts may find an alternative source of knowledge in a sophisticated understanding of the operation of theoretical presuppositions upon the perceptions and beliefs of political actors and upon the actions and policy options which follow from those perceptions and commitments. Attention to the theoretical constitution of facticity and to the dimensions of political strife which derive therefrom may afford policy analysts firmer ground for policy predictions than can be afforded by techniques dependent on the myth of the given.

8

The Political Cast of Policy Presuppositions: The Case of Workfare

IT HAS been suggested that theoretical presuppositions have a distinctive political cast. Through the perceptions they engender, the valuations they sanction, the evidence they accredit, and the explanations they warrant, theoretical presuppositions endorse a substantive conception of reality. Incorporated in policy proposals, divergent theoretical presuppositions legitimize particular forms of belief, modes of action, and orders of being which are far from neutral or value free. For this reason, it is important that policy analysis engage in sustained examination of the implications of contentious policy presuppositions for particular forms of life. Policy presuppositions must be judged on the basis of the world they would produce if significant numbers of people acted in accordance with their precepts.

This chapter will explore the political cast of the theoretical presuppositions which inform workfare programs in the United States. It will suggest that any effort to consider the implications of contentious policy presuppositions for determinate forms of life must move beyond the range of assessments routinely incorporated in policy analysis.[1] Although consideration of the internal consistency of policy objectives, of the adequacy of designated means to achieve policy goals, and of the efficiency of implementation strategies are important elements in a theoretically sophisticated policy analysis, they are not sufficient to illuminate the political implications of contentious policy presuppositions. Policy analysis attuned to the politics of the theoretical constitution of facticity must investigate the contours of the world and the character of life which specific policy presuppositions would make possible.

Workfare: The Legislation and Its Legitimation

Workfare, a government program which requires recipients of public assistance to 'work off' the value of their benefits through unpaid labor in community service projects, has been hailed as the "welfare reform of the 1980s."[2] In 1977, in a series of amendments to the Food Stamp Act, Congress first established workfare demonstration projects which required food stamp recipients "to work at public service jobs in return for their household's food stamp benefits."[3] The Omnibus Budget Reconciliation Act of 1981 extended the concept of workfare to additional social welfare programs by permitting states to establish Community Work Experience Programs (CWEP) in conjunction with Aid to Families with Dependent Children (AFDC), Aid to Families with Dependent Children/Unemployed Parent (AFDC/UP) and General Assistance.[4] CWEP requires participants to 'earn' their welfare benefits by working a specified number of hours in projects which serve a useful public purpose. The exact number of hours is calculated on the basis of the value of the household's benefits divided by the prevailing minimum wage. The CWEP legislation stipulates that earning the benefits must take the form of a *quid pro quo* exchange based on unpaid labor, that participants are not entitled to any salary or reimbursement for training expenses, although provision for transportation costs to the job site is allowed. Failure to complete the requisite number of hours of unpaid labor results in termination of benefits to the household. In 1983, the Reagan Administration again expanded the scope of workfare by altering the status of CWEP from an option for the states to a requirement: every state must now implement some form of workfare as a component of its welfare policy.[5]

Proponents of workfare have noted that the primary reasons for incorporating a mandatory work requirement in public assistance programs are to "encourage recipient identification with the labor market, provide recipients with a work history and develop the discipline necessary for accepting employment in the regular economy."[6] For this reason, workfare requirements are targeted at the "able-bodied," "employable" poor; exemptions are allowed for those who are physically or mentally unfit for work, for mothers who have children under the age of three, and for individuals who are already employed for eighty or more hours per month. Thus, workfare derives its justification from a particular conception of poverty, one which explains the causes of poverty in terms of the attitudes and the psychology of the poor. On this view, the problem to be addressed in any successful welfare policy is the mindset of the "professional poor who have adopted welfare as a way of life,"[7] who intentionally waste their skills and talents by willfully refusing to work.

The assumptions underlying this conception of poverty have been developed systematically in an essay published in *The Public Interest*. Claiming that it is impossible to explain the high rates of unemployment among disadvantaged groups "by appealing to lack of jobs, discrimination or other social conditions over which the disadvantaged have no control,"[8] Lawrence Mead suggests that the problem of poverty must be understood in terms of the poor's unwillingness to accept the jobs which are available to them. The underdevelopment of the work ethic is the fundamental problem of the poor. Mead links this pervasive moral problem to twenty years of welfare programs that "merely give things to their recipients . . . [which] support recipients while expecting nothing in return. Specifically, welfare programs contain no effective requirements that recipients work in return for their benefits."[9] According to Mead, in direct contrast to the market, which reinforces the work ethic by rewarding individuals' efforts and contributions to society, welfare undermines the value of such reciprocity by severing the connection between benefits and obligations. To rectify this problem, Mead argues that welfare programs "should try to assure recipients the same balance of rights and obligations that non-dependent people face in their daily lives. The needy should be supported, but they should also be expected to work, if employable, to stay in school, if young, to obey the law and so on. This is the only way these programs can support and justify, rather than tacitly undercut, the civic sense their clients need to progress in American society."[10] Thus, workfare must replace welfare in order to ensure the future prosperity of the currently disadvantaged members of society and to facilitate their integration into the mainstream of American life.

Acknowledging that the success of workfare requires the exercise of authority, and at times coercion, over welfare recipients, Mead offers a legitimation of the policy consonant with popular concepts in public administration. "Low wage work is no longer a 'private good,' something the individual will seek spontaneously because it benefits him. Rather, it has become a 'public good,' something in which society as a whole has an interest, for reasons of moral or social integration, but which may not serve individual interests. Like other public goods, it now has to be produced using government authority rather than through the dynamic of individual interest operating in the marketplace. Government must now obligate program recipients to work rather than just entice them. What is obligatory cannot simply be offered as a choice—it has to be enforced by sanctions, in this case, loss of the welfare grant."[11]

Once poverty is understood in terms of particular debilitating attitudes held by the poor, workfare as a social policy designed specifically to alter individual attitudes toward work, emerges as an appropriate remedy to the contemporary welfare crisis. Proponents of workfare suggest that this new welfare program will generate a host of benefits for individual welfare recipients and for society. Requiring welfare recipients to work regularly will help them to cultivate a work habit as they overcome fears of not being able to compete in a job market. On-the-job experience in public service projects will increase welfare recipients' feelings of self-worth and self-confidence as they realize they are contributing something valuable to their communities. The dependency bred by reliance on government hand-outs will be supplanted by a growing sense of self-sufficiency as workfare participants gain a sense of mastery in their job assignments. The gradual accrual of job experience will enhance the marketable skills and hence the employability of workfare participants. Over time, the regular exposure to the world of work, coupled with confidence and the acquisition of marketable skills, will facilitate the individual's transition from workfare to permanent paid employment in the private sector. Thus, the long-term consequence of workfare will be a reduction in state and federal expenditures for welfare as the total number of recipients is reduced due to job placements. State and federal governments will also realize immediate reductions in their welfare expenditures as those recipients who are unwilling to assume their workfare responsibilities are terminated from the welfare rolls. Workfare also produces an additional residual benefit: reduction in the stigma associated with welfare. As the rolls are purged of welfare "cheats," workfare participants will encounter a new respect as the American public recognizes that the poor "have earned" the benefits they receive.[12]

Lest the success of workfare appear to rest on excessively optimistic assessments of the effect of unpaid community work experience on individual attitudes and behavior, proponents of workfare hasten to add that workfare also possesses a deterrent capacity. The introduction of CWEP in 1981 was accompanied by sharp restrictions in the provisions governing eligibility for AFDC. Work incentives, introduced in 1967, which had allowed welfare recipients to deduct the first thirty dollars of monthly earnings plus one third of the remaining earnings from the estimate of need and consequent determination of benefit levels, were restricted to use in the first four months of employment and disallowed thereafter. Moreover, the 1981 reforms placed a limit on work-related expenses (seventy five dollars per month) and child care expenses ($160 per child per month) that could be used to calculate need and income. As a result of these restrictions which affect the working poor, some 500,000 AFDC families (eleven percent of the case load) became ineligible for assistance, and an additional 300,000 families had their benefits reduced.[13] Reducing benefits while simultaneously requiring recipients to work off the benefits received was intended to deter people from seeing welfare as an alternative to work. The image of welfare as a "pre-paid life-time vacation plan"[14] would be permanently replaced by a conception of welfare as minimal subsistence support which would be "administered with a sufficient degree of harshness and limitation in benefits that people who could work would be happy to get off and those who did work would stay off."[15] Thus an adequate understanding of workfare must include an awareness of both its positive incentives, that is, the opportunity for the poor to develop work skills and habits, self-esteem and confidence, and a basic marketability; and its deterrence capabilities, or the assignment of individuals to menial jobs without pay as a condition for the receipt of minimal subsistence benefits. Both its potential to increase the employability of the poor and its deterrent effect have played a central role in legitimizing the policy.

Assessing Policy Presuppositions

To assess the merits of workfare, it is important to begin with an examination of the assumptions upon which the program is based, the internal consistency of the program's objectives, and the adequacy of the mechanisms established to achieve the policy's goals. The most fundamental assumptions underlying workfare concern the nature and causes of poverty. Workfare is premised on the 'pathological' theory of poverty, which explains poverty in terms of the characteristics, or 'defects' of the poor themselves.[16] In the contemporary United States, this view is associated with a constellation of beliefs about capitalism, the function of the market, and the sphere of individual freedom and responsibility. At the center of these beliefs lies the notion that upward social mobility is possible for any individual who possesses determination, energy, and a willingness to expend effort. Economic success is the market's reward for hard work. But if success is within the reach of any hard-working individual, if individual effort is all that stands between the rich and the poor, then the poor are peculiarly responsible for their own fate. Those who choose to live in ignominious conditions by willfully refusing to take advantage of the opportunities which the free market affords are morally reprehensible. On this view, 'laziness,' or unwillingness to work, is a form of moral defect for which the poor should be held strictly accountable.[17]

Is the pathological theory an adequate account of poverty? An examination of the demographic characteristics of the poor suggests that the pathological theory is fundamentally flawed. More than two-thirds of the poor in the contemporary United States are unable to work because of age, disability, or caretaking responsibilities for preschool children. Forty-eight percent of the households with pretransfer incomes below the poverty line are headed by individuals age sixty-five or older; another twelve percent are headed by disabled individuals; seven percent are headed by women with children younger than six. Of the remaining households below the poverty line, seven and a half percent are headed by persons who work full-time year round, but whose incomes do not meet family subsistence needs; 20.4% are headed by part time-workers; and five percent are headed by students.[18] Moreover, recent studies of AFDC recipients, the group of the poor most frequently discussed in terms of the pathological theory of poverty, indicate that the belief that AFDC household heads do not work or will not work is simply mistaken. Seventy percent of AFDC households have at least one earner during the years on welfare: in forty percent of these households, it is the head who earns the income, in the remainder, the earnings are those of older children within the household.[19] Further, there is much greater movement between welfare and work than the pathological theory admits. Only a small proportion of households receiving public benefits remain on welfare for long periods of time.[20] The vast majority resort to welfare to upgrade their total income because their earnings from work are inadequate or because they are temporarily unemployed.

A number of studies of the attitudes of the poor toward work also challenge the pathological theory's accuracy. "In answer to the question, 'Do the poor want to work?', research on the work orientations of the poor has concluded that yes, the poor do want to work. The work ethic is upheld strongly by AFDC recipients and work plays an important role in their life goals."[21] Indeed, results from the most comprehensive study on the attitudes of the poor towards work "unambiguously indicate that AFDC recipients, regardless of sex, age or race, identify their self-esteem with work as strongly as do the non-poor. . . . Despite their adverse position in society and their past failures in the labor force, these persons clearly upheld the work ethic and voiced strong commitments toward work."[22]

In summary then, the pathological theory of poverty underlying the workfare policy rests upon a number of misconceptions. Contrary to the pathological view, the able-bodied poor share the American commitment to the work ethic, and they do work. Their problem is not one of attitude but of inadequate pay or inadequate employment. The market economy has not afforded these individuals the mythologized avenues of upward social mobility. And recent research suggests that even in an expanding economy, the market will not provide an escape from poverty for these individuals in the future. "The evidence from the recent past suggests that economic growth will not raise the earnings of the poor enough to enable many of them to escape poverty without government assistance. The major factor contributing to the reduction of poverty since 1966 seems to have been the growth in government transfers, which offset increases in poverty resulting from demographic changes and high unemployment rates. Economic growth *per se* seems to have had little effect."[23]

Proponents of workfare have repeatedly emphasized the dual objectives of the program: 1) to increase the employability of the poor by inculcating work habits and work motivation, by teaching marketable skills, and by increasing self-esteem; and 2) to use mandatory labor in menial jobs to deter the able-bodied poor from resorting to welfare. To ask if these two objectives are internally consistent is to ask if they can be accomplished simultaneously without undermining each other.

The first objective of workfare can best be understood as an attempt to *constitute*, or create, a productive member of the workforce. The constitution of such a worker implies not only the transmission of particular work skills, but also the inculcation of a commitment to work that is sufficiently powerful to serve as a continuing motive to work. Within market economies, the development of such a work commitment has been related to the intrinsic rewards of the work (the inherently satisfying nature of the activity) and to the extrinsic rewards of the work (the level of pay, prestige, power, or perquisites the work affords). Thus, the work motive of the typical worker is fueled by: 1) the intrinsic value of the work, which overrides concern with extrinsic rewards; 2) the extrinsic rewards, which offset any negative aspects of the work activity itself; or 3) the optimal situation, in which the intrinsic value of the work is accompanied by favorable extrinsic rewards.

The second objective of workfare emphasizes deterrence capability by requiring as a condition for the receipt of minimal subsistence benefits that welfare recipients perform tasks sufficiently onerous that no worker would ever be attracted to the welfare alternative. It would appear highly improbable that a job sufficiently onerous to satisfy the worker deterrence objective could simultaneously satisfy the worker constitution objective. To achieve the desired deterrence effect, workfare must minimize the intrinsic value of mandatory job assignments. And the workfare format, unpaid labor in exchange for minimal subsistence benefits, precludes the use of extrinsic rewards to offset the unpleasant aspects of the required labor. What remains instead of the intrinsic and extrinsic rewards of work is a program of forced labor operating under the sanction of starvation (forfeiture of benefits). While such a program would serve as a considerable deterrent to employed workers, it is incapable of fostering self-esteem or of providing an additional incentive to work for welfare recipients already imbued with the work ethic. On the contrary, it is likely to breed hostility and resentment among its involuntary participants.

The incompatibility of workfare's dual objectives becomes manifest when the program rhetoric is translated into attempts to implement the policy. A number of evaluation studies conducted in conjunction with the experimental workfare programs authorized under the Food Stamp Act reveal a clear disjuncture between program objectives and the means adopted to achieve those objectives.[24] For example, to achieve either its worker constitution objective or its worker deterrence objective, workfare must be implemented uniformly; the work requirements must be applied to all eligible welfare recipients. Yet in practice, every workfare program has been characterized by enormous selectivity in the imposition of work requirements upon welfare recipients. Local administrators have used broad discretion in determinimg who should work at what job and under what conditions, as well as who should be exempted "for good cause." Indeed, a recent survey of workfare program administrators indicated widespread confusion among administrators about the rules governing workfare participation: while ten to fifteen percent of local administrators claimed that the imposition of the work requirement was governed by rules relating to the category or characteristics of clients; an equal proportion claimed that no rules governed workfare, that it was simply up to the administrator to decide when to impose the work requirement.[25] As a consequence of both confusion and discretion, workfare requirements are typically imposed on nine to eleven percent of welfare recipients,[26] a percentage small enough to undermine the achievement of program objectives, yet significant enough to raise questions concerning unconstitutional discrimination in the application of the program.[27]

According to the rhetoric of proponents of workfare, the public service assignments of workfare participants should serve a useful community purpose and afford opportunities for the development of marketable skills. Indeed, the legislation creating CWEP stipulates that "Community Work Experience Programs shall be limited to projects which serve a useful public purpose in fields such as health, social service, environmental protection, education, urban and rural development and redevelopment, welfare, recreation, public facilities, public safety and daycare."[28] In practice, however, the great majority of welfare recipients have been placed in low-level maintenance and clerical positions.[29] "Jobs such as cutting grass, picking up trash, washing dishes, mopping and waxing floors, driving senior citizen vans, moving furniture, assisting the dog catcher and doing general office work are typical."[30] Evaluation studies note that workfare program administrators have made no effort to offer participants jobs that use skills they already possess, nor have administrators made placements that enable participants to acquire marketable skills. Moreover, workfare assignments tend to be in unskilled jobs, precisely the kind of jobs which are prone to elimination during periods of economic recession.[31] Thus, even if performance in these unskilled jobs is considered a form of 'skills training,' the acquired skills are not marketable because equivalent employment is not readily available in the regular workforce.[32] Pursuit of the deterrence objective justifies such menial job placements for workfare participants, but these placements are incompatible with the goal of creating an employable worker. Several evaluation studies suggest that placing workfare participants in jobs which require few job skills actually lessens their chances of obtaining employment which affords sufficient income to escape poverty. A workfare participant who succeeds in finding a job in the workplace equivalent to the workfare assignment will earn too little to support a household. The welfare rolls will not be reduced because government transfers will still be required to supplement an inadequate income.[33]

Proponents of workfare have emphasized the importance of work as a mechanism to heighten the self-esteem of the poor. Although the precise relationship between individual experience, social values, and self-esteem is not thoroughly understood by existing psychological theories, there are good reasons to challenge any view which postulates the development of self-esteem as an automatic response to work, regardless of the nature of the work or the conditions under which the work is performed. Under the rubrics of workfare, work is mandatory as a condition for the receipt of welfare benefits. Individual participants have no choice in job assignments and no control over the conditions under which they work. In many instances, workfare participants are required to work side by side with individuals who are receiving salaries for performing the same tasks. Evaluation studies indicate that paid employees tend to denigrate workfare participants both for being unable to secure paid employment, and for agreeing to "work for nothing."[34] Thus, workfare participants must contend with the onus of mandatory menial labor, with complete lack of control over their work lives, with interactions with program administrators who dictate the conditions of their existence, and with coworkers who stigmatize them for complying with a policy over which they have no control. Such an array of forces can scarcely be expected to contribute to the self-esteem of the average individual. Nor should it be expected that these negative forces could be offset by the fact that workfare "makes a contribution to the community." The menial nature of the workfare assignments (leaf-raking, dish-washing, floor-mopping, etc.) coupled with their involuntary status, tend to undermine any sense of pride associated with performance of a public service. Finally, the sense of being a victim of an inequitable system is bound to constrain the development of self-esteem among workfare participants. The individuals who are required to participate in workfare programs know that they are not the only persons who receive economic benefits from the government. They comprise a small fraction of welfare recipients. The dollar value of their subsistence benefits is miniscule in comparison to the value of government benefits accorded to corporations, businesses, farmers, home-owners, in the form of investment credits, price supports, tax deductions, and direct services. Yet they alone are singled out and required to perform punitive public service to pay back their benefits. Awareness of the fundamental unfairness of this requirement is likely to color workfare participants' assessments of the workfare experience, and reactions informed by this sense of victimization are not likely to be consonant with high self-esteem.

The practices associated with implementing workfare are conducive to achieving the program's deterrent objective: no human being would embrace the opportunity to comply with workfare's punitive provisions; but they are singularly at odds with the more benign objectives emphasized in the rhetoric of program advocates. Workfare does not provide meaningful public service opportunities for the poor; it does not afford training or marketable skills; and it does not contribute to the self-esteem of individuals who are committed to the work ethic but who stand in desperate need of permanent employment at a decent wage. Moreover, if the pathological theory of the poor is incorrect; if people resort to welfare because the labor market does not provide enough jobs for all who desire them, then the deterrent objective of workfare degenerates into a cruel policy of punishing the poor for fluctuations in the labor market over which they have no control.[35]

Based on an erroneous theory of poverty, workfare cannot reduce the welfare rolls; it simply intensifies the burdens imposed upon the poor as a condition of survival. Evaluation studies indicate that workfare has not generated the predicted savings in welfare expenditures due to reductions in the case loads.[36] On the contrary, they indicate that the administrative costs associated with workfare registration, screening, job placement, supervision and imposition of sanctions, make the program more expensive than previous welfare policies.[37]

Assessing Policy Implications

Application of some of the standard techniques of policy analysis to the case of workfare suggests that workfare is a troubled policy. It is founded on erroneous assumptions concerning the causes of poverty. It embodies incompatible objectives: its goal of constituting employable workers for an advanced industrial economy is undermined by its commitment to serve as a deterrent. In addition, the means adopted to implement workfare are incapable of achieving the program's objectives: the menial labor assigned to participants cannot increase their self-esteem or equip them with marketable skills; the deterrent objective cannot be achieved because high unemployment rates and inadequate incomes continue to increase the ranks of the poor; and the high administrative costs of the program increase rather than decrease governments' welfare expenditures.

Taken in consort, these defects raise serious questions about the desirability of workfare as a welfare policy. Yet they do not exhaust the possibilities for systematic examination of workfare, for they do not touch the question of the implications of workfare for determinate orders of being. The remaining section of this chapter will investigate the political cast of the presuppositions which inform workfare, focusing on the form of life that would be created if these presuppositions gained popular assent. It will suggest that the assumptions underlying workfare support social relations which intensify the imposition of discipline, diminish individual freedom, and legitimize increasing use of a range of subtle mechanisms of social control.

Critics of workfare have identified a number of undesirable consequences which follow from widespread adoption of the policy. It has been suggested that the availability of the unpaid labor of a group of persons who possess no employment rights "will be used by employers to lower payrolls, will reduce the effective prevailing wage rate, and will keep workers now in the lowest-paid, lowest status jobs from asserting their rights to traditional employment benefits."[38] On this view, controlling the work habits of the unemployed is also a way to discipline the labor force by lowering workers' expectations and demands, thereby contributing to increases in profits. It has also been suggested that politicians' emphasis upon the pathological theory of povery and workfare as an appropriate remedy to the welfare crisis, reinforces popular belief in the free market economy and in the possibility of upward social mobility. Thus, the dissemination of this conception of poverty sustains the productivity of working Americans by fostering the illusion of success.[39] But workfare also has a profound effect on work life in America by foreclosing debate about the fundamental meaning of work for an individual, about the relationship between work, self-definition, and self-determination, and about the relation between the character of work performed and the constitutive principles of a society. As the rhetoric of workfare is popularized and internalized, the question of the relation between work and freedom is subverted. The very notion that people should be free, individually and collectively, to examine the nature of work and to choose to accept or to restructure the conditions of work life in contemporary society is supplanted by a profound resignation to the prevailing patterns of debilitating employment as the only conceivable option.

The theoretical presuppositions which inform workfare envision a world in which welfare recipients are 'deviants' who must be subjected to rules, habits, and commands in order to transform and improve them, to make them productive members of society.[40] The pathological theory of poverty's equation of unemployment with willfull deviance legitimizes bureaucratic intervention to 'normalize' and reconstitute the personalities of those who fall outside advanced industrial definitions of useful employment. The attitudes and identities of the poor must be subjected to management techniques for the sake of their own rehabilitation.

To accomplish the prescribed reconstitution of the poor, bureaucrats must subject the everyday behavior of those who do not conform to prevailing conceptions of work to constant surveillance. Administrators with the power to judge must assess the needs and capacities of the workfare participants. Adequate evaluation of individual potential and on-the-job performance necessitates that each case be monitored, inspected, and appraised in meticulous detail. Each individual must be judged in terms of punctuality, regularity of attendance, constancy of effort, attention or inattention to detail, enthusiasm, zeal, level of cooperation, deportment, responsiveness to constructive criticism, and attitude toward authority. Individuals must be evaluated in terms of progress made and future potential, as well as in comparison with the performance of their peers, an agenda for evaluation which has no limit. All assessments must be compiled in a permenent document which "captures and fixes the individual" by determining individual aptitude and ability and by indicating the possible uses which might be made of the person.[41] The long-term goal is not simply to accustom the individual to uninterrupted supervision and judgment, to the continual exercise of authority over every aspect of daily life, but to inscribe the dominant standard of judgment in the individual's own consciousness. To reconstitute the person as subject (as one who is subjected), is to produce an "individual who assumes responsibility for his [her] own constraint, an individual who becomes the principle of his [her] own subjection."[42]

The individual who has been subjected does not ask questions about what kinds of work might be more fulfilling, more interesting, or more conducive to developing one's full potential. The subjected individual obeys.[43] The individual who has been normalized does not conceive of work as a means of achieving dignity or as a means of expressing creativity; work is accepted as a form of discipline which extorts the body's forces in order to optimize the capacities which society finds useful. The individual who has been subjected to the rigors of discipline accepts "technical mutation,"[44] the modification of the individual to fit the needs of society, as a condition of survival. The disciplined individual does not challenge the proliferation of administrators who function as technicians of behavior and engineers of conduct in their quest to produce a population that is both docile and capable.[45] The normalized subject accepts that an "exhaustive disciplinary apparatus [that] assumes responsibility for all aspects of the individual, physical training, aptitude for work, everyday conduct, moral attitude, state of mind," constitutes an unalterable element in the natural order of things.

Workfare incorporates many of the hallmarks of discipline: it conceives of the individual psyche as an object to be managed and controlled; it legitimizes the adoption of administrative techniques to correct individual attitudes and dispositions; it defines work as menial labor devoid of creative, expressive, or developmental potential; it construes individual compliance with the demands of an advanced industrial economy as a virtue; it condones local administrators' increasing surveillance of the daily activities of the poor; it warrants the accumulation of detailed documentation concerning the noncriminal activities of a significant proportion of the population; and it endorses punitive sanctions for nonconformity to types of work accredited by the corporate sector.

Implementation of workfare will necessarily implicate the poor more thoroughly in an intricate web of discipline. But the fact that workfare could be embraced as a popular welfare reform in the 1980s suggests the extent to which Americans have already succumbed to the dictates of discipline. When intolerable constraints on personal freedom are depicted in the sanitized language of rehabilitation and the public nods wholehearted assent; when a conception of work stripped of all but its meanest properties, is wielded as a weapon against the poor and not a word is spoken in protest; when conformity to the norm of the subjugated producer is conflated with human excellence and the slightest deviations from that norm are treated as punishable offences; then the imperatives of discipline have already constricted the public imagination.

Discipline is a method of power "whose operation is not ensured by right but by technique, not by law but by normalization, not by punishment but by control . . . employed on all levels and in forms that go beyond the state and its apparatus."[46] It derives its legitimacy from its promise to integrate all people into the mainstream of society, and from its potential for maximizing efficiency and heightening productivity. It operates under the auspices of the ideal of self-restraint, the *sine qua non* of a functioning democratic order. Yet despite its allegiance to the beneficent goals of the liberal capitalist society, the underside of discipline is rife with illiberal consequences.

The disciplined society breeds passivity and disengagement,[47] it silences alternative viewpoints and stifles public debate; it fosters inhumane policies of which workfare is a prime example. In structuring the world according to its own imperatives, discipline seeks to control "not only what people do, but what they are, will be, may be,"[48] by controlling what they are capable of imagining themselves to be.

Discipline celebrates a world in which self-constrained bodies voluntarily serve the demands of efficiency. In adopting the work ethic as a vehicle, discipline trades upon deeply rooted commitments; it capitalizes upon unquestioned assumptions. In deploying the rhetoric of freedom, self-direction, and self-restraint, it masks the mechanisms of social control and the forces of subjugation on which it depends. But as the punitive policies of surveillance and normalization associated with workfare make clear, the appeal to benign principles simply camouflages the development and legitimation of a disciplinary apparatus that diminishes rather than heightens individual freedom. The presuppositions which sustain the policy of workfare would create a world in which, "Work is the providence of the modern peoples; it replaces morality, fills the gaps left by beliefs, and is regarded as the principle of all good."[49] It is important to consider in detail the desirability of such a world. Policy analysis that identifies the underside of the commitments which inform workfare, illuminating the unsavory political cast of the policy and the erroneous assumptions on which it rests, may help to facilitate systematic examination of the merits of the world envisioned by such contentious policy presuppositions.

9

Science, Scientism, and Democracy: A Return to the Theoretical Issues

RECENT discussions of policy analysis have generated two markedly different accounts of the nature of that endeavor. The dominant view conceives policy analysis as a technical discipline in which skilled professionals use scientific techniques to provide value-free prescriptions for achieving politically designated ends. In contrast to this optimistic appraisal, critics have suggested that technocratic policy inquiry is a form of scientism that operates to privatize and depoliticize, thereby contributing to the destruction of public discourse, and with it, the possibility of democratic decision-making.

The evidence adduced to support the vision of policy analysis as science in service to democracy draws heavily on a conception of science that emphasizes a narrow role for the policy expert within the decision-making process. Developed within empiricist and positivist traditions, this conception of science restricts the attention of the analyst to a limited set of empirical questions which can be answered by careful application of scientific methods to the data at hand. Conscientious observance of the fact/value dichotomy ensures that the policy prescriptions produced through systematic empirical inquiry derive their force from the accuracy of their predictions and the utility of the technical information which they afford. They neither infringe upon nor supplant the valuative judgments and choices which remain the responsibility of political decision-makers. Restricted to the factual realm, policy science can perform its task as handmaiden of democracy precisely because it knows and respects the limits of rational inquiry; it knows that in the realm of values, politics, not science, holds sway.

The arguments sustaining the conception of policy science as a technical resource for decision-makers accept that reason can operate reliably only in the sphere of value-free facts. This conviction serves both to define and to accredit the activity of scientific policy analysis as an inquiry firmly rooted in empirical observation and deriving its authority therefrom. But it also demarcates a legitimate role for policy analysis within democratic systems. The positivist conception of reason thus serves dual purposes within the policy literature: it provides an epistemological justification for particular strategies of empirical investigation within policy analysis, and it legitimizes a narrowly circumscribed role for the policy expert in the democratic decision-making process, a role which derives its authority from the facts, but which does not impede the political determination of ends.

The positivist conception of reason affords policy analysts a method and a mission. Moreover, it grants policy science immunity against the charge of scientism. By classifying the claims concerning scientism within the realm of the valuative, and by invoking the equation of valuation and arbitrary preference, policy science can discount the value-laden critique as irrational; but it can do so only at an exacting cost. Using the fact/value dichotomy to discredit valuative discourse allows the dismissal of the critique of scientism only by definitional fiat. The immediate consequence of this strategy is the admission that there is no way to assess the arguments advanced by the critics of scientism on their merits, an admission that reason cannot be brought to bear upon the most pressing questions concerning the nature of policy inquiry.

The consequence of the repudiation of all valuation as subjective preference is not only that the nature of policy analysis cannot be rationally assessed, but that there can be no rational debate on any personal, professional, or political questions that involve values. A consistent commitment to a positivist conception of reason, then, precludes the possibility of rational deliberation on the most important political issues confronting contemporary polities. A consistent commitment to positivism reduces the options for political decision-making to pluralist negotiation, cynical manipulation, or brute force. But the constriction of reason, which results in this drastic reduction of the possible forms of political life, is mandated by interlocking positivist assumptions concerning reality, not by an unmediated grasp of reality in itself.

The assumptions that provide epistemological warrant for empirical policy analysis are highly contentious. Indeed, the conceptions of science, explanation, and prediction, as well as the instrumental conceptions of theory and rationality, the correspondence theory of truth, the fact/value dichotomy, and emotivist notions of value upon which policy science rest, have been discredited by recent work in the philosophy of science.[1] These problematic notions represent various manifestations of an attempt to deal with the problems of human fallibility, the finitude of individual perception, and the contingency of events. They are important facets of a sustained effort to rescue knowledge from the foibles of human knowers and the intractability of contingent affairs. But despite the worthy ambitions which inspire them, positivist precepts and the empirical techniques that they engender fail to achieve their designated objectives. Neither the propensity to err nor the partiality of individual perspectives can be eliminated by carving the world into disparate realms bearing the labels 'facts' and 'values.' The formative contribution of theoretical presuppositions to perception and cognition cannot be eradicated by claims that facts are given or unproblematic. The valuative dimension of scientific discourse cannot be expunged by a simple denial of its existence. The role of creativity and judgment in rationality cannot be removed either by the assumption that the truth concerning factual matters is manifest or by the belief that reality can be grasped without the mediation of the human mind. The problem of human knowledge cannot be resolved by stipulative definitions which restrict the operation of reason to a narrow sphere of means-ends calculations. The problem of induction cannot be circumvented by appeals to criteria of verifiability or falsifiability, or by characterizing contentious claims as "laws" of social life. The truth of scientific models cannot be proven by their capacity to produce desired results, for power and truth remain discrete and disparate concepts. The problem of contingency cannot be eliminated by the conflation of explanation and prediction. And the possibilities for future political life cannot be determined solely by the evidence of past and present political relations.

The assumptions underlying empirical policy science provide an account of human knowledge which is seriously flawed both by excessive optimism concerning the possibility of factual knowledge, and by excessive pessimism concerning the possibility of rational assessment of valuative claims. The scope of reason is far more expansive than empiricist and positivist conceptions admit, and the conclusions of human inquiry are far more contentious than positivist and empiricist approaches acknowledge. Informed by erroneous epistemological assumptions and overly simplistic solutions to the problem of human knowledge, the methods prescribed for empirical policy analysis by empiricist and positivist presuppositions rest upon a range of mistakes which have been brought to light by the detailed critiques advanced by presupposition theories of science.

If the insights of presupposition theories of science have seriously challenged the epistemological foundation of the methods of empirical policy analysis, they raise equally important questions about the role accorded policy analysts within democratic systems. For the mission of empirical policy analysis presupposes a division of labor between policy experts and political decision-makers that depends on the fact/value dichotomy. But if that dichotomy rests upon an overly facile conception of facts, an erroneous conception of values, and a misconception of the power of reason, then important questions must be asked about using that dichotomy to sustain the mission of policy analysis.

It has been suggested that facts and values have far more in common than their dichotomous treatment admits.[2] Both facts and values are theoretically constituted propositions, which acquire their meaning in the context of particular human practices. Both derive their force from the theoretically mediated evidence and arguments advanced in their support. Both can be assessed only through rational deliberation upon various considerations pertaining to their theoretical origins, the depth of their insights, their practical utility, and their political implications. These commonalities, as well as the common problems they engender, are masked by the ideal of value-free policy inquiry. The belief that the policy scientist can free facts from all traces of the valuative and provide the truth about a determinate range of neutral facts pertinent to political decision-making overlooks the theoretical constitution of the empirical realm and the inevitable contestability of all cognitive accounts concerning that realm.

The neglect of the theoretical dimension has important implications for the role of the policy analyst in a democratic polity. For the legitimacy accorded policy scientists is parasitic on beliefs sustained by the discredited fact/value dichotomy, beliefs that make scientific prescriptions appear more simple and straightforward than they are and which make political choices appear more arbitrary and irrational than they are. In concentrating attention on the quest for scientific proofs pertaining to 'factual' matters, empirical policy analysis masks both the valuative dimension of its own technical discourse, and the fallibility of its prescriptions. But more importantly, in wielding the fact/value dichotomy so as to heighten the authority of science while denigrating valuative discourse as arbitrary and irrational, empirical policy analysis endorses technocratic solutions to political problems. For when the options for political decision are artificially limited to either scientific evidence or arbitrary choice, it is only reasonable to prefer technical grounds for decisions. Thus, the neglect of the theoretical constitution of facticity gives science far more weight in the political process than is warranted by its status as one fallible cognitive practice among others.

Rather than keeping science within its legitimate sphere, the fact/value dichotomy deployed by empirical policy analysts subtly sustains the displacement of politics by science. It does so by holding out a promise of incontrovertible truth, which is both impossible and distortive of the political process. By promising a proof which is impossible, the scientific rhetoric of policy analysis endorses the repudiation of all decision criteria that fall short of certainty; in cultivating a desire for the indubitable, it denies the rationality of deliberative choice; in confusing the question of proof with the question of political choice, it unduly constricts the sphere of political freedom. For the matters of deliberation and choice concerning the form of life to be pursued by particular communities cannot be resolved by the introduction of scientific proofs. The central questions of politics do not conform to an illusory model of knowledge in which there is one and only one correct position supported by an uncompromising logic derived from the necessity of truth. To insist that public policy be premised upon such illusory promises not only truncates democratic political processes, but it concentrates power in the hands of self-certifying technocrats whose claims of value-neutrality camouflage the political cast of their contentious prescriptions.

The insights of presupposition theories of science challenge not only the epistemological justification of the methods of empirical policy analysis and the legitimation of the political mission of policy analysts, but also policy science's immunity from the charge of scientism, for that immunity presupposes the validity of the emotivist conception of values and the instrumental conception of reason which presupposition theorists have impugned. Without the support of the mutually reinforcing presuppositions of positivism, the attempt to discredit the charge of scientism by recourse to stipulative definition appears as one more manifestation of the scientistic pretense that what science cannot prove, humans cannot know. Indeed, as long as policy science continues to disseminate discredited positivist doctrines as indubitable truth, the charge of scientism retains its force. As long as policy analysts uncritically appropriate the rhetoric of science, promote the image of political issues as technical questions best handled by experts, assert their political authority on the grounds of value-free expertise, and promulgate the emotivist conception of values as a means to accredit their authority while simultaneously denigrating alternative modes of political decision-making, the charge of scientism has much to commend it.

The charge of scientism will continue to haunt the discipline as long as policy science is promoted as a form of objective political problem-solving superior to, and therefore preferable to, democratic deliberation. The force of the charge cannot be dispelled by recourse to positivist principles which insist that the rational consideration of theoretically constituted and value-permeated presuppositions is impossible, unnecessary, arbitrary, subjective, or impractical, for all of these claims have been systematically and repeatedly refuted.[3] Positivist presuppositions are mutually reinforcing, self-validating, and self-perpetuating, but persistent appeals to positivism cannot undermine the charge of scientism, for it is precisely the validity of positivist precepts which are at issue in this debate. If policy analysis is to avoid dogmatism, vicious circularity, and question-begging, it must move on to other ground.

Douglas Amy has offered a number of explanations for policy science's tenacious commitment to positivist principles which move beyond positivist presuppositions to disciplinary and political concerns. He has suggested that despite its intellectual flaws, positivism provides multiple advantages to the profession. It sustains an image of a value-free, apolitical, technical advisor which enhances the employment prospects of members of the profession. It delimits the scope of policy inquiry in such a way that analysts can offer advice to clients without questioning the desirability of clients' norms or challenging the legitimacy of clients' interests; it preserves and protects the status quo. It affords politicians a technical rhetoric with which to 'sell' policy proposals, and provides a ready scape-goat if policies fail. It affords a mechanism by which to generate value-laden prescriptions while simultaneously obscuring their political cast. Moreover, it reinforces the style of decision-making and the ideology of the American political system.[4] Should this catalogue of self-serving concerns constitute the rationale for the perpetuation of positivist principles within policy analysis, it lends credibility to the charge of scientism. For it suggests that the discipline clings to a flawed epistemology not because of honest mistakes, not because of a sincere commitment to an erroneous system of belief, but rather because of a cynical and willful adherence to distortions that promote political advantage.

New Directions for Policy Analysis

The arguments advanced by presupposition theories of science leave little hope for redeeming positivism. Thus they provide compelling reasons for reconsidering the theoretical underpinnings of policy analysis. The detailed and trenchant criticisms of the positivist conceptions of science and knowledge, however, do not create a methodological void. On the contrary, they provide rich insights for redirecting policy analysis. They offer a sophisticated understanding of diverse cognitive practices, reclaiming the manifold resources of rationality for use in policy inquiry. Moreover, they suggest an agenda for policy analysis involving the sustained investigation of the theoretical presuppositions which shape policy prescriptions and circumscribe political options.

A policy analysis informed by presupposition theories of science would require the reorientation of the discipline's methods and mission. It would require that the rhetoric of science be displaced by the rhetoric of practical reason, that the language of deliberation and judgment supplant the language of scientific laws. It would necessitate more systematic investigation of the theoretical constitution of facticity, rather than acquiescence in the myth of the given. It would mandate constant questioning of the political cast of cognitive claims and detailed consideration of the political implications of tacit theoretical presuppositions.

In return for such a reconceptualization of the field, policy analysis would gain a more expansive conception of politics, derived from the recognition of the essentially contentious nature of theoretical claims. For an understanding of the influence of contestable theoretical presuppositions upon perception and cognition, as well as upon action, heightens awareness of the ground of intractable political disputes, of the scope of the politically actionable, as well as of the limits of the politically acceptable. In addition, it generates an alternative conception of explanation that takes the complexity of perceptual and cognitive processes into account and an alternative basis for policy prediction rooted in the relation between beliefs and action.[5]

A revised policy analysis attuned to the theoretical dimension of policy questions rests on a more sophisticated epistemological theory than positivism. But the conception of cognition as a human practice affords policy analysis no false promises concerning the transcendence of fallibility or finitude. In endorsing the employment of a variety of deliberative techniques developed in a number of cognitive traditions to facilitate the examination of evidence and the analysis of arguments pertinent to policy prescriptions, post-postivist theorists offer policy analysts no monopoly on truth. Critical scrutiny of contending claims and careful analysis of theoretical commitments can illuminate error, distortion, mystification, misperception, misunderstanding, mistaken beliefs, fallacious arguments, and contentious propositions, but it cannot escape the conditions of human cognition.

Theoretically sophisticated policy analysis is premised upon the recognition that in a world of contingency populated by finite minds, fallibility is inescapable. Guided by this recognition, it repudiates any claim of ahistorical and universal validity for its analyses. Instead of transcendent claims, post-positivist policy analysis derives its justificatory force from its capacity to illuminate the contentious dimensions of policy questions, to explain the intractability of policy debates, to demonstrate the deficiencies of alternative policy proposals, to identify the defects of supporting arguments, and to elucidate the political implications of contending prescriptions. In its systematic investigation of the contentious assumptions sustaining the constitution of perception, cognition, facticity, evidence, arguments, explanations, and options, post-postivist policy analysis can surpass positivist policy analysis because more is examined and less is assumed.

If post-positivist presupposition theories of science offer policy analysis an alternative epistemology, a revised rhetoric, and a reoriented methodology, they also suggest a different role for policy analysts in the political process. The fundamental task of theoretically informed policy analysis is to identify the dimensions of contention surrounding policy questions. Examining the conceptual and methodological assumptions that structure the constitution of facticity, the generation of evidence, the development of arguments, and the identification of policy alternatives can illuminate the forces circumscribing policy choices. But the identification and rational assessment of these issues cannot eliminate political choice itself. Policy analysis attuned to the politics of theoretical presuppositions can expand the scope of political possibility by increasing awareness of the dimensions of contestation and, hence, the range of choice, but it cannot dictate what is to be done in a particular policy domain. If post-positivist policy analysis is to avoid scientistic pretentions, it must accept a limited role in the political process. If it is to avoid the hubris of technocracy, it must refuse to substitute its rational judgments for the choices of members of the political community.

Awareness of the partiality and fallibility of individual perspectives suggests that there will always be many views concerning appropriate political choices for particular communities. Recognition of the subtle as well as the overt political casts of policy prescriptions suggests that none of the policy proposals generated in particular contexts will be neutral or value-free. An understanding of the scope of political choice in human affairs suggests that there will always be alternative ways to pursue identical ends, and there will always be many ends worth pursuing. A grasp of the intricacy of political commitments and the complex conditions of political choice suggests that well-intentioned individuals who confront political choices in good faith may reach markedly different conclusions concerning ultimate political objectives and immediate political strategies to promote those objectives. The methodology of post-positivist policy analysis is designed to comprehend this complexity in order to elucidate the contours of policy debates. But this very sophistication with respect to the manifold dimensions of potential conflict precludes simplistic notions that rational argument could dispel all causes of contention. Sophistication suggests that scientistic solutions to political problems are every bit as naive and authoritarian as the dreams of philosopher-kings.

Policy analysts who devote energy and intellect to the systematic investigation of specific policy areas will undoubtedly conclude that they know best what ought to be done; and, in many instances, the force of reason will be on their side. But neither conviction nor reason warrants the substitution of the policy analyst's will for political choice. Democracy has never guaranteed the rule of reason, nor is it likely to do so. If discussions of democracy are not to deteriorate into a cynical rhetoric devised to mask manipulation and control, policy analysts cannot accord themselves unwarranted authority on the basis of depth of understanding, superior insight, or technical expertise.

In the effort to illuminate the political dimensions of perception and cognition, the influence of theoretical assumptions upon choice and action, and the contentious character of scientific policy prescriptions, post-positivist policy analysis invokes a more participatory conception of democracy. In attempting to dispel the technocratic mystique, post-positivist policy inquiry deprives decision-makers of the facile claim that there is only one scientific solution to pressing political problems. But in so doing, it provides a more comprehensive analysis of the dimensions of political dispute, of the stakes involved and of the implications of alternative policy options. By investigating the theoretical constitution of policy alternatives, policy analysts can supplant the hegemony of science and restore recognition of the importance of political choice. By encouraging policy-makers and citizens to engage in rational deliberation upon the options confronting the political community, post-positivist policy analysis can contribute to an understanding of politics which entails collective decision-making about a determinate way of life. In illuminating the precise grounds upon which specific decisions are made, post-positivist policy analysis can facilitate awareness of the character of the world which is being shaped and of viable alternatives. Rather than encouraging resignation to fate or blind submission to the status quo, post-positivist policy analysis can contribute to the choice of a way of life.

Critics of scientism have charged that the policy studies disciplines are deeply implicated in a political process that privatizes and depoliticizes citizens as it reinforces elite decision-making. Little in the education or practice of policy scientists prepares them to engage that charge. On the contrary, the rhetoric of policy science supports unbounded confidence in the possibility of technical solutions for social and political problems. Systematic training in quantitative analysis without any consideration of the problematic positivist foundations of the discipline reinforces belief in the feasibility of value-free policy prescriptions. Governments' demands for cost-benefit analyses provide a rationale for the certification of a cadre of experts who can perform a needed public service. And images of the profession, whether cast in terms of the noble 'handmaiden of democracy', or the more pragmatic 'hired gun,' depict a legitimate role for analysts within liberal democratic polities.

An understanding of the theoretical constitution of the empirical realm can illuminate dimensions of policy analysis which give force to the charge of scientism. The language of science, the terms of art, the technical vocabulary of policy inquiry construct a political universe. What is at issue is not passive observation or neutral description, but the active constitution of the political domain. When the 'laws' of social science establish that democratic elitism is the only viable form of democracy, when 'science' certifies that technical solutions exist for political problems, when pragmatism dictates that pluralism is the only realistic mechanism for policy-making, when reason 'proves' that moral principles are irrational preferences impervious to argument or alteration, what is being asserted is far more than a neutral scientific description of the given phenomena. The seemingly unproblematic concepts which constitute the foundation of the policy sciences accredit a particular conception of reality with a determinate political cast. The theoretical assumptions and methodological commitments which inform policy research not only define a field of inquiry, but also actively shape the contemporary understanding of political possibility.[6]

Discredited positivist precepts offer an illusive immunity against the charge of scientism, an immunity which precludes critical reflection on the nature of policy inquiry and its role in contemporary politics. Protection from criticism is purchased at the price of the prohibition of systematic rational inquiry. Such a restrictive intellectual and political agenda is not the only option available. Theoretically sophisticated policy analysis provides an alternative which is broad in its scope, critical in its orientation, and rich in potential.

The scope for such a reoriented policy analysis is as expansive as the domain of the contentious. The resources available for rational analysis of policy questions are as rich as the multiplicity of intellectual techniques devised in the history of human cognition to facilitate deliberative judgment. The promise of post-positivist policy inquiry is also impressive for it offers a form of analysis that is more human and less heroic, more sophisticated and less deceived, more critical and less covetous of control, more tolerant of democracy and less committed to technocracy. In eschewing reductionism, methodological mystification, and unwarranted claims of authority, postpositivist policy analysis is less prone to the problems of scientism. In recognizing the scope of human freedom, the expanse of the politically contestable and the legitimacy of collective determination of political ends, theoretically sophisticated policy analysis affords a mode of assessment consonant with diversity and respectful of the irreducible plurality of human affairs. Confining its endeavors to the elucidation of the contentious, it promises explanations, predictions, and evaluations of policy options consistent with the conditions of human cognition and conducive to the cultivation of democracy.

Notes

CHAPTER 1

1. G. David Garson has suggested that much of the debate concerning contemporary policy analysis simply replays conflicts developed in the discipline of political science between the proponents of rational comprehensive decision-making and the proponents of pluralism. "From Policy Science to Policy Analysis: A Quarter Century of Progress," in *Policy Analysis: Perspectives, Concepts and Methods*, ed. William Dunn (Greenwich, Ct.: J.A.I. Press, 1986). For arguments which link policy studies to particular facets of the American liberal tradition, see Lawrence Herson, *The Politics of Ideas: Political Theory and American Public Policy* (Homewood, Ill.: Dorsey Press, 1984); and Raymond Seidelman and Edward Harpham, *Disenchanted Realists: Political Science and the American Crisis 1884–1984* (Albany: SUNY Press, 1985). For arguments which relate policy inquiry to the *Methodenstreit* of Max Weber and his contemporaries, see Bruce Jennings, "Interpretive Social Science and Policy Analysis," in *Ethics, the Social Sciences and Policy Analysis*, ed. Daniel Callahan and Bruce Jennings (New York: Plenum Press, 1983); and Paul Healy, "Interpretive Policy Inquiry: A Response to the Limitations of the Received View," *Policy Sciences* 19(1986):381–396.

2. Much of the discussion in the policy literature of the intricacies of political decision-making in republican systems was anticipated by Aristotle in his discussion of "mixed constitutions" in *The Politics*, ed. and trans. Ernest Barker (London: Oxford University Press, 1958); by Machiavelli in the *Discourses*, ed. and trans. Leslie J. Walker (London: Routledge and Kegan Paul, 1950); and by Adam

Smith in *An Inquiry into the Nature and Causes of the Wealth of Nations*, ed. R. H. Campbell and A. S. Skinner (Oxford: Clarendon Press, 1976) and in *Moral and Political Philosophy*, ed. H. W. Schneider (New York: Hafner, 1948).

3. For discussions of the importance of Galilean and Newtonian conceptions of science for contemporary quantitative research, see W. H. Werkmeister, "Social Science and the Problem of Value," and W. T. Couch, "Objectivity and Social Science," both in *Scientism and Values*, ed. Helmut Schoek and James Wiggins (Princeton, N.J.: D. van Nostrand Company, 1960). For discussion of the intellectual heritage of the conceptions of reason and science assumed in contemporary policy studies, see Alasdair MacIntyre, *After Virtue* (Notre Dame: University of Notre Dame Press, 1981) 51–52, 72–84.

4. It is important to note that policy assessment studies are frequently discussed in terms of policy evaluation. The meaning of *evaluation* in this context is typically construed narrowly to refer to the extent to which policy objectives are achieved, the efficiency with which they are achieved, and the calculation of certain cost-benefit ratios related to their achievement. For discussions of the methods of policy evaluation, see Michael Carley, *Rational Techniques in Policy Analysis* (London: Heinemann, 1980); William Dunn, *Public Policy Analysis* (Englewood Cliffs, N.J.: Prentice Hall, 1981); Duncan MacRae and James Wilde, *Policy Analysis for Public Decisions* (N. Scituate, Ma.: Duxbury, 1979); Stuart Nagel, *Public Policy: Goals, Means, Methods* (New York: St. Martins, 1983); Edward Quade, *Analysis for Public Decisions* (New York: Elsevier, 1982); and Edith Stokey and Richard Zeckhauser, *A Primer for Polciy Analysis* (New York: Norton, 1978).

5. It should be noted that empiricism itself is a doctrine with a long history. I am grateful to John Nelson for reminding me that the conception of empiricism rooted in trial and error experimentation which was advanced by the ancient Greeks and Romans varies in important respects from the Baconian empiricism discussed in this paragraph and the logical empiricism which has dominated the policy sciences in the twentieth century and which is discussed in greater detail later in this volume.

6. For interesting arguments concerning the political dimensions of these precepts of scientific methodology, see W. Van den Daele, "The Social Construction of Science," in *The Social Production of Scientific Knowledge*, ed. E. Mendelsohn, P. Weingart, R. Whit-

ley (Dordrecht: D. Reidel, 1977); Sandra Harding, *The Science Question in Feminism* (Ithaca: Cornell University Press, 1986); as well as the sources sited in note 3.

7. In contrast to the popular belief that empiricist methodology is neutral, Sheldon Wolin has argued that methodology is more accurately understood as "mind engaged in the legitimation of its own political activity." He provides a detailed discussion of this understanding of methodology in the context of Weber's conception of social science in "Max Weber: Legitimation, Method, and the Politics of Theory," *Political Theory* 9(1981):401–424.

CHAPTER 2

1. For a helpful guide to the underlying issues in this debate, see G. David Garson, "From Policy Science to Policy Analysis: A Quarter Century of Progress," in *Policy Analysis: Perspectives, Concepts and Methods*, ed. William N. Dunn (Greenwich, Ct.: J.A.I. Press, 1986) 3–22.

2. See for example, Grover Starling, *The Politics and Economics of Public Policy* (Homewood, Ill.: The Dorsey Press, 1979); and Harry Hatry, et. al., *Program Analysis for State and Local Government* (Washington, D.C.: The Urban Institute, 1976); Randall Ripley, *Policy Analysis in Political Science* (Chicago: Nelson-Hall Publishers, 1985).

3. Aaron Wildavsky, *Speaking Truth to Power: The Art and Craft of Policy Analysis* (Boston: Little, Brown and Company, 1979); Charles Lindblom and David Cohen, *Usable Knowledge: Social Science and Social Problem Solving* (New Haven: Yale University Press, 1979).

4. For a defense of the position that policy analysis can and should be value free, see Thomas R. Dye, *Understanding Public Policy*, 2d ed., (Englewood Cliffs, N.J.: Prentice-Hall, 1975). For arguments that policy analysis cannot be altogether value-free, but that it can escape ideological bias, see Randall Ripley, *Policy Analysis in Political Science* (Chicago: Nelson-Hall Publishers, 1985); Stuart Nagel, *Contemporary Public Policy Analysis* (Tuscaloosa: University of Alabama Press, 1984); and Jeanne Guillemin and Irving Horowitz, "Social Research and Political Advocacy" in *Ethics, The Social Sciences and Policy Analysis*, ed. Daniel Callahan and Bruce Jennings (New York: Plenum Press, 1983) 187–211. For a helpful review of di-

verse arguments that policy analysis cannot be value-free, see Rita Mae Kelly, "Trends in the Logic of Policy Inquiry: A Comparison of Approaches and a Commentary" *Policy Studies Review* 5(1986):520–528.

5. This tripartite schema is developed by Martin Bulmer, *The Uses of Social Research: Social Investigation in Public Policy Making* (London: Allen & Unwin, 1982), Chapter 2. Bulmer discusses these alternatives in terms of the conceptual relations between knowledge and policy. For a related discussion cast in terms of a developmental dialectic, see Douglas Torgerson, "Between Knowledge and Politics: Three Faces of Policy Analysis," *Policy Sciences* 19 (1986):33–59.

6. I. L. Horowitz and J. E. Katz, *Social Science and Public Policy in the United States* (New York: Praeger, 1975). For a discussion of which of these approaches generates research that the government is more likely to use, see R. A. Scott and A. R. Shore, *Why Sociology Does Not Apply: A Study of the Use of Sociology in Public Policy* (New York: Elsevier, 1979).

7. Charles Merriam, *Systematic Politics* (Chicago: University of Chicago Press, 1945) 337.

8. Harold Lasswell, "The Policy Orientation," in *The Policy Sciences: Recent Developments in Science and Method,* ed. Harold Lasswell and Daniel Lerner (Stanford: Stanford University Press, 1951) 3.

9. Harold Lasswell, *A Preview of Policy Science* (New York: Elsevier, 1971) 13.

10. Erve Chambers, "The Cultures of Science and Policy," in *Policy Analysis: Perspectives, Concepts and Methods,* ed. William N. Dunn (Greenwich, Ct.: J.A.I. Press, 1986), 104.

11. Nagel, *Contemporary Public Policy Analysis,* xiii.

12. Ripley, *Policy Analysis in Political Science,* 206.

13. Duncan MacRae, Jr., *The Social Function of Social Science* (New Haven: Yale University Press, 1976) 306.

14. Wildavsky, 255; see also 256–7, 278.

15. Michael McPherson, "Imperfect Democracy and the Moral Responsibilities of Policy Advisors," in *Ethics, The Social Sciences*

and Policy Analysis, ed. Daniel Callahan and Bruce Jennings (New York: Plenum Press, 1983) 76. In recognition of the conflicts which may arise among these competing obligations, a good deal of attention has been devoted in recent years to the question of "ethical dilemmas in policy analysis." In addition to the anthology edited by Callahan and Jennings, Stuart Nagel has devoted a chapter to this topic in *Contemporary Public Policy Analysis* (129–148); both Wildavsky (252–278) and MacRae (33–52, 77–306) deal extensively with this issue; Rosemarie Tong has written a book on the subject, *Ethics in Policy Analysis* (Englewood Cliffs, N.J.: Prentice-Hall, 1986); William Dunn has produced two anthologies which present alternative views on the topic, *Values, Ethics and The Practice of Policy Analysis* (Lexington, Ma.: D.C. Heath & Company, 1983) and *Policy Analysis: Perspectives, Concepts and Methods* (Greenwich, Ct.: J.A.I. Press, 1986); and several recent articles have called for the establishment of a "Code of Ethics" for policy analysts. See, for example, Donald Warwick and Thomas Pettigrew, "Toward Ethical Guidelines for Social Science Research in Public Policy," in Callahan and Jennings, 335–368; Peter Brown, "Ethics and Policy Research," in *Policy Analysis* 2 (1976): 325–340; and Guy Benveniste, "On a Code of Ethics for Policy Experts," in *Journal of Policy Analysis and Management* 3 (1984):561–572.

16. In contrast to the optimism of classical philosophy concerning the human capacity to understand the "Laws of Nature," i.e., the principles governing the order and operation of the universe, Thomas Hobbes argued unrelentingly that humans can have certain or "scientific" knowledge only of those subjects of which we are the cause, whose construction is in our power or depends upon our arbitrary will. Put simply, Hobbes claimed that we can know only what we make. Since we do not make natural forces, they are, strictly speaking, unintelligible to us. For this reason, natural science is and must always remain hypothetical. Humans invent theories about nature, hypothetical constructs to help us gain mastery over natural phenomena. The appropriate criterion for judging such theories is pragmatic: a good theory is one which enables humans to conquer and control nature. Hence the notion of 'instrumental rationality,' reason is an instrument which enables humans to achieve the ends which they devise for themselves; it is a tool which facilitates the satisfaction of desires. On Hobbes' view, there is far greater hope for a science of politics than for natural science, precisely because humans create political systems and can therefore understand the principles

of their operation. For a full discussion of these issues, see *Leviathan*, originally published in 1651.

17. In both *A Treatise of Human Nature* (1739) and *An Enquiry Concerning Human Understanding* (1748), David Hume deployed the weapons of reason against the metaphysical and epistemological claims of Rationalism. In brief, Hume suggested that humans could achieve knowledge only in two areas: relations of ideas, and matters of fact. Arguing that humans can have certain, *a priori* knowledge only of relations of ideas, i.e., of tautologies or analytic statements which are true by definition, Hume demonstrated that precisely because of their character as *a priori* relations of ideas, such statements can give us no knowledge about the empirical world. Knowledge of matters of fact, which is *a posteriori*, i.e., dependent upon observation and induction, is always tentative and fragile for it is based upon limited and incomplete evidence concerning a contingent realm which could change at any moment. Moreover, claims concerning matters of fact are premised upon correlations ('constant conjunctions') of observed phenomena, not upon causal ('necessary') connections and as such, are highly fallible. Turning to questions of moral principles, Hume argued that moral judgments are neither relations of ideas nor matters of fact. Hence they cannot be known either *a priori* or *a posteriori* and they cannot be deductively or inductively inferred from statements of fact; thus, there is a logical gulf between the *is* and the *ought*. Hume argued that morals involved questions of feeling or sentiment rather than reason or knowledge. Hume's legacy is one of mitigated skepticism, for although he identified serious problems with induction, the only method available for gaining knowledge about the empirical world, he nevertheless recognized that humans must act on the basis of fallible knowledge. As a practical matter, he recommended reliance upon custom and tradition to compensate for the fragility of reason.

18. Between 1830 and 1842, Auguste Comte created the six volume opus, *Positive Philosophy*, which advanced a theory of knowledge, a philosophy of history, and a program for social reform. In brief, Comte argued that the human mind developed from a primitive phase of theological interpretation through a stage of metaphysical speculation to a mature stage of 'positive' or scientific understanding. While the pre-scientific periods were characterized by abstract speculation concerning human origins and purposes, the era of positivism restricted its epistemological enquiries to the realm of the 'positive,' denoting 'real' or 'actual' existence. By relying solely upon observable

facts and the relations which hold among observed phenomena, scientific positivism could discover the laws which governed empirical events. Once established, these laws could provide the foundation for the scientific reform of society.

19. Formed in 1924 under the leadership of Moritz Schlick, the Vienna Circle of Logical Positivists or Logical Empiricists was committed to the development of a philosophy of science based upon the logic derived from the *Principia Mathematica* by Whitehead and Russell (3 vols., 1910–13; 1925). Perhaps best known in the United States through the works of Carnap and Hempel, the central doctrine of the positivist verification theory of meaning is that a contingent proposition is meaningful if and only if it can be empirically verified, i.e., if there is an empirical method for deciding if it is true or false. Propositions which fail this test must be rejected as nonsense.

20. Max Weber, *The Methodology of the Social Sciences*, ed. and trans. Edward Shils and Henry Finch (New York: Free Press, 1949) 17.

21. Eugene Meehan, "Philosophy and Policy Studies" *Policy Studies Journal* 2 (1973) :43–44.

22. The positivist assumptions concerning science that sustain this debate will be considered in detail in the following chapter.

23. Arguments inspired by Weber's conception of rationalization surfaced in the "end of ideology" debates in the 1950s and 1960s. For a clear presentation of this view, see Robert Lane, "The Decline of Politics and Ideology in a Knowledgeable Society," *American Sociological Review* 31 (5):650–663. It is not clear that Weber would have greeted the displacement of politics with as much enthusiasm as some of the participants in this later debate, for Weber continued to link the possibility of freedom to the scope of political choice. For discussions of Weber's ambivalence toward the process of rationalization, see Richard Bernstein, "The Rage Against Reason," *Philosphy and Literature* 10 (1986) :186–210; and Sheldon Wolin, "Max Weber: Legitimation, Method and the Politics of Theory," *Political Theory* 9 (1981) :401–424.

24. Weber, *The Methodology of the Social Sciences*, 10.

25. Weber suggested a division of labor between social scientists and philosophers in which social scientists would use empirical techniques to identify the indispensable means to established ends, the practical consequences of various proposals, and the inevitable re-

percussions of specific policies, while philosophers would use the
tools of logic to consider the internal consistency of policy values, the
compatibility of various policy objectives, and the logical implications of policy proposals for empirical relations (18–20). But there
is no reason that well-trained policy analysts could not combine these
tasks in their effort to subject policy proposals to systematic inquiry.

26. Weber, *Methodology*, 18.

27. Weber, *Methodology*, 20.

28. Weber, *Methodology*, 21.

29. 'Pareto optimality' is a principle devised by Vilfredo Pareto
to assess the efficiency of distributions of goods and of modes of production. The principle holds that a configuration is efficient whenever it is impossible to change it so as to make some persons (at least
one) better off without simultaneously making other persons (at least
one) worse off. Thus a distribution of commodities is efficient if there
exists no possible redistribution of these goods that improves the circumstances of at least one individual without disadvantaging
another. An organization of production is efficient if there is no way to
alter inputs so as to produce more of some commodity without producing less of another. Pareto discusses this principle of efficiency in
Chapter VI, §53 of *Manuel d'économie politique* (Paris, 1909). A translation of the relevant passages can be found in A. N. Page, *Utility
Theory: A Book of Readings* (New York: John Wiley, 1968) 38ff.

30. Ripley, *Policy Analysis*, 90.

31. For an argument that the differences between social science
and policy analysis are sufficiently significant to undermine the analogy between 'pure' and 'applied' science, see Mark Moore, "Social Science and Policy Analysis: Some Fundamental Differences" in Callahan and Jennings, 271–291.

32. Harold Lasswell, *The Future of Political Science* (New York:
Atherton, 1963).

33. For a survey of such responses, see Thomas Murray, "Partial
Knowledge" in Callahan and Jennings, 305–331.

34. Randall Ripley has suggested that the chances of utilization
of technical knowledge increase when: "(1) the ruling paradigms of
the agency or program being studied are not challenged; (2) there is
lack of involvement or interest by Congress; (3) when bureaucrats
have either neutrality toward or a shared commitment to the use of

empirically derived knowledge in decision-making; and (4) when the researcher and the sponsor are engaged in a 'clinical' relationship. *Policy Analysis in Political Science*, 193–6. For additional discussions, see Carol Weiss, *Using Social Research in Public Policy Making* (Lexington, Ma.: D.C. Heath, 1977); and R. A. Scott and A. R. Shore, *Why Sociology Does Not Apply: A Study of the Use of Sociology in Public Policy* (New York: Elsevier, 1979).

35. B. R. Fry and M. E. Tompkins, "Some Notes on the Domain of Public Policy Studies," *Policy Studies Journal* 6 (1978) :306.

36. Martin Tolchim, "Regulation and the Economist," *New York Times*, November 20, 1983: F 4.

37. The Executive Order was discussed in an article in the *New York Times*, November 6, 1981 and is cited in David C. Paris and James F. Reynolds, *The Logic of Policy Inquiry* (New York: Longman, 1983) 105, note 6. It is important to note that in certain areas, such as Occupational Safety and Health, Congress has legislated that cost-benefit calculations *cannot* be the sole criterion used in assessing pending regulations. For a discussion of this restriction, see Mark Sagoff, "Values and Preferences," *Ethics* 96 (1986): 301–316.

38. For an excellent critique of data and conclusions generated by cost-benefit analyses in the context of issues pertaining to solid waste management and the SST decision, see Ida Hoos, *Systems Analysis in Public Policy: A Critique* (Berkeley, University of California Press, 1972).

39. For systematic discussions of problems in these areas, see Warwick and Pettigrew, "Toward Ethical Guidelines for Social Science Research in Public Policy" in Callahan and Jennings; Robert Backoff and Barry Mitnick, "Reappraising the Promise of General Systems Theory for the Policy Sciences" in Dunn (1986); Chapters 4 and 5 in Paris and Reynolds, *The Logic of Policy Inquiry*; and the insightful studies of a range of policy areas in Part II of Shotland and Marks, *Social Science and Social Policy*.

40. Wildavsky, *Speaking Truth*, 16.

41. Bulmer, *Social Research* 45; see also Wildavsky, pp. 8–11; Lindblom and Cohen, 31.

42. Lindblom and Cohen, 91.

43. Lindblom and Cohen, 86–95; Tong, 14–29; Paris and

Reynolds, 118–123; Bulmer, 45, and Wildavsky, 8–17.

44. Although the pluralist commitments of Wildavsky and Lindblom are clearly expressed in their works on policy questions, there is far less clarity manifested in their direct discussions of "knowledge." For example, in *Usable Knowledge*, Lindblom and Cohen note (quite unobjectionably) that "ordinary knowledge" is highly fallible; but they then go on to suggest that "we shall call it knowledge even if it is false. Whether it is true or false, knowledge is knowledge to anyone who takes it as a basis for some commitment or action," 12. They then suggest that because ordinary knowledge (whether or not it is true) provides a basis for action, it should be characterized as "authoritative knowledge." Having thus conflated ordinary knowledge with authoritative knowledge by definitional fiat, they then go on to claim that ordinary knowledge is preferable to the knowledge generated by "professional social science inquiry" because decision-makers act on ordinary knowledge but they tend to ignore the information afforded by professional social science inquiry. In brief, ordinary knowledge is preferable because whether it is true or false, it is authoritative. Surely this account strains credulity, if not the principle of noncontradiction.

The introduction of an elementary philosophical distinction between knowledge and belief and a brief treatment of the relation between belief and action could rescue Lindblom and Cohen from this muddle. Perhaps then, philosophy is not as useless as contemporary social scientists have been led to believe.

45. The phrase is drawn from the classic work of Harold Lasswell, *Politics: Who Gets What, When, How* (New York: P. Smith, 1950); the view is advanced by Lindblom and Cohen, 88; and Wildavsky, 115–140.

46. Consonant with the realism of applied pluralism, there is a marked diminution in expectations concerning the nature of such political successes. On this view, the pragmatic education of decision-makers must prepare them for the recognition that "in actual historical fact, the 'solution' to many social problems is simply continuing suffering" (Lindblom and Cohen, 91). For in the political fray, many "problems are not so much solved as superceded" (Wildavsky, 83). Indeed, "political knowledge" seems to commend the abandonment of excessive expectations concerning democracy. Democratic ideals must not be allowed to blind policy makers to "one of the

paradoxes of political democracy in the nationstate, still not widely appreciated, that its ordinary citizens have good reason to feel almost as impotent as the citizens of an authoritarian regime. For insofar as genuine democracy is approximated, power is equally distributed among millions of citizens with the consequence that no single citizen enjoys more than a tiny, nearly useless share" (Lindblom and Cohen, 69). An enlightened public policy under such conditions will strive "to create more choices for people," choices which will increase their freedom in the private realm (Wildavsky, 269). For "to sacrifice private life on the altar of citizen participation seems excessive" (Wildavsky, 257).

47. Cook, "Postpositivist Critical Multiplism," 36; and Murray, "Partial Knowledge," 330.

48. Wildavsky, 19.

49. David Truman, "The Politics of New Collectivism," cited in Shin'ya Ono, "Limits of Bourgeois Pluralism" in *Apolitical Politics*, ed. Charles McCoy and John Playford (New York: Thomas Crowell Company, 1967) 116.

50. The notion of the 'Invisible Hand' is advanced by Adam Smith to illustrate the means by which the free market transforms the pursuit of private interest into public benefits. Smith notes that: "As every individual, therefore, endeavors as much as he can both to employ his capital in the support of domestic industry and so to direct that industry that its produce may be of the greatest value; every individual necessarily labors to render the annual revenue of society as great as he can. He generally, indeed, neither intends to promote the public interest, nor knows how much he is promoting it. By preferring the support of domestic to that of foreign industry, he intends only his own security; and by directing that industry in such a manner as its produce may be of the greatest value, he intends only his own gain, and he is in this, as in many other cases, led by an invisible hand to promote an end which was no part of his intention. Nor is it always the worse for society that it was not part of it. By pursuing his own interest he frequently promotes that of the society more effectually than when he really intends to promote it." *An Inquiry into the Nature and Causes of the Wealth of Nations*, ed. Bruce Mazlish (New York: Bobbs-Merrill, 1961) 166.

51. Wildavsky has argued that the pluralist model of policy-

making institutionalizes skepticism and thereby helps to save society from excesses. He accuses the planning model of institutionalizing dogmatism (205–211).

52. Cook, 59.

53. For a stinging critique of incrementalism, see Robert Goodin, *Political Theory and Public Policy* (Chicago: University of Chicago Press, 1982) 19–38.

54. For critical discussions of the role of *homo economicus* within pluralism and within political science more generally, see Fred Dallmayr, *Beyond Dogma and Despair* (Notre Dame, Ia.: University of Notre Dame Press, 1981) 43-68; and Nancy Hartsock, *Money, Sex and Power* (Boston: Northeastern University Press, 1985) Part I.

55. For discussions of the inadequacy of the assumptions of *homo economicus* as a model of policy-making, see Graham Allison's classic work, *Essence of Decision.* For an insightful discussion of the inappropriateness of this model as an explanation of political behavior more generally, see Donald Moon, "The Logic of Political Inquiry: A Synthesis of Opposed Perspectives," *Handbook of Political Science,* Vol. 1, ed. Fred Greenstein and Nelson Polsby (Reading, Ma.: Addison-Wesley, 1975).

56. For an excellent comparison of some of the similarities between cost-benefit analysis and incrementalism, see Paris and Reynolds, 95–136.

57. Garson, 9–10.

58. Pluralists have adopted the market model quite explicitly; systems analysts incorporate the same model tacitly. For an insightful analysis of the extent to which systems analysis is premised upon the market's equilibrium model, see José Sorzano, "David Easton and the Invisible Hand," *American Political Science Review* 69 (1975) :91–106.

59. Helmut Schoek and James Wiggins have traced the original use of scientism as a critical and derogatory term to Max Scheler's *Die Wissenformen und die Gesellschaft* (Leipzig, 1926). For an extensive discussion of the growing concern over scientism in the late 1950s and early 1960s, see Schoek's and Wiggins's *Scientism and Values* (Princeton: D. Van Nostrand Company, 1960).

In more recent years, the conception of scientism has entered academic discussions largely through the works of Jürgen Habermas.

See, for example, *Toward a Rational Society: Student Protest, Science and Politics*, trans. Jeremy Shapiro, (Boston: Beacon Press, 1970); *Knowledge and Human Interests*, trans. Jeremy Shapiro (Boston: Beacon Press, 1971); *Legitimation Crisis*, trans. Thomas McCarthy (Boston: Beacon Press, 1975) and *Communication and the Evolution of Society*, trans. Thomas McCarthy (Boston: Beacon Press, 1979). For a helpful introduction to the work of Habermas, see Thomas McCarthy, *The Critical Theory of Jürgen Habermas* (Cambridge, Ma.: M.I.T. Press, 1978); and Seyla Benhabib, *Critique, Norm and Utopia* (New York: Columbia University Press, 1986).

60. Gerald Holton, "Modern Science and the Intellectual Tradition," *Science* CXXXI (April 22, 1960) : 1191.

61. Richard Weaver, "Concealed Rhetoric in Scientistic Sociology," in Schoek and Wiggins, 83–99.

62. Laurence Tribe, "Policy Science: Analysis or Ideology," *Philosophy and Public Affairs* 2 (1972): 66–110.

63. Fred Kramer, "Policy Analysis as Ideology" *Public Administration Review* 35 (1975): 509–517.

64. Theodore Lowi, "The Politics of Higher Education: Political Science as a Case Study," in *The Post-Behavioral Era: Perspectives on Political Science*, ed. George Graham and George Carey (New York: McKay Company, 1972). See also his "Decision Making vs. Policy Making: Toward an Antidote for Technocracy" *Public Administration Review* 30 (1970): 318–319.

65. John Ladd, "Policy Studies and Ethics" *Policy Studies Journal* 2 (1973): 42–3; see also his "Ethics of Participation" in *NOMOS XVI: Participation*, ed. J. Roland Pennock and John W. Chapman (New York: Atherton Press, 1975) 98–125.

66. Paris and Reynolds, 48, 90, 177. See also Frank Fischer, *Politics, Values and Public Policy: The Problem of Methodology* (Boulder: Westview Press, 1980) 8, 45, 193.

67. Habermas' theory of cognitive interests is cited frequently in this literature, although the extent to which Habermas' position is embraced varies markedly. Habermas has identified three distinct cognitive interests which guide human endeavors: a technical interest related to humans' efforts to sustain their material existence and improve the conditions in which they live and work is manifested in the efforts of the empirico-analytic sciences to achieve mastery and

control over nature and the environment; a practical interest rooted in interpersonal contacts and communicative interactions which strive toward mutual understanding is embodied in the principles of the historical-hermeneutic disciplines; and an emancipatory interest linked to the human desire to be free from ideological mystifications and institutional practices which perpetuate domination is manifested in critical philosophical reflection. On Habermas' view, scientism is an ideology which conflates all knowledge with technical interests, and which reduces all modes of cognition to those techniques characteristic of the empirico-analytic sciences. For a full discussion of these points, see *Knowledge and Human Interests*. For examples of the application of Habermas' view to questions of policy analysis, see Paris and Reynolds, 191–250, and Fischer, 77–99. For more critical treatments of Habermas in the context of contemporary policy debates, see Fred Dallmayr, "Critical Theory and Public Policy" in Dunn (1986), 41–67; and Kai Nielsen, "Emancipatory Social Science and Social Critique," in Callahan and Jennings, 113–157.

68. For a detailed discussion, see Habermas, *Toward a Rational Society*.

69. Nielsen, 125.

70. Nielsen, 124.

71. Thomas Nagel, *The View From Nowhere* (New York: Oxford University Press, 1986) 9.

72. Ibid.

73. Herbert Reid and Ernest Yanarella, "Political Science and the Postmodern Critique of Scientism and Domination," *Review of Politics* 37 (1975): 286–316. The conception of privatization operative here involves more than recent attempts to dismantle state power either through the sale of public corporations or through a system of "contracting-out" public services to private companies, it refers to a process through which the public realm is undermined by the destruction of the beliefs necessary for its successful operation. The details of this process are discussed further below.

74. Richard Bernstein, *Beyond Objectivism and Relativism: Science, Hermeneutics and Praxis* (Philadelphia: University of Pennsylvania Press, 1983) 150.

75. Alasdair MacIntyre, *After Virtue* (Notre Dame, Ia.: University of Notre Dame Press, 1981) 102.

76. Carol Weiss, "Ideology, Interests and Information: The Basis of Policy Decisions" in Callahan and Jennings, 219. For an overview of this literature, see also Carol Weiss, *Using Social Research in Public Policy Making* (Lexington, Ma.:D.C. Heath, 1977).

77. For a helpful introduction to noncognitivism as well as to the particular theory of emotivism, see W. D. Hudson, *Modern Moral Philosophy* (New York: Anchor Books, 1970). For an excellent discussion of these issues in the context of policy analysis, see Alex Michalos, "Technology Assessment, Facts and Values" in Dunn (1986) 69–91.

78. For a summary of the diverse defects of emotivism, see Alasdair MacIntyre, *After Virtue* 12–19. For documentation of emotivism's resiliance within social science, see David Warwick, *The Teaching of Ethics in the Social Sciences* (Hastings-on-Hudson, N.Y.: Institute of Society, Ethics and the Life Sciences, 1980).

79. MacIntyre, 21.

80. Robert Bellah, Richard Madsen, William Sullivan, Ann Swidler, and Steven Tipton, *Habits of the Heart: Individualism and Commitments in American Life* (New York: Harper and Row, 1985) 65.

81. Bellah et al., 75.

82. Bellah et al., 78.

83. Bellah et al., 6.

84. Bellah et al., vi-vii. See also William E. Connolly, *Appearance and Reality in Politics* (Cambridge University Press, 1981) 145.

85. Bernard Williams, *Ethics and the Limits of Philosophy* (Cambridge: Harvard University Press, 1985) 156.

86. Williams, 159. Williams points out that this suspension of assessment is *not* equivalent to a non-relativistic morality of universal toleration.

87. MacIntyre; 22, 68.

88. Fred Dallmayr, *Beyond Dogma and Despair*, 2.

89. It might be argued that one of the most obvious manifestations of privatization is the ascendency of the private eye in popular culture. From Remington Steele, Simon and Simon, Spenser, the Equalizer, and MacGyver to Moonlighting, Magnum, and the "new"

Mike Hammer, tales of the private investigator dominate prime time television. In all these instances, as well as in their film and pulp fiction counterparts, the private eye, or more appropriately, the "Private I," is the individual who does what the public authorities (police, F.B.I., government) cannot do. Whether the specific assignment involves solving crimes, bringing criminals to justice, protecting the innocent, satisfying desires for retribution or vengeance, or fighting communism and making the world safe for further pursuit of subjectively determined ends, the "Private I" (working alone or in consort with a trusted associate) accomplishes precisely what the official representatives of the people have failed to do. The efficacy of the individual in opposition to the incompetence of collective endeavors is the unmistakeable subtext in the unending episodes of these series.

90. Sagoff, 312.

91. Tong, 58.

92. Tong, 222. See also the essays in Charles McCoy and John Playford, eds. *Apolitical Politics* (New York: Thomas Crowell, 1967), J. Peter Euben, "Political Science and Political Silence," in *Power and Community*, ed. Philip Green and Sanford Levinson (New York: Random House, 1969) 3–58, and Robert Bellah, "Social Science as Practical Reason" in Callahan and Jennings, 37–64.

93. Dallmayr, *Beyond Dogma and Despair*, 241. See also Vic George and Paul Wilding, *Ideology and Social Welfare* (London: Routledge and Kegan Paul, 1976).

94. This phrase is borrowed from David Hume who argued that "reason is and ought only to be the slave of the passions." *A Treatise on Human Nature*, ed. L. A. Selby-Bigge (Oxford: Clarendon Press, 1975) 415, 470.

95. Henry Kariel, "Social Science as Autonomous Activity" in Schoek and Wiggins, 253.

96. Kariel, 251.

97. For a full discussion of this concept, see William E. Connolly, "Toward Theoretical Self-Consciousness" in *Social Structure and Political Theory*, ed. William E. Connolly and Glen Gordon, (Lexington, Ma.: D.C, Heath, 1974).

98. Kramer, 514. See also, Paris and Reynolds, 203–261; and

Martin Rein, *Social Science and Public Policy* (New York: Penguin, 1976).

99. Christian Bay, "Politics and Pseudo-Politics: A Critical Evaluation of Some Behavioral Literature" *American Political Science Review* 59 (1965): 39–51.

100. Martin Bulmer advocates the "enlightenment model" in *The Uses of Social Research;* Martin Rein endorses "a value critical approach" in *Social Science and Public Policy;* and Douglas Torgerson suggests a "postpositivist paradigm" in "Between Knowledge and Politics." Paul Healy prescribes a similar method under the label, "interpretive policy inquiry," in "Interpretive Policy Inquiry: A Response to the Limitations of the Received View," *Policy Sciences* 19 (1986): 381–396.

101. Kenneth Prewitt, "Subverting Policy Premises," in Callahan and Jennings, 293–304.

102. M. Janowitz, *Sociological Models and Social Policy* (Morristown, N.J.: General Learning Systems, 1972) 5–6.

103. Healy, 386.

104. Torgerson, 35.

105. Several surveys of policy analysts have revealed a good deal of disagreement concerning their understanding of their endeavors. Arnold Meltsner has documented support for two quite different conceptions embraced by analysts, that of the "politician" and that of the "entrepreneur," in *Policy Analysts in the Bureaucracy* (Berkeley: University of California Press, 1976) 48. Elizabeth Howe and Jerome Kaufman have documented a different division between those analysts devoted to a "value-committed" stance and those committed to a "value-neutral" stance in "Ethics and Professional Practice" (Dunn [1983], 9–31). Such disagreements suggest that a consensus might be quite elusive.

CHAPTER 3

1. Martin Rein, *Social Science and Public Policy* (New York: Penguin, 1976) 87.

2. The relation between issues in the philosophy of science and

debates in the policy literature may represent part of the legacy policy analysis inherits from the social sciences. The dispute within the policy literature between the applied social science and the applied pluralist model of policy analysis is parasitic upon a long established debate within behavioral political science, which is itself parasitic on a debate within the philosophy of social science concerning the nature of science. For a detailed discussion of the relationship between positivism in the philosophy of science and behavioralism in political science, see John Gunnell, *Between Philosophy and Politics* (Amherst: University of Massachusetts Press, 1986). For a treatment of these issues in the context of social science more generally, see Richard Bernstein, *The Restructuring of Social and Political Theory* (Philadelphia: University of Pennsylvania Press, 1976).

3. William Dunn, *Values, Ethics and the Practice of Policy Analysis* (Lexington, Ma.: D.C. Heath, 1983) 1.

4. Frank Fischer, *Politics, Values and Public Policy: The Problem of Methodology* (Boulder, Co.: Westview Press, 1980) 2.

5. Max Weber, *The Methodology of the Social Sciences*, trans. and ed. Edward Shils and Henry Finch (New York: Free Press, 1949) 4.

6. Among the leading positivist philosophers of science were R. Carnap, P. Frank, C.G. Hempel, R. von Mises, E. Nagel, O. Neurath and M. Schlick. In the works of these philosophers, there are, of course, extensive differences on a number of important topics. In the following section, I shall attempt to provide a brief overview of positivism which for the sake of simplification will ignore most of the issues which engendered the greatest debate among these thinkers. For more detailed treatments of positivism, see A. J. Ayer, ed. *Logical Positivism* (New York: Free Press, 1959); Victor Kraft, *The Vienna Circle*, trans. A. Pap (New York: Philosophical Library, 1952); and J. Joergenson, *The Development of Logical Empiricism* Vol. II, No. 9 of the *International Encyclopedia of Unified Science* (Chicago: University of Chicago Press, 1951).

7. For this reason, the positivist model of science is often referred to as the "Naturalist Model" in the context of the social sciences; it models social science on practices drawn from the natural sciences. For an example of this terminology in use, see D. Moon, "The Logic of Political Inquiry: A Synthesis of Opposed Perspectives," *Handbook of Political Science*, Vol. I, pp. 131-217. This model is also described in terms of "Empirical Theory," terminology which emphasizes the ori-

gin of the model in empirical observation. For an example of this approach, see Richard Bernstein, *The Restructuring of Social and Political Theory.*

8. Randall Ripley, *Policy Analysis in Political Science* (Chicago: Nelson-Hall Publishers, 1985) 9.

9. J. S. Coleman, *Policy Research in the Social Sciences* (Morristown, N.J.: General Learning Press, 1972); David Hoaglin et al., *Data For Decisions: Information Strategies for Policymakers* (Cambridge, Ma.: Abt, 1982); S. Nagel, *Public Policy: Goals, Means and Methods* (New York: St. Martin's, 1984); and M. White et al., *Managing Public Systems: Analytic Techniques for Public Administration* (N. Scituate, Ma.: Duxbury, 1980).

10. Thomas Dye, *Understanding Public Policy,* 2d edition (Englewood Cliffs, N.J.: Prentice-Hall, 1975); Stuart Nagel, *Contemporary Public Policy Analysis* (Tuscaloosa: University of Alabama Press, 1984).

11. Popper's most important works include *The Logic of Scientific Discovery* (New York: Basic Books, 1959), *Conjectures and Refutations: The Growth of Scientific Knowledge,* 4th ed. rev. (London: Routledge and Kegan Paul, 1972) and *Objective Knowledge: An Evolutionary Approach* (Oxford: Clarendon Press, 1972).

12. On Hume's view, 'necessity' does not lie in the facts but rather in a custom or habit of the mind to impose a notion of causality upon the constant conjunctions which are perceived. Thus Hume provides a psychological account of necessity as a means to supplement his empiricist theory of knowledge.

13. The correspondence theory of truth holds that a statement (proposition, idea, thought, belief, opinion) is true if that to which it refers (corresponds) exists; thus truth lies in correspondence with facts.

14. This model of social science is itself heavily influenced by a model of social life drawn from Adam Smith's model of market relations.

15. The quotation is drawn from *Conjectures and Refutations,* 52. For examples of Popper's own efforts to employ a mode of rational analysis for the assessment of social and political theories analogous to the hypothetico-deductive model, see *The Open Society and Its*

Enemies, 2 vols., rev. ed. (Princeton: Princeton University Press, 1950); and *The Poverty of Historicism* (Boston: Beacon Press, 1957).

16. For an insightful discussion of the difficulties related to various attempts to define positivism, as well as for arguments concerning the propriety of placing Popper within the positivist camp, see Norman Stockman, *Anti-positivist Theories of the Sciences: Critical Rationalism, Critical Theory and Scientific Realism* (Dordrecht: D. Reidel, 1983).

17. See for example, Moon, 143–187.

18. Stockman, 76. See also Harold Brown, *Perception, Theory and Commitment: The New Philosophy of Science* (Chicago: Precedent Publishing Company, 1977) 65–75.

19. Thomas D. Cook, "Postpositivist Critical Multiplism" in *Social Science and Social Policy*, ed. R. L. Shotland and M. M. Marks (Beverly Hills: Sage Publications, 1985) 21–62; W. N. Dunn, *Public Policy Analysis: An Introduction* (Englewood Cliffs, N.J.: Prentice-Hall, 1981); C. E. Lindblom and D. K. Cohen, *Usable Knowledge: Social Science and Social Problem Solving* (New Haven: Yale University Press, 1979); A Wildavsky, *Speaking Truth to Power: The Art and Craft of Policy Analysis* (Boston: Little, Brown, 1979).

20. Cook, 53; Wildavsky, 15; W. N. Dunn, A. Cahill, M. Dukes, A. Ginsberg, "The Policy Grid: A Cognitive Methodology for Assessing Policy Dynamics," in *Policy Analysis: Perspectives, Concepts and Methods*, ed. W. N. Dunn (Greenwich, Ct.: J.A.I. Press, 1986) 355–375.

21. Cook, 53; Wildavsky, 35, 59.

22. Cook, 59; Wildavsky, 59; Lindblom and Cohen, 88.

23. Cook, 45, 54; Wildavsky, 115–140, 205–211.

24. Cook, 45–46; Lindblom and Cohen, 45, 95–100; Wildavsky, 271–278; Duncan MacRae, *The Social Function of Social Science* (New Haven: Yale University Press, 1976) 5–29, 77–106; Fischer, *Politics, Values and Public Policy* (Boulder, Co.: Westview Press, 1980) 99–164; David Paris and James Reynolds, *The Logic of Policy Inquiry* (New York: Longman, 1983) 203–249.

25. Lindblom and Cohen, 95–100; Wildavsky, 115–140.

26. It has become something of a standard operating procedure to invoke the work of Thomas Kuhn, most notably *The Structure of Scientific Revolutions*, 2d ed. enl. (Chicago: University of Chicago Press, 1970), as an example of presupposition theory. But Kuhn has been so used and abused in contemporary social science, I prefer to refrain from that practice. For detailed discussions of the troublesome appropriations of Kuhn's work by social scientists, see Richard Bernstein, *The Restructuring of Social and Political Theory* (Philadelphia: University of Pennsylvania Press, 1976) 84–103. The following discussion will draw instead from the works of Stockman and Brown, cited above, as well as from Michael Polanyi, *Personal Knowledge* (Chicago: University of Chicago Press, 1958); Richard Bernstein, *Beyond Objectivism and Relativism* (Philadelphia: University of Pennsylvania Press, 1983); John Gunnell, *Between Philosophy and Politics* (Amherst: University of Massachusetts Press, 1986); Willard C. Humphreys, ed., *Perception and Discovery* (San Francisco: Freeman, Cooper, 1969); and Frederick Suppe, ed., *The Structure of Scientific Theories*, 2d ed. (Urbana: University of Illinois Press, 1977).

27. Hanson, cited in Humphreys, 61. 28.

28. For an excellent introduction to these views, see the discussion of perception and theory in Brown, 81–144.

29. Eliseo Vivas, "Science and the Studies of Man," in *Scientism and Values*, ed. Helmut Schoek and James Wiggins (Princeton, N.J.: D. van Nostrand Company, 1960), 76.

30. Thomas Murray, "Partial Knowledge," in *Ethics, The Social Sciences and Policy Analysis*, ed. Daniel Callahan and Bruce Jennings (New York: Plenum Press, 1983), 319–320, 321.

31. Bernard Williams, *Ethics and the Limits of Philosophy* (Cambridge, Ma.: Harvard University Press, 1985) 138.

32. Moon, 146; Brown, 38–48; Stockman, 73–76.

33. Brown notes that Popper himself came to acknowledge that there can be no conclusive disproof of a theory for reasons such as these, 69–75.

34. For an interesting discussion of this evidence in relation to the persistence of sexism is science, see Sandra Harding, *The Science Question in Feminism* (Ithaca: Cornell University Press, 1986).

35. Moon, 146–147. For a full discussion of the problematic relation between explanation and prediction in the context of Hempel's work, see Brown, 51–57.

36. Stockman, 81–82.

37. Brown, 75.

38. Brown, 108.

39. For a helpful discussion of theoretical presuppositions in relation to traditions, preunderstandings, and prejudgments, see Bernstein, *Beyond Objectivism and Relativism*, 113–167.

40. In *Beyond Objectivism and Relativism*, Bernstein characterizes this erroneous conclusion as the "myth of the framework," 84.

41. *Ibid.*, 92. See also Brown, 93–94; Stockman, 79–101; Gunnell, 66–68.

42. This phrase is borrowed from Wilfred Sellars, *Science, Perception and Reality* (New York: Humanities Press, 1963) 164. For a helpful introduction to Sellars's views, see Gibson Winter, *Elements for a Social Ethic: Scientific and Ethical Perspectives on Social Process* (New York: Macmillan, 1966) 61–166; Bernstein, *The Restructuring of Social and Political Theory*, 121–135, and Gunnell, *Between Philosophy and Politics*, 68–90.

43. Williams, 140.

44. Brown, 93.

45. Brown, 148–152; Bernstein, *Beyond Objectivism and Relativism*, 54–78.

46. Hans Albert, *Treatise on Critical Reason*, trans. Mary Varney Rorty (Princeton: Princeton University Press, 1985) 169.

47. It might be argued that the identification of the values incorporated into alledgedly 'value-free' policy studies has been the only growth industry for political theorists in the past several decades. For examples of this work, see Charles Taylor, "Neutrality in Political Science," *Philosophy, Politics and Society*, 3d series, ed. Peter Laslett and W. G. Runciman (London: Basil Blackwell, 1978); W. G. Runciman, *Social Science and Political Theory* (Cambridge: Cambridge University Press, 1963); Martin Rein, *Social Science and Public Policy* (New York: Penguin, 1976); Martin Bulmer, *The Uses of Social Research: Social Investigation in Public Policy Making* (London: Allen and

Unwin, 1982); Donald Warwick and Thomas Pettigrew, "Toward Ethical Guidelines for Social Science Research in Public Policy," in *Ethics, The Social Sciences and Policy Analysis*, ed. Daniel Callahan and Bruce Jennings (New York: Plenum Press, 1983); R. Lance Shotland and Melvin Marks, *Social Science and Social Policy* (Beverly Hills: Sage, 1985); Robert Goodin, *Political Theory and Public Policy* (Chicago: University of Chicago Press, 1982); David Paris and James Reynolds, *The Logic of Policy Inquiry* (New York: Longman, 1983); Frank Fischer, *Politics, Values and Public Policy* (Boulder: Westview Press, 1980); Laurence Tribe, "Policy Science: Analysis or Ideology," *Philosophy and Public Affairs* 2(1972): 66–110; Ellen Paul and Philip Russo, Jr., *Public Policy: Issues, Analysis and Ideology* (Chatham, N.J.: Chatham House Publishers, 1982).

48. Dunn, 1981, 1983, 1986; Yehezkel Dror, "Some Features of a Meta-Model for Policy Studies," in *Policy Studies Journal* 3(1975): 245–250; Lindblom and Cohen, *Usable Knowledge* (New Haven: Yale University Press, 1979); Wildavsky, *Speaking Truth to Power* (Boston: Little, Brown, 1979); Stuart Nagel *Contemporary Public Policy Analysis* (Tuscaloosa: University of Alabama Press, 1984); Randall Ripley, *Policy Analysis in Political Science* (Chicago: Nelson-Hall Publishers, 1985).

49. Murray, "Partial Knowledge," in Callahan and Jennings, 325.

50. Rita Mae Kelly, "Trends in the Logic of Policy Inquiry: A Comparison of Approaches and a Commentary," in *Policy Studies Review* 5(1986): 520, 527.

51. This metaphor is borrowed from Fred Dallmayr, "Critical Theory and Public Policy," in Dunn (1986) 49.

52. Ripley, 17.

53. There is a good deal of overlap among these three approaches in the policy literature; however, to facilitate explication and analysis, in the following discussion I shall treat these strategies independently.

54. Douglas Amy, "Why Policy Analysis and Ethics are Incompatible," *Journal of Policy Analysis and Management* 4(1984): 574.

55. Ruth Hanft, "Use of Social Science Data for Policy Analysis and Policymaking," in Callahan and Jennings, 261.

56. Paul and Russo, 4.

57. *Ibid.*

58. Hanft, 254, 261. See also the detailed prescriptions of Warwick and Pettigrew, "Toward Ethical Guidelines for Social Science Research in Public Policy," in Callahan and Jennings, 335–368.

59. Nagel, 1984, 136–137.

60. Kevin Kearns, "The Analytic Hierarchy Process and Policy
Argumentation," in Dunn (1986), 333–354.

61. *Ibid.*

62. Michael Carley, "Into the Snakepit: Value Weighting
Schemes in Policy Analysis," in Dunn (1986), 269–279; Stephen Linder, "Efficiency, Multiple Claims and Moral Values," in Dunn (1986),
281–299; H. J. Einhorn and W. McCoach, "A Single Multi-attribute
Procedure for Evaluation," *Behavioral Science* 22(1977): 270–282.

63. Dunn et al., "The Policy Grid: A Cognitive Methodology for
Assessing Policy Dynamics," in Dunn (1986), 355–375.

64. The 'forensic model' of adversarial debate advanced by Duncan MacRae in *The Social Function of Social Science* has been inf-
luential in shaping many of these proposals; however, since MacRae's
own treatment of values in policy analysis goes well beyond strategies
of value identification, his work will be discussed in a later section on
normative policy analysis. For proponents of adversarial strategies,
see Hanft, 269; Allan Mazor, "Science Courts," *Minerva* 17(1977): 2–
4; Cook, 45–46; Warwick and Pettigrew, 358.

65. Cook, 53.

66. Cook, 53. It should be pointed out that efforts to institutionalize adversarial procedures in order to promote benign outcomes is a recurrent motif in pluralist thought. Drawn from Smith's
model of the market, which posits that under conditions of perfect
competition, the pursuit of private vices can be transformed into public benefits, this notion resurfaces in Madison's defense of the design
U.S. Constitution on the grounds that it can wed private interest to
public office, thereby allowing ambition to counteract ambition
while preventing the encroachment of government upon the lives of
citizens, as well as in the classic arguments of the pluralist paradigm
which posit that the pursuit of private interests produces a system of
political bargaining and compromise which ensures that moderate
policy is always the outcome of the policy process. Cook's application

of this notion to policy research draws upon this older tradition, as well as upon Popper's employment of this model as a mechanism to promote objectivity in science.

67. See, for example, Shotland and Marks, 14; Cook, 54–59; Ripley, 17, 200.

68. Paul and Russo, 3–9, Wildavsky, 271–272.

69. Edward Shils, *The Calling of Sociology and Other Essays on the Pursuit of Learning* (Chicago: University of Chicago Press, 1980) 366–367.

70. Stuart Nagel, 1984, 142–143.

71. Ripley, 175–186.

72. The most systematic contributions to this debate have been advanced by Martin Rein, *Social Science and Public Policy* (New York: Penguin, 1976) and "Value Critical Policy Analysis" in Callahan and Jennings, 83–110; Duncan MacRae, *The Social Function of Social Science* (New Haven: Yale University Press, 1976); Frank Fischer, *Politics, Values and Public Policy* (Boulder: Westview Press, 1980) and "Practical Discourse in Policy Argumentation" in Dunn (1986) 315–332; and David C. Paris and James F. Reynolds, *The Logic of Policy Inquiry* (New York: Longman, 1983). Other contributors include Douglas Amy, "Why Policy Analysis and Ethics Are Incompatible," *Journal of Policy Analysis and Management* 3(1984): 573–591 and "Teaching the Moral Analysis of Policy Issues" *News for Teachers of Political Science* 36(1983): 1, 6; Charles Anderson, "The Place of Principles in Policy Analysis" *American Political Science Review* 73(1979): 711–723; Robert Bellah, "Social Science as Public Philosophy" in *Habits of the Heart* (New York: Harper and Row, 1985) 297–307 and "Social Science as Practical Reason," in Callahan and Jennings, 37-64; Martin Bulmer, *The Uses of Social Research: Social Investigation and Public Policy Making* (London: Allen & Unwin, 1982) and "The British Tradition of Social Administration" in Callahan and Jennings, 161–185; Gregory Daneke, "Ethics in Public Policy Education" in Dunn (1983) 125-136; Paul Healy, "Interpretive Policy Inquiry: A Response to the Limitations of the Received View," *Policy Sciences* 19(1986): 381–396; Lawrence Herson, *The Politics of Ideas: Political Theory and American Public Policy* (Homewood, Ill.: Dorsey Press, 1984); Bruce Jennings, "Interpretive Social Science and Policy Analysis," in Callahan and Jennings, 3–35; Douglas Torgerson, "Between Knowledge and Politics: Three Faces of Policy Analysis"

Policy Sciences 19(1986): 33–59 and "Interpretive Policy Inquiry: A Response to its Limitations," *Policy Sciences* 19(1986): 397–405.

73. MacRae provides detailed discussions of the normative dimensions of cost-benefit analysis and pluralist models of politics; Fischer advances thorough critiques of behavioral and post-behavioral methods in policy analysis; Paris and Reynolds provide systematic criticisms of both the applied social science and applied pluralist approaches to policy inquiry; and Rein provides detailed studies of the value presuppositions of particular arguments and techniques employed in social policy research.

74. Rein, 72–85; MacRae, 77–98; Fischer, 99–164; Paris and Reynolds, 203–249. These authors typically acknowledge that their recommendations for normative policy analysis are heavily indebted to Max Weber's arguments concerning the potential contributions of logical analysis to policy studies. A comparison of the passages noted here with Weber's discussion in *The Methodology of the Social Sciences*, ed. and trans. Edward Shils and Henry Finch (New York: Free Press, 1949) 18–20, will reveal the extent of this debt. For a brief discussion of Weber's views, see chapter 2, 17–18.

75. For a systematic explication of prescriptivism, see R. H. Hare, *The Language of Morals* (London: Oxford University Press, 1952), and *Reason and Freedom* (Oxford: Clarendon Press, 1963). For a discussion which situates prescriptivism in the context of twentieth century discussions of meta-ethics, see W. D. Hudson, *Modern Moral Philosophy* (New York: Anchor Books, 1970).

76. Fischer (1980) 83, 97, 150, (1986) 321; MacRae, 5, 7, 67; Rein, (1976) 71, 169; Paris and Reynolds, 5, 69–70, 210–213; Anderson, 722.

77. Rein, (1976) 38–39, 71, 92, 251–254; Fischer (1980) 48, 164, 190, (1986) 322; MacRae, 5, 12, 52, 73, 80, 306; Paris and Reynolds, 1, 27, 210–211, 219, 233.

78. The most systematic discussion of rational and irrational ideologies is presented by Paris and Reynolds, who suggest that an understanding of the ideological nature of all policy prescriptions can provide insights into an alternative 'logic' of policy inquiry, 201–261. Although the language of the argument varies to some extent, similar views can be found in Fred Kramer, "Policy Analysis as Ideology," *Public Administration Review* 35(1975): 509–517; Frederic G. Raemer, "Principles of Ethics and the Justification of Policy," in *Policy Analysis: Presepctives, Concepts, Methods*, ed. William N. Dunn (Green-

wich, Ct.: J.A.I. Press, 1986); and Carol Weiss, "Ideology, Interests and Information: The Basis of Policy Decisions," in *Ethics, the Social Sciences and Policy Analysis*, ed. Daniel Callahan and Bruce Jennings (New York: Plenum Press, 1983).

79. Paris and Reynolds, 207, 210.

80. *Ibid.* 209. The Popperian flavor of this distinction is unmistakeable, see also 213–228.

81. *Ibid.*, 235.

82. For helpful discussions of ideology critique, see Stockman, 234–255; and Seyla Benhabib, *Critique, Norm and Utopia* (New York: Columbia University Press, 1986).

83. The claims concerning empirical science which are advanced by Paris and Reynolds are instructive on this point. They note that in contrast to ideologies, scientific theories "are uniquely proved by empirical data" (211). Indeed, they claim that "scientific theories are fully determined by proximate evidence and conclusive argument . . . the reasons for them are not just good but fully adequate" (210).

84. For a systematic demonstration of the role of theory in incrementalist (applied pluralist) approaches to policy analysis, see Robert Goodin, *Political Theory and Public Policy* (Chicago: University of Chicago Press, 1982) 19–38; for similar demonstrations with respect to applied social science models, see W. Runciman, *Social Science and Political Theory* (Cambridge: Cambridge University Press, 1963), and Rosemarie Tong, *Ethics in Policy Analysis* (Englewood Cliffs, N.J.: Prentice-Hall, 1986).

85. Wayne Leys, *Ethics for Policy Decisions: The Art of Asking Deliberative Questions* (New York: Prentice-Hall, 1952) 11. In this volume, Leys provides an exhaustive overview of the possible uses of diverse ethical theories for policy-making. For an abbreviated treatment of these possibilities, see Peter Brown, "Ethics and Policy Research," in *Policy Analysis* 2(1976): 325–340, and "Ethics and Public Policy: A Preliminary Agenda," in *Policy Studies Journal* 7(1978): 132–136.

86. The eclectic model is drawn from the detailed discussions provided by Leys.

87. Arguments for utilitarianism were forcefully presented by Max Weber in "Politics as A Vocation," *From Max Weber: Essays in*

Sociology, trans. Hans Gerth and C. Wright Mills (New York: 1946). For more recent arguments, see Goodin, chapters 1, 5, 12; Vincent Vacarro, "Cost Benefit Analysis and Public Policy Formulation," in *Ethical Issues in Government*, ed. Norman Bowie (Philadelphia: Temple University Press, 1981) 146–163. Utilitarianism is also endorsed by MacRae, 274, and by Fischer, 155–165.

88. For critiques of utilitarianism, see Alasdair MacIntyre, "Utilitarianism and Cost/Benefit Analysis: An Essay on the Relevance of Moral Philosophy to Bureaucratic Theory," in *Ethical Theory and Business*, ed. Tom Beauchamp and Norman Bowie (Englewood Cliffs, N.J.: Prentice-Hall, 1979); Albert Weale, *Political Theory and Social Policy* (London: MacMillan, 1983) 11–17; Don Herzog, *Without Foundations: Justification in Political Theory* (Ithaca, N.Y.: Cornell University Press, 1985) 108–154; and Tong, 82–84. For rebuttals of these attacks, see Goodin, chapters 3, 5; and Tom Beauchamp, "The Moral Adequacy of Cost-Benefit Analysis As the Basis for Government Regulation of Research," in *Ethical Issues in Government*, ed. Norman Bowie (Philadelphia: Temple University Press, 1981) 163–176.

89. For examples of the application of deontological principles to policy issues, see M. Cohen, T. Nagel, and T. Scanlon, eds., *Rights and Wrongs of Abortion* (Princeton: Princeton University Press, 1974); *War and Moral Responsibility* (Princeton: Princeton University Press, 1974); and *Equality and Preferential Treatment* (Princeton: Princeton University Press, 1977). For a general discussion of the merits of contractarian principles for social policy, see Weale, *Political Theory and Social Policy*.

90. Gibson Winter, *Elements for a Social Ethic: Scientific and Ethical Perspectives on Social Process* (New York: MacMillan, 1966).

91. Kai Nielsen, "Emancipatory Social Science and Social Critique," in Callahan and Jennings, 113–157.

92. Paris and Reynolds, 240–245.

93. Tong, 86–104. Among the virtues for policy experts identified by Tong are honesty and candor, competence and diligence, loyalty and discretion.

94. Guy Benveniste, "On a Code of Ethics for Policy Experts," *Journal of Policy Analysis and Management* 3(1984): 561–572; Warwick and Pettigrew, "Toward Ethical Guidelines for Social Science Re-

search in Public Policy," in Callahan and Jennings, 335–368; Tong, chapters 5–7; Goodin, chapters 3, 12; Leys, part II.

95. For examples of this work, see Tom L. Beauchamp, ed., *Ethics and Public Policy* (Englewood Cliffs, N.J.: Prentice-Hall, 1975); William Blackstone and Robert Heslep, eds. *Justice and Preferential Treatment* (Athens, Ga.: University of Georgia Press, 1977); Norman Bowie, ed. *Ethical Issues in Government* (Philadelphia: Temple University Press, 1981); M. Cohen, T. Nagel and T. Scanlon, eds., *Rights and Wrongs of Abortion* (Princeton: Princeton University Press, 1974); M. Cohen, T. Nagel, and T. Scanlon, eds. *War and Moral Responsibility* (Princeton: Princeton University Press, 1974); M. Cohen, T. Nagel, and T. Scanlon, eds. *Equality and Preferential Treatment* (Princeton: Princeton University Press, 1977); Barry Gross, ed., *Reverse Discrimination* (New York: Prometheus Books, 1977); Amy Gutmann and Dennis Thompson, eds., *Ethics and Politics* (Chicago: Nelson-Hall Publishers, 1984); Tom Regan and Donald Van de Veer, eds., *And Justice for All* (Totowa, N.J.: Rowman and Littlefield, 1982); Steven Rhoads, ed., *Valuing Life: Public Policy Dilemmas* (Boulder, Co.: Westview Press, 1980); William Rowe, ed., *Energy Risk Management* (New York: Academic Press, 1979); and Kristin Schrader-Frechette, *Nuclear Power and Public Policy* (Dordrecht: D. Reidel, 1980).

96. Among the journals which publish articles concerning ethics and public policy are *Philosophy and Public Affairs, Ethics, Social Theory and Practice, Political Theory, Monist,* and *Journal of Applied Philosophy.*

97. This term was used by Robert Goodin, who devotes a good deal of attention to the obstacles which particular philosophical styles raise for policy analysts, 8–18.

98. The books by Leys, Runciman, Winter, and Tong are good examples of this effort.

99. Winter, 167–174, 215–219; Runciman, 85, 174–175; Goodin, 4, 26–28.

100. Goodin, 4.

101. Goodin, for example, accepts the hypothetico-deductive model as appropriate for social scientific theories, and expresses great optimism concerning the potential contributions of mathematical and computer models for the identification of intervention strategies

that can facilitate rational comprehensive planning within policy analysis, 26–28.

CHAPTER 4

1. For alternative accounts of facts and values, see Richard Bernstein, *Beyond Objectivism and Relativism* (Philadelphia: University of Pennsylvania Press, 1983); Harold Brown, *Perception, Theory and Commitment: The New Philosophy of Science* (Chicago: Precedent Publishing Company, 1977); William E. Connolly, *Appearance and Reality in Politics* (Cambridge: Cambridge University Press, 1981); John Gunnell, *Between Philosophy and Politics* (Amherst: University of Massachusetts Press, 1986); Mary Hesse, *Revolutions and Reconstructions in the Philosophy of Science* (Brighton: Harvester Press, 1980); Alasdair McIntyre, *After Virtue* (Notre Dame: University of Notre Dame Press, 1981); Norman Stockman, *Anti-Positivist Theories of Science: Critical Rationalism, Critical Theory, and Scientific Realism* (Dordrecht: D. Reidel, 1983); Bernard Williams, *Ethics and the Limits of Philosophy* (Cambridge, Ma.: Harvard University Press, 1985).

2. This confusion between classificatory decisions concerning types of claims (i.e., 'factual' or 'valuative') and epistemological justifications of certain claims as correct has been discussed in detail in an excellent article by Alex Michalos, "Technology Assessment, Facts and Values," which orginally appeared in *Philosophy and Technology*, ed. P. T. Durbin and F. Rapp (Dordrecht: D. Reidel, 1983) and is reprinted in *Policy Analysis: Perspectives, Concepts and Methods*, ed. Willian N. Dunn (Greenwich, Ct.: J.A.I. Press, 1986) 69–91. The following discussion draws heavily upon the arguments advanced by Michalos. It should be noted that in discussing the initial question of classifying a claim as empirical or normative, Michalos describes the task in terms of making an ontological distinction between facts and values. Because I believe that this assumes precisely what needs to be proven (as will be argued in detail below), I prefer to discuss the process in terms of a conventional classification rather than an ontological classification.

3. Michalos, 72.

4. Michalos, 74.

5. Paul Healy has shown that no choice among alternative

means to a particular end is possible unless some evaluative criteria are employed. Moreover, despite empirical analysts' claim that the sole criterion invoked is efficiency, that criterion is always supplemented by other values of which the analysts are typically unaware. As evidence for this claim, Healy notes that adherence to efficiency calculations would generate policy recommendations which no analyst would endorse. For example, within the context of health policy, the most efficient means to reduce health care costs significantly might well be extermination of the weakest 5% of the population. That policy analysts do not routinely recommend this option is testament to the operation of other values, whether they be described in terms of respect for persons, commitments to equality, fairness, or the value of human life, they certainly transcend mere efficiency. See "Interpretive Policy Inquiry: A Response to the Limitations of the Received View," *Policy Sciences* 19(1986):381-396. For insightful discussions of this form of equivocation and its consequences for policy analysis, see Laurence H. Tribe, Corrine S. Schelling, and John Voss, eds., *When Values Conflict: Essays on Environmental Analysis, Discourse and Decision* (Cambridge, Ma.: Ballinger, 1976).

6. Michalos, 74.

7. Michalos, 77.

8. Williams, 132–133.

9. For a more detailed treatment of this problem, see the discussion of Popper's critique of the verification criterion of meaning in the previous chapter.

10. For a more detailed presentation of these points, see the discussion of presupposition theories of science in the previous chapter.

11. The problem of relativism has been the subject of extensive debate in recent years. For detailed arguments that relativism does not pose a major threat to the acquisition of knowledge after the abandonment of the fact/value dichotomy, see Bernstein, *Beyond Objectivism and Relativism*; Stanley Cavell, *The Claim of Reason* (New York: Oxford University Press, 1979); Frank Cunningham, *Objectivity in Social Science* (Toronto: University of Toronto Press, 1973); James Fishkin, *Beyond Subjective Morality* (New Haven: Yale University Press, 1984); John Gunnell, *Between Philosophy and Politics*; Don Herzog, *Without Foundations: Justification in Political Theory* (Ithaca: Cornell University Press, 1985).

12. Michalos, 71.

13. John Pollack, "A Theory of Moral Reasoning," *Ethics* 96(1986):506–523; 508.

14. See, for example, the arguments of Mary Hesse, *Revolutions and Reconstructions in the Philosophy of Science*, 63–110; and Richard Bernstein, *Beyond Objectivism and Relativism*, 30–34, 51–108.

15. The following discussion has been influenced by Richard Bernstein, *Beyond Objectivism and Relativism*; Harold Brown, *Perception, Theory and Commitment*; Stanley Cavell, *The Claim of Reason*; William Connolly, *The Terms of Political Discourse* (Lexington, Ma.: D.C. Heath, 1974), *Appearance and Reality in Politics*, and "Where the Word Breaks Off," (unpublished manuscript); Fred Dallmayr, *Beyond Dogma and Despair* (Notre Dame: University of Notre Dame Press, 1981) and *Language and Politics* (Notre Dame: University of Notre Dame Press, 1984); John Gunnell, *Between Politics and Philosophy*; Alasdair MacIntyre, *After Virtue*; Hannah Pitkin, *Wittgenstein and Justice* (Berkeley: University of California Press, 1972); Michael Polanyi, *Personal Knowledge: Towards a Post-Critical Philosophy* (Chicago: University of Chicago Press, 1958); Norman Stockman, *Antipositivist Theories of the Sciences*; and Bernard Williams, *Ethics and the Limits of Philosophy*.

16. For a detailed discussion of a range of conceptions of theory which includes but goes far beyond the three noted here, see Gunnell, *Between Politics and Philosophy*.

17. Gunnell, 72.

18. For a discussion of this process in the context of the 'culture' or 'tradition' of natural science, see Polanyi, 112; for a treatment that encompasses both the natural sciences and the humanities, see Bernstein, Parts II and III.

19. Dallmayr, *Language and Politics*, 3–5.

20. Bernstein, 140.

21. Gibson Winter, *Elements for a Social Ethic: Scientific and Social Perspectives on Social Process* (New York: Macmillan, 1966), 61.

22. Williams, 140.

23. Connolly, *Appearance and Reality in Politics*, 110; Charles

Taylor, "Neutrality in Political Science," in *Philosophy, Politics and Society*, ed. P. Laslett and W. Runciman (London: Basil Blackwell, 1978).

24. John Grunnell, *Between Philosophy and Politics*, 65, 72, 83.

25. Polanyi, 60. For an insightful discussion of the tacit presuppositions which sustain behavioral methods in the social sciences and their relation to the American liberal tradition, see Gunnell, 26–40.

26. Bernstein, 93; Williams, 113.

27. Polanyi, 289–291.

28. Polanyi, 60. For a related discussion in the context of Gadamer's work, see Bernstein, 145.

29. For helpful discussions of this point, see Alexander Nehamas, "Untruth as a Condition of Life," in Nietzsche: *Life As Literature* (Cambridge, Ma.: Harvard University Press, 1985) 43–74; and Don Herzog, *Without Foundations: Justification in Political Theory* (Ithaca: Cornell University Press, 1985) 231–236.

30. Nehamas, 55.

31. Dallmayr, *Beyond Dogma and Despair*, 265–279; Brown, 93–94.

32. The criteria identified below are discussed in detail and are employed in an assessment of alternative theoretical interpretations of the American political system by William Connolly, *Appearance and Reality in Politics*, 8, 85 and *passim*.

33. This phrase was introduced by W. B. Gallie, "Essentially Contested Concepts," *Proceedings of the Aristotelian Society* 56(1956):167–199. For a detailed discussion of such concepts in the context of political life, see William E. Connolly, *Terms of Political Discourse* (Lexington, Ma.: D.C. Heath, 1974).

34. For a discussion of a variety of sources of possible disagreement consistent with rational decisions concerning theoretical formulations, see Williams, 133–153.

35. For an intriguing discussion of some of the most fundamental presuppositions which have shaped Western cognitive practices since the 17th century, see Michel Foucault, *The Order of Things: An Archaeology of the Human Sciences* (New York: Vintage Books, 1973).

36. Gunnell has pointed out that it is only the consistent deployment of positivist assumptions which generates the conclusion that "facts and theories are both myths and the reality which is supposed to underlie and verify both is inaccessible," 78.

37. Bernstein characterizes this mistake as one more manifestation of the "myth of the framework," 84–85.

38. Bernstein, 128.

39. Bernstein has noted that "we become fools of history if we think that by an act of will we can escape the prejudgments, practices, and traditions that are constitutive of what we are," 167.

40. Nehamas, 65.

41. For an interesting discussion of rhetorical strategies common to the natural sciences, the social sciences, and the humanities, see John S. Nelson, Allan Megill, and Donald N. McCloskey, eds., *The Rhetoric of the Human Sciences* (Madison: University of Wisconsin Press, 1987).

42. For an insightful discussion of practices and their relations to traditions and institutions, see Alasdair MacIntyre, *After Virtue*, 175–181.

43. For a detailed discussion of the typical demarcations between the natural sciences and the human sciences and of the recent abandonment of these inadequate distinctions, see Mary Hesse, *Revolutions and Reconstructions in the Philosophy of Science*, 63–110; and Bernstein, *Beyond Objectivism and Relativism*, 30–34, 52–108.

44. Pitkin, 237.

45. Insightful discussions of the differences between the natural sciences and ethics can be found in Pitkin, 219–239, and Williams, 132–153; discussions of natural sciences and the social sciences are provided by Bernstein, *The Restructuring of Social and Political Theory* (Philadelphia: University of Pennsylvania Press, 1976); MacIntyre, 77–101; Habermas, *Knowledge and Human Interests*, trans. Jeremy Shapiro (Boston: Beacon Press, 1971); and Hesse, Introduction and Part III. It has been pointed out that in attempting to rescue social science from the grip of scientism, Habermas has uncritically accepted the positivist account of natural science as essentially correct. For a full discussion of this problem see R. Keat and J. Urry, *Social Theory as Science* (London: Routledge and Kegan Paul, 1975), and

Normon Stockman, *Antipositivist Theories of Science* (Dordrecht: D. Reidel, 1983). One might add that Habermas is not alone in failing to challenge the positivist understanding of scientific knowledge and in failing to subject the positivist conceptions of theory, explanation, and the "empirical" to critical scrutiny. A willingness to accept the positivist vision of natural science has become something of a hallmark of the contemporary age.

46. The conception of politics operative in this passage is drawn from William Connolly's *Terms of Political Discourse*. Connolly suggests that politics is an ongoing process of contestation among "persons and groups who share a range of concepts, but share them imperfectly and incompletely." On this view, politics "involves the clash that emerges when appraisive concepts are shared widely but imperfectly, when actual understanding and interpretation is possible but in a partial and limited way, when reasoned argument and coercive pressure commingle precariously in the endless process of defining and resolving issues," 6, 10, 40.

CHAPTER 5

1. An earlier version of this chapter appeared as "The Affirmative Action Debate and Conflicting Conceptions of Individuality," in *HYPATIA*, a special issue of the *Women's Studies International Forum* 7(5):335–347, Fall, 1984.

2. Title VII of the Civil Rights Act of 1964 and Executive Orders 11246 and 11375 are the foundation of the government's Affirmative Action program. In essence, the program requires that job opportunities be publicly advertised, that the criteria for hiring employees be related to job performance, that sex, race, and ethnicity may not be used as criteria for employment unless it can be demonstrated that they are legitimate occupational requirements and that employers make a good faith effort to recruit qualified women and minority candidates. Although Title VII specifically prohibits the use of quotas and the lowering of standards in order to give preferential treatment to minority and women applicants, implementation efforts by the Office of Federal Contract Compliance (OFCC) within the Department of Labor have included the establishment of "numerical objectives" for minority employment within a specified time frame.

3. Preferential treatment refers to the policy of counting minority status or female sex as additional qualifications when considering

applicants for employment, promotion, or admission to higher education. Thus, given two competent candidates for a job, one a white male and one a black male, the policy of preferential treatment would suggest that the black male has an additional qualification and, therefore, ought to be hired.

4. Reverse discrimination is a label frequently given to the policy of preferential treatment. Although popularized in the course of the *Bakke* case, the phrase incorporates several contentious assumptions. For instance, the term "reverse discrimination" implies that white males have rights to certain educational and employment opportunities which are being violated when women or minorities are admitted or hired. In a meritocratic, capitalist society, no particular individual ever has a right to any job or university slot. Further, using the term "discrimination" to describe the case of white men who are no longer permitted to take advantage of opportunities created by racism and sexism, suggests that the current experience of white men is indistinguishable from the oppression experienced by women and minorities, a suggestion which could not be substantiated by any detailed analysis of these experiences. Despite the questionable implications of the phrase, "reverse discrimination" is used in this chapter in order to convey accurately the views of those who use the label.

5. Ellen Wood argues in *Mind and Politics* (Berkeley: University of California Press, 1972) that commitment to individualism as a social doctrine is compatible with two divergent interpretations of individuality, which she dubs 'dialectical individualism' and 'metaphysical individualism.' While there are some similarities between my conceptions of socialized individualism and atomistic individualism and Wood's two conceptions, I refrain from adopting her terminology for I doubt that the assumptions underlying the debate discussed in this paper reflect the depth of commitment to distinct world views which her analysis suggests. Operating solely within the confines of contemporary American culture, I wish to suggest simply that there exist at least two different ways of understanding what it means to be an individual, and that these different understandings have social policy implications. For a comprehensive analysis of individualism, see Steven Lukes, *Individualism* (New York, Harper and Row, 1973).

6. Much has been written about the atomistic conception of the individual and its relation to liberal theory. For examples of such analyses, see C. B. Macpherson, *The Political Theory of Possessive Individualism* (Oxford, Clarendon Press, 1962); Roberto Unger, *Know-*

ledge and Politics (New York: Free Press, 1975); Zillah Eisenstein, *The Radical Future of Liberal Feminism* (New York: Longman, 1981); and Mark Weaver, "The Concept of Mind and Political Theory." Ph.D. Dissertation, University of Massachusetts (Amherst), May 1980.

7. For an analysis of the social and psychological consequences of accepting these assumptions, see Michael Lewis, *The Culture of Inequality* (New York: New American Library, 1978) and Richard Sennett and Jonathan Cobb, *The Hidden Injuries of Class* (New York: Alfred A. Knopf, 1972).

8. F. A. Hayek, "Individualism: True and False," *Individualism and Economic Order* (Chicago: University of Chicago Press, 1948) 24.

9. *Ibid.*

10. Weaver, 197. The conception of socialized individualism is developed in the works of a number of contemporary critical theorists. For an overview of this work, see Fred Dallmayr, *Beyond Dogma and Despair* (Notre Dame: University of Notre Dame Press, 1981).

11. Thomas Sowell, "Affirmative Action Reconsidered," *The Public Interest* (Winter, 1976); and Sidney Hook, "The Bias of Anti-Bias Regulations," *Measure* #14 (October, 1971) base their arguments against affirmative action on this premise. These and a number of similar articles are included in *Reverse Discrimination*, ed. B. R. Gross (Buffalo, New York: Prometheus Books, 1977).

12. Sowell, 119.

13. Hook, 89.

14. Richard A. Lester, *Anti-Bias Regulations of Universities: Faculty Problems and Their Solutions* (New York: McGraw Hill, 1974).

15. Sowell, 119–120. Sowell does not actually include statistical tables to support this summary statement, and one wonders what data he used. F. K. Barasch provides statistical evidence to support just the opposite claim about female academicians' publishing records and professional qualifications in "HEW, The University and Women," *Dissent* (Summer, 1973).

16. Sowell, 129.

17. Hook, 90. In *Fair Game: Inequality and Affirmative Action*, (San Francisco: W. H. Freeman and Company, 1979), John Livingston

cites several other factors which have been advanced to explain racial inequality: (1) genetic inferiority, (2) the "recent" arrival of blacks in the U.S. and insufficient time for their full assimilation into the "melting pot" of American culture (3) the comparative youth of the black population—the median age of black Americans at the last census was 23 years, too young to have acquired the years of education and experience requisite to high level posts, and (4) the values of different ethnic groups which accord priority to the development of different aptitudes and consequently predispose individuals to choose different sorts of career goals (53–55). Except for the claim of genetic inferiority, all of these could be subsumed under the category of "objective forces"; genetic inferiority would be rejected by those who accept an atomistic conception of the individual because it violates the fundamental assumption that all individuals have equal natural assets, which is necessary to the justification of competition as a fair method of distribution.

18. Miro M. Todorovich, "Discrimination in Higher Education: A Debate on Faculty Employment," *Civil Rights Digest* (Spring, 1975); also in Gross, 34.

19. Hook, 95.

20. Todorovich, 37–38.

21. Hook, 20.

22. William T. Blackstone, "Reverse Discrimination and Compensatory Justice," in *Social Justice and Preferential Treatment*, ed. W. T. Blackstone and R. D. Heslep (Athens, Ga.: University of Georgia Press, 1977).

23. Lee Nisbet, "Affirmative Action—A Liberal Program?" in Gross, 52.

24. Todorovich, 38.

25. *Korematsu v. United States* (323 U.S. 214, 1944) sustained a pernicious classification (that which legitimated the internment of Japanese Americans during World War II) based upon race or ancestry despite the strict scrutiny test on the grounds of war-time emergency.

26. *Dunn v. Blumstein* (405 U.S. 330, 363–4, 1972).

27. *Regents of the University of California v. Bakke* (438 U.S. 265, 1978). The text of the Bakke decision which I have used in this analysis is that printed in *The United States Law Week*, 46 LW 4896

(June 27, 1978). The page references in the following notes refer to this copy of the decision.

28. *Ibid.*, 4906.

29. The study, by S. Sleeth and R. Mishell, was published in the *New England Journal of Medicine* 297(21):1146–1148 on November 24, 1977. The reference appears in footnote 47, p. 4907 of the Court decision.

30. *Bakke*, 4906.

31. *Ibid.*, 4904.

32. *Ibid.*, 4906–7.

33. *Ibid.*, 4907. (Emphasis added).

34. *Ibid.*, 4903.

35. *Ibid.*, 4909.

36. It is interesting to note that it is not just scholars and jurists who believe that success depends solely upon individual will and effort. Survey research conducted by the National Opinion Research Center (NORC) indicates that as recently as 1977, 65% of the white individuals interviewed attributed the economic disadvantage experienced by blacks to the moral failings of individual blacks: "most blacks just don't have the motivation or will power to pull themselves up out of poverty." For a review of NORC data, see Seymour Martin Lipset and William Schneider, "An Emerging National Consensus," *New Republic,* October 15, 1977, 8–9.

37. *Wygant v. Jackson Board of Education* (476 U.S. ___ 1986). The text of this decision can be found in *U.S. Law Week* 54 LW 4479 (May 19, 1986). *Wygant* involved a policy concerning reductions in force worked out in contract negotiations between a Michigan school board and the teachers union. The policy, which had the support of black and white teachers, provided that in order to preserve the presence of black teachers in the schools during a period of teacher layoffs, some nonminority teachers would be laid off while minority teachers with less seniority were retained. The lower courts had found this contract constitutionally permissible, the Supreme Court reversed these lower court decisions.

38. *Wygant,* 4479.

39. *Johnson v. Transportation Agency, Santa Clara County,*

California. The text of this decision can be found in *United States Law Week* 55 LW 4379 (March 24, 1987).

40. *Ibid.*, 4390–4391.

41. *Ibid.*, 4391.

42. *Ibid.*, 4393.

43. *Ibid.*, 4394. The "Weber sense" refers to job categories which have been segregated as a result of intentional and systematic exclusion proven by judicial or administrative investigation.

44. *Ibid.*, 4391.

45. *Ibid.*

46. *Ibid.*, 4392. 4394.

47. *Ibid.*, 4395.

48. *Ibid.*, 4396.

49. Tom L. Beauchamp, "The Justification of Reverse Discrimination," in Blackstone and Heslep, 90.

50. A series of Court decisions concerning Title VII of the Civil Rights Act of 1964 have sustained the use of statistical evidence showing underrepresentation as sufficient to establish a *prima facie* case of discrimination. See, for example, *United States v. Iron Workers Local 86; United States v. Hayes International Corp.; United States v. United Brotherhood of Carpenters and Joiners.*

51. Alan H. Goldman, "Affirmative Action," in *Equality and Preferential Treatment*, ed. Cohen, Nagel and Scanlon (Princeton: Princeton University Press, 1977) 194.

52. The Supreme Court ruled that underutilization (i.e., a comparison based upon calculations concerning those in the labor force who possess the relevant qualifications) constituted the appropriate measure to establish a *prima facie* case of discrimination for jobs which require specialized training in *Hazelwood School District v. U.S.*, 433 U.S. 299 (1977). Unfortunately, the requirement of this more stringent standard is often misunderstood, in part because the Supreme Court continues to refer to this as a demonstration of "underrepresentation." For an example of the use of underutilization to make a case for the existence of discrimination against women, see F. K. Barasch, "HEW, the University and Women," *Dissent* (Summer) 1973.

53. Given the suspicious circumstances surrounding the causes of underutilization, both EEOC officials and the courts have laid the burden of proof of nondiscrimination upon employers. Given a *prima facie* case of discrimination, it becomes the burden of the person or institution accused of discrimination to convince the court that minorities or women are underutilized for reasons other than discrimination. *United States v. Iron Workers Local 86*, 443 F. 2d. 544 (9th Circuit, 1971), cert. denied, 404 U.S. 984, 92 S. Ct. 447, 30 L. Ed.2d. 367 (1971).

54. Virginia Held, "Reasonable Progress and Self-Respect" in *Ethics and Public Policy*, ed. Tom L. Beauchamp (Englewood Cliffs, New Jersey: Prentice-Hall, 1975) 33.

55. Livingston, 182.

56. Louis Katzner, "Reverse Discrimination," in *And Justice For All*, ed. Tom Regan and Donald Van De Veer (Totowa, New Jersey: Rowman and Littlefield, 1982) 75.

57. Livingston, 120–128; Held, 33–34.

58. Veronica Nieva and Barbara Gutek, "Sex Effects on Evaluation," *Academy of Management Review* 5 (1980):267–276.

59. Beauchamp, "The Justification of Reverse Discrimination," in Blackstone and Heslep, 110.

60. Graham Hughes, "Reparations for Blacks," in *Ethics and Public Policy*, 26.

61. Livingston, 38.

62. Judith Jarvis Thompson, "Preferential Hiring," in Cohen et. al., 36.

63. Livingston, 132.

64. J. Stanley Pottinger, "The Drive Toward Equality," *Change Magazine* 4(October 1972) reprinted in Gross, 49.

65. Howard A. Glickstein, "Discrimination in Higher Education: A Debate on Faculty Employment," in Gross, 30.

66. J. Stanley Pottinger, "Affirmative Action," *New York Times*, 18 December, 1971.

67. Livingston, 32.

68. Letter to the Editor, *New York Times*, quoted in Nisbet, 52.

69. For an example drawn from the medical profession, see P. B. Price et al., "Measurement of Physician Performance," *Journal of Medical Education* 39(1964):203. Price et al. found no correlation between student grades in undergraduate or medical school and physician performance on medical school faculties, as board-certified specialists, or as urban or rural general practitioners.

70. Glickstein, 29.

71. Held, 34.

72. *Bakke*, 4912.

73. *Ibid.*, 4923.

74. *Ibid.*, 4931.

75. *Ibid.*, 4918.

76. *Ibid.*, 4912.

77. *Ibid.*, 4919–4920.

78. *Ibid.*, 4912.

79. *Steelworkers v. Weber*, 443 U.S. 193 (1979).

80. *Ibid.*, 208.

81. *Johnson v. Transportation Agency, Santa Clara County, California*, 55 LW 4380, 4386.

82. *Ibid.*, 4385.

83. *Ibid.*

84. *Ibid.*, 4386, note 17.

85. *Ibid.*, 4385. To substantiate this point, Justice Brennan pointed out that the Agency's personnel data clearly indicated that the vast majority of promotions were being awarded to men and that the petitioner himself had been awarded such a promotion since this case had been initiated (4385, note 15).

86. *Ibid.*, 4386.

87. *Ibid.*, 4387.

88. *Ibid.*

89. *Ibid.*, 4388.

90. *Ibid.* In formulating this broad vision, Justice Stevens drew his language from Sullivan's article, "The Supreme Court—Comment, Sins of Discrimination: Last Term's Affirmative Action Cases," 100 *Harvard Law Review* 78, 96 (1986).

91. For a detailed examination of the extent to which liberal presuppositions drawn from the works of John Locke involve a denial of human biology, see Alison Jaggar, *Feminist Politics and Human Nature* (Totowa, New Jersey: Rowman and Allanheld, 1983) 38–48.

92. This point has been made by Louis Dumont in "The Modern Conception of the Individual: Notes on Its Genesis and that of Concomitant Institutions," *Contributions to Indian Sociology* VIII(1965):13–61 and in *Homo Hierarchicus: The Caste System and Its Implications*, trans. Mark Sainsbury (London: Weidenfeld and Nicolson, 1970). See also Lukes, 146–157.

93. Thomas Hobbes, one of the first theorists to develop the atomistic conception of the individual, recognized clearly the implications of his determinist assumptions for a conception of freedom. Thus, he rejected notions of free will as "words without meaning, that is to say, absurd." *Leviathan* (New York: Bobbs-Merrill, 1958) 47.

94. Both John Livingston and Virginia Held have suggested that the perpetuation of racial and sexual inequality poses a threat to the legitimacy of the democratic order in the U.S. See Livingston, 186–199, and Held, 39–40.

CHAPTER 6

1. An earlier version of this chapter appeared as "Violence and the Politics of Explanation: Kampuchea Revisited," *Journal of Applied Philosophy* 2(1985):69–83.

2. In the late 1960s, Cambodia was invaded by North Vietnamese, South Vietnamese, and U.S. armed forces, and served for several years as the main battleground of the Vietnam War. For a more detailed account of these invasions, see Peter Poole "Communism and Ethnic Conflict in Cambodia 1960–1975," in *Communism in Indochina*, ed. Zasloff and Brown (Lexington, Ma.: D.C. Heath, 1975). Kampuchea was invaded again by the North Vietnamese in 1978 and 1979. For accounts of these developments, see Karl Jackson "Cambodia 1978: War, Pillage and Purge in Democratic Kampuchea" *Asian Survey* 19(1): 72–84, and Justus van der Kroef, "Cambodia: From

Democratic Kampuchea to People's Republic," *Asian Survey* 19(8): 731–750.

3. Between 1969 and August 1973, the U.S. dropped 539,129 tons of bombs on Cambodia. For a fuller account, see William Shawcross, *Sideshow: Nixon, Kissinger and the Destruction of Cambodia* (New York: Simon and Schuster, 1979).

4. Lon Nol, aided by Sirik Matak, overthrew Norodom Sihanouk in March 1970. There is also evidence that during the period of 1975–1977, the Vietnamese infiltrated assassination teams into Kampuchea, backed abortive coups, and fought against consolidation of power in the hands of Pol Pot. For a discussion of these events, see Karl Jackson, 77. In 1979, Vietnamese-backed Heng Samrin overthrew Pol Pot.

5. By 1972, the battle in Cambodia had devolved into a "genuine civil war" between Lon Nol's forces supported and supplied by the United States and a coalition of Khmer Rouge and Khmer Rumdos (Sihanoukists) supplied by China and North Vietnam. For a review of the civil war, see J. Davidson, *Indochina: Signposts in the Storm* (Singapore: Longman Malaysia, 1979) 167.

6. For a description of the revolutionary program of the Khmer Rouge, see Timothy Carney, *Communist Party Power in Kampuchea: Documents and Discussion*, Data Paper 106, Southeast Asia Program, Cornell University, 1977. For conflicting descriptions of the implementation of that program, see Francois Ponchaud, *Year Zero* (New York: Holt, Rinehart and Winston, 1977); and Hildebrand and Porter, *Cambodia: Starvation and Revolution* (New York: Monthly Review Press, 1976).

7. The best description of Pol Pot's purges of both Vietnamese sympathizers and Chinese Cultural Revolution sympathizers from the ranks of the Khmer Rouge is provided by Ben Kiernan, "Conflict in the Kampuchean Communist Movement" *Journal of Contemporary Asia* 10(1–2):7–74.

8. Claims about the prevalence of terrorism and summary executions by the Khmer Rouge after their April 1975 victory vary markedly from one author to the next. For the most extreme statements, see, Barron and Paul, *Murder of a Gentle Land* (Readers Digest Press, 1977). This book received a second printing under the title, *Peace With Horror* (Hodder and Stoughton, 1977). For a thorough critique of this volume, see Noam Chomsky and Edward S. Herman,

After the Cataclysm: Post War Indochina and the Reconstruction of Imperial Ideology. (Boston: Southend Press, 1979) 135–294.

9. Since the 1979 invasion of Kampuchea by Vietnamese forces and the institution of Heng Samrin's regime, Pol Pot's Khmer Rouge army has resumed guerilla activity in an effort to oust the Vietnamese from Kampuchean soil. It is estimated that as many as twelve factions of Cambodian exiles of diverse ideological bents have organized troops for guerilla activities along the Thai border. For a discussion of these developments, see Roger Kershaw, "Multipolarity and Cambodia's Crisis of Survival: A Preliminary Perspective on 1979, *Southeast Asian Affairs 1980* (Singapore: 1980). It is worth noting that since the Vietnamese-backed coup of 1979, the United States has become a champion of Pol Pot at the United Nations, insisting that Pol Pot is the sole legitimate representative of Kampuchea.

10. Sheldon Simon, "Cambodia: Barbarism in a Small State Under Seige," *Current History* (December 1978) 197; Ponchaud, 192; Barron and Paul, 43–61.

11. Justice van der Kroef, "Cambodia: From Democratic Kampuchea to People's Republic," *Asian Survey* 19(8):747.

12. Norodom Sihanouk, *War and Hope: The Case for Cambodia* (New York: Pantheon Books, 1980) 83.

13. Wilfred Burchett, *The China, Cambodia, Vietnam Triangle* (Chicago: Vanguard Books, 1981) 47.

14. Two recent works raise serious challenges to the veracity of refugee accounts of Khmer Rouge behavior. See Gavan McCormack, "The Kampuchean Revolution 1975–1978: The Problem of Knowing the Truth," *Journal of Contemporary Asia* 10(1–2):75–118 and Chomsky and Herman, 135–294.

15. Barron and Paul as well as Ponchaud have made much of the translation of Angka Leou as "the Organization on High" or "Higher Organization," implying an anonymous power of absolute proportions, devoid of any notion of accountability for its actions. In this respect, it is interesting to note that all the military cables which gave official sanction to U.S. secret bombing of Cambodian targets in 1969 stipulated that these orders too had come from "Highest Authority," a thinly veiled reference to the White House. See Shawcross, p. 21.

16. For the most complete account of these atrocities, see Barron and Paul, 40–42.

17. Simon, "Cambodia: Barbarism in a Small State Under Seige," 197.

18. The following account is drawn from Barron and Paul, *Murder in a Gentle Land*; and *Peace with Horror*, 43–61.

19. *Ibid.*, p. 46.

20. *Ibid.*

21. *Ibid.*, p. 47.

22. *Ibid.*, 61. Barron and Paul note that this is "obviously a matter of conjecture," nevertheless, it is the only explanatory conjecture advanced in their 234 page book. Thus it deserves to be treated as a serious hypothesis.

23. Kiernan, "Conflict in the Kampuchean Communist Movement."

24. I do not want to suggest that psychological factors are always or necessarily irrelevant to an explanation of socio-political events. However, I do believe that amateur attempts to psychoanalyze particular individuals on the basis of scanty information and to use such speculative accounts to explain social crises are fundamentally flawed, as the case of Khieu Samphan so clearly illustrates.

25. Van der Kroef, "Cambodia: From Democratic Kampuchea to Peoples Republic," 747.

26. Ponchaud, xvi.

27. Carney, 11.

28. Peter Poole, "Cambodia 1975: The GRUNK Regime," *Asian Survey* 16(1):24. Poole attributes this conclusion to "foreign observers." See also Karl Jackson, "Gone to Pot," *Asian Survey* 18(1):90; Donald Kirk, "Revolution and Political Violence in Cambodia 1970–1974," in Zasloff and Brown, 223; and Ponchaud, 22, 50, 118.

29. Kirk, p. 223.

30. Carney, 6.

31. Most notably Ponchaud, whose work will be discussed in greater detail later. In "Political Ideology in Democratic Kampuchea," *Orbis* 22(4): 1007–1032, Justus van der Kroef refers to the Khmer Rouge program as "Socialism without a blueprint," and

Carney's work identifies Khmer objectives which are not related to traditional Marxist-Leninism in general.

32. Ponchaud, 21.

33. *Ibid.* Marx, of course, had relied upon an urban industrial economy as the breeding ground for the revolutionary consciousness of the proletariat; he had little use for the "idiocy of rural life."

34. Ponchaud, 120.

35. *Ibid.*, 72, 102.

36. Kiernan, "Conflict in the Kampuchean Communist Movement," *passim.*

37. Kiernan, "Cambodia in the News: 1975–1976, *Melbourne Journal of Politics* (1976) and Kiernan, "Social Cohesion in Revolutionary Cambodia," *Australian Outlook* (December 1976), cited in Chomsky and Herman 226–227. Sheldon Simon also discusses differences in goals and strategies among segments of the revolutionary movement in "The Khmer Resistance: External Relations, 1973–1974," in Zasloff and Brown, 199.

38. Donald Kirk, "Revolution and Political Violence in Cambodia," 220.

39. Richard Dudman, *Forty Days with Enemy* (Liveright, 1971); Karl Jackson, 78; Sihanouk as cited in Shawcross, 390–1.

40. Chomsky and Herman, 150.

41. David Chandler, "The Tragedy of Cambodian History," *Pacific Affairs* 52(3):411.

42. For a graphic description of the South Vietnamese Army's brutalities toward the Khmer population, see Shawcross, 174.

43. Mairon Kirsch Leighton, "Perspectives on the Vietnamese Cambodian Border Conflict," *Asian Survey* 18(5):448–457 and Karl Jackson "Cambodia 1978: War, Pillage and Purge . . ." *Asian Survey* 19(1):77.

44. Kiernan, "Conflict in the Kampuchean Communist Movement," *Journal of Contemporary Asia* 10(12):8, 13, 14, 35.

45. *Ibid.*, 20, 49.

46. *Ibid.*, 35, 64.

47. Wilfred Burchett, *The China, Cambodia, Vietnam Triangle* (Chicago: Vanguard, 1981) 233.

48. *Ibid.*, 38–42.

49. *Ibid.*, 65.

50. *Ibid.*, 227–229.

51. Norodom Sihanouk's most recent analysis of the Kampuchean situation lays blame for the current suffering on the unchecked conflict between two types of Communism, yet he does not suggest that this is primarily an ideological dispute. *War and Hope: The Case for Cambodia* (Pantheon, 1981).

52. This suspicion has been nurtured by Vietnamese behavior. For example, Vietnamese actions during the Geneva Conference of 1953–1954 have been interpreted by the Cambodians as an outright betrayal, as has the Vietnamese withdrawal of military assistance from the Khmer Rouge in 1973 as part of an effort to force Kampuchea to negotiate a settlement to the civil war (a precondition set by Kissinger for U.S. aid to Vietnamese reconstruction). For detailed discussion of these events, see Shawcross, 48 and 281.

53. In many respects, Burchett's volume epitomizes the view from Hanoi. For a more balanced depiction of the perceptions and misperceptions on both sides, see Huynh Kim Khanh, "Into the Third Indochina War," *Southeast Asian Affairs* 1980, 331.

54. Marion Kirsch Leighton casts doubt on the proxy war explanation of the conflict in "Perspectives on the Vietnam-Cambodian Border Conflict," *Asian Survey* 18(5):450.

55. For the best discussion of the influence of these international actors on the current conflict, see Roger Kershaw, "Multipolarity and Cambodia's Crisis of Survival," *Southeast Asian Affairs 1980*.

56. George Hildebrand and Gareth Porter, *Cambodia: Starvation and Revolution* (New York: Monthly Review Press, 1976).

57. *Ibid.*, 19–33.

58. *Ibid.*, 41.

59. *Ibid.*, 44.

60. *Ibid.*, 87.

61. *Ibid.*, 57–86. Hildebrand and Porter stress the importance of

the irrigation network constructed under Khmer Rouge supervision, which enabled the Kampucheans to produce two to three rice crops per year rather than the customary production of one crop.

62. Poole, Carney, and Chomsky all discuss the excesses which may be attributable to the inexperience and inflexibility of these young soldiers.

63. Shawcross, 148.

64. Ibid., 87.

65. Chomsky and Herman, ix.

66. Ibid., 218.

67. Ibid., 219. It is interesting to note in this respect the intensification of bombing after the Vietnamese-U.S. Paris Accords were signed.

68. Ibid., 222.

69. Thus, I disagree with Chomsky's and Herman's conclusion that the marked deficiencies of available accounts of events in Indochina signify an intentional effort to select, modify, or sometimes invent 'facts' in order to create an image of events which suits the ideological requirements of dominant social groups (293).

70. This distance need not be measured in miles. It could just as easily suggest the vast cultural differences between an upper middle-class suburban household and life in an inner-city ghetto. For a lucid analysis of political violence in the United States, see H. L. Nieburg, *Political Violence: The Behavioral Process* (New York: St. Martin's Press, 1969).

71. For a more detailed analysis of this conception of action, see Hannah Arendt, *The Human Condition* (Chicago: University of Chicago Press, 1958).

72. Ernest Nagel, *The Structure of Science*, 2d ed. (Indianapolis: Hackett, 1979), 447. For arguments which arrive at similar conclusions, see Richard Bernstein, *The Restructuring of Social and Political Theory* (Philadelphia: University of Pennsylvania Press, 1976) 24–45; Charles Lindblom and David Cohen, *Usable Knowledge* (New Haven: Yale University Press, 1979), 73–75; Alasdair MacIntyre, *After Virtue* (Notre Dame: University of Notre Dame Press, 1981), 84–101; J. Donald Moon, "The Logic of Political Inquiry: A Synthesis of Op-

244 NOTES

posed Perspectives," *Handbook of Political Science* Vol. 1, 131–217; W. G. Runciman, *Social Science and Political Theory* (Cambridge: Cambridge University Press, 1963), 3–11, 110–135; Aaron Wildavsky, *Speaking Truth to Power* (Boston: Little, Brown & Company, 1979), 8–16.

73. MacIntyre, 86–87.

CHAPTER 7

1. This phrase is borrowed from Clifford Geertz, "Blurred Genres: The Refiguration of Social Thought," *American Scholar* 49(1980): 165–179.

2. This chapter draws on arguments developed in two earlier publications: "The Ideological Prism and the Conceptualization of Human Rights," *Politics and Policy* 5(1985):1–11; and "Ideological Immunity: The Soviet Response to Human Rights Criticism," *Universal Human Rights* 2(1980):67–84.

3. Hugo Bedau, "International Human Rights," in *And Justice For All*, ed. Tom Regan and Donald Van De Veer (Totowa: New Jersey: Rowman and Littlefield, 1982), 300.

4. *Ibid.*

5. Jack Donnelly, "Human Rights and Human Dignity: An Analytic Critique of Non-Western Conceptions of Human Rights," *Americn Political Science Review* 76(2):303–316; 303.

6. *Ibid.*, 312.

7. Tracy Strong, "Taking Rank With What Is Ours: American Political Thought, Foreign Policy and the Question of Rights," in *The Politics of Human Rights*, ed. Paula Newberg (New York: New York University Press, 1980), 33–64.

8. A. Pollis and P. Schwab, eds, *Human Rights: Cultural and Ideological Perspectives* (New York: Praeger, 1980), xiii.

9. Eddison J. M. Svobgo, "Human Rights: A Third World View," in *Human Rights and American Foreign Policy*, ed. Donald Kommers and Gilbert Loescher (Notre Dame: University of Notre Dame Press, 1979), 93.

10. *Ibid.*, 81–82.

11. Harry Scoble and Laurie Wiseberg, "Problems of Comparative Research on Human Rights," in *Global Human Rights*, ed. V. Nanda, J. Scarritt, and G. Shepherd (Boulder, Colorado: Westview Press, 1981), 148.

12. Richard Falk, "Theoretical Foundations of Human Rights," in *The Politics of Human Rights*, ed. Paula Newberg, 72.

13. Paula Newberg, "Introduction," *The Politics of Human Rights*, 2.

14. David Riesman, "Human Rights: Competing Ideals," in *Human Rights and U.S. Foreign Policy*, ed. Barry Rubin and Elizabeth Spiro (Boulder, Colorado: Westview Press, 1979), 71.

15. Robert Johnson, "Human Rights in the 1980s: Revolutionary Growth or Unanticipated Erosion," *World Politics* 35(2):286.

16. Pollis and Schwab, 13–14.

17. Bedau, 297.

18. Two articles are especially good in their survey and criticisms of the range of human rights justifications advanced by philosophers: Robert Young, "Dispensing with Moral Rights," *Political Theory* 6(1):63–74; and Lawrence Becker, "Individual Rights," in *And Justice For All*, 197–216.

19. The most systematic attempt to link rationality to rights is Alan Gewirth's *Reason and Morality* (Chicago: University of Chicago Press, 1978). Several critics have noted that Gewirth's attempt generates a conception of *goods*, not a conception of rights. See the review of *Reason and Morality* by Henry Veatch in *Ethics* 89:404–414; and James Fishkin, *Beyond Subjective Morality* (New Haven: Yale University Press 1984), 91–94. Cogent criticisms of Gewirth's approach have also been advanced by Alasdair MacIntyre, *After Virtue* (Notre Dame: University of Notre Dame Press, 1981), 63–65; and by Bernard Williams, *Ethics and the Limits of Philosophy* (Cambridge, Ma.: Harvard University Press, 1985), 54–63.

20. For a full discussion of this issue, see Lawrence Becker, 208–210.

21. For a full discussion of these examples, see Hugo Bedau, 298–299.

22. This definition is advanced by Becker, 203.

23. This conception is developed by Terry Pinkard in "Models of the Person," *Canadian Journal of Philosophy* 10(4):623–635.

24. The claim that conceptions of human rights reflect assumptions about human nature and human interests which are culturally and historically variable does not necessarily entail relativism. To reject absolutist expectations with respect to moral reasoning is not to reject all standards of objectivity. For a cogent discussion of the alternatives to absolutism and relativism, see Fishkin, *Beyond Subjective Morality*, and Richard Bernstein, *Beyond Objectivism and Relativism* (Philadelphia: University of Pennsylvania Press, 1983).

25. For a synopsis of the assumptions which inform the atomistic conception of the individual, see chapter 5, 97–99.

26. Arguments concerning human equality grounded in rationality can be found in John Locke, *The Second Treatise of Civil Government* (New York: Hafner Press, 1947), 122–128. Arguments for equality based on survival capabilities are advanced by Jean Jacques Rousseau, "A Discourse on the Origin of Inequality," *The Social Contract and Discourses* (New York: E.P. Dutton & Co., 1950), 199–234. Arguments concerning equality rooted in a psychology of unlimited desires and a roughly equal capacity to kill were developed by Thomas Hobbes, *Leviathan* (New York: Bobbs Merrill, 1958), 86–104. It should be noted that in each of these instances, the recognition of "universal" equality pertained only to the male of the human species. For discussions of the exclusion of women from these formulations, see Susan Moller Okin, *Women in Western Political Thought* (Princeton: Princeton University Press, 1979); and Martha Lee Osborne, *Women in Western Thought* (New York: Random House, 1979).

27. The following discussion will be restricted to an analysis of the problem of political order, but atomistic assumptions create similar problems for the problem of economic order. Thus it could be shown that it is the particular assumptions of atomistic individualism that necessitate the search for impersonal mechanisms to regulate individual action in the economic sphere, and which culminate in the liberal defense of the market.

28. In the most recent reformulation of the liberal creed, John Rawls has referred to these basic civil rights and liberties as primary goods which enable individuals to achieve their private ends, whatever they may be. He argues that the provision of equal rights and liberties to all citizens not only facilitates achievement of their own

privately determined ends, but also frees individuals from the tyranny of social expectations in the choice of private goals. See *A Theory of Justice* (Cambridge, Massachusetts: Belknap Press, 1971), 92–93, 442, and Rawls, "Fairness to Goodness," *Philosophical Review* 84:536–554.

29. Rita Hauser, "Human Rights: A First World View," in *Human Rights and American Foreign Policy*, ed. Donald Kommers and Gilbert Loescher, 87.

30. *Ibid.*, 89.

31. For arguments that the assumptions of classical liberalism have been incorporated in the self-understanding of individuals in the contemporary United States, see C. B. Macpherson, *The Life and Times of Liberal Democracy* (London: Oxford University Press, 1977); Michael Lewis, *The Culture of Inequality* (New York: New American Library, 1978); Robert Bellah et al., *Habits of the Heart* (New York: Harper and Row, 1985); and the discussion in chapter 5 of this book. For a direct discussion of these liberal assumptions and the conception of human rights advanced in western liberal democracies, see John T. Wright, "Human Rights in the West: Political Liberties and the Rule of Law," in *Human Rights: Cultural and Ideological Perspectives*, ed. Pollis and Schwab, 19–31.

32. Karl Marx, *The German Ideology*, reprinted in Robert Tucker, ed. *The Marx-Engels Reader*, 2d ed., (New York: W. W. Norton, 1978), 148–155; cf. *The Grundrisse* in Tucker, ed., 222–223. All page references in the following notes will refer to the Tucker anthology. For secondary sources on Marx's view of human nature, see P. Walton, A. Gamble, and J. Coulter, "The Image of Man in Marx," *Social Theory and Practice* 1(2):69–84; Edward Andrew, "Work and Freedom in Marcuse and Marx," *Canadian Journal of Political Science* 3(2):241–256; Adam Schaff, *Marxism and the Human Individual* (New York: McGraw Hill, 1970); I. Fetscher, "Karl Marx on Human Nature," *Social Research* 40:443–467; A. Sohn Rothel, "Mental and Manual Labor in Marxism" in *Situating Marx*, ed. P. Walton and S. Hall (London: Human Context Books, 1974); and J. J. O'Rourke, *The Problem of Freedom in Marxist Thought* (Dordrecht: D. Reidel, 1974).

33. *The Grundrisse*, 224–240.

34. *The German Ideology*, 155–158.

35. Marx insisted that history has no intrinsic meaning other

than the production of goods to satisfy needs, and through that process, the generation of new needs. Thus, he argued that historians who wish to discuss progress, regress, or repetition must necessarily impose an "extraneous standard" upon history, and he noted that his own account of the development of societies from ancient communal through feudal to capitalist should be understood in this light. *The German Ideology*, 165–193.

36. For Marx's account of the achievements of capitalism, see *The Communist Manifesto*, especially 475–479.

37. These defects are first presented in *The Economic and Philosophic Manuscripts of 1844*, 70–81; and are elaborated upon in *Wage, Labor and Capital*, 203–217; *The Grundrisse*, 248–267; and *Capital*, 344–438.

38. *Capital*, 303–312.

39. *Economic and Philosophic Manuscripts of 1844*, 70–77.

40. *Capital*, 326; *The German Ideology*, 164.

41. *Economic and Philosophic Manuscripts of 1844*, 81–93; *The German Ideology*, 160.

42. *The German Ideology*, 197.

43. *The German Ideology*, 191; *Communist Manifesto*, 484.

44. Lenin "Preliminary Draft of the Theses on the National and Colonial Questions," (June 1920) *Selected Works* (Moscow: Foreign Languages Publishing House, 1943), Vol. X, 231–232.

45. Reflecting the belief that emancipation from exploitation constitutes the most fundamental human right, the Soviet Constitution lists the right to labor, that is, to receive guaranteed work and remuneration for work, first among the enumerated basic rights, liberties, and duties of citizens of the USSR. The subsequent rights enumerated are: the right to rest, to free health care, to material security in old age, illness, and cases of disability, the rights to housing, to education, to the use of cultural achievements, to freedom of scientific, technical, and artistic creation, the rights to participate in the administration of state affairs, to submit proposals on improving their activities, and to criticize shortcomings in work. The Soviet Constitution places the rights most frequently enshrined in bourgeois constitutions in a context which allows for clear restriction of these rights should they be put to non-socialistic uses: "In accordance with

the working peoples' interests and for purposes of strengthening the socialist system, USSR citizens are guaranteed freedom of speech, of the press, of assembly, of mass meetings, and of street processions and demonstration." The language of the introductory clause provides ample grounds upon which to rescind these rights, for it states that they "may not be used to the detriment of the working people's interests," or "to weaken the socialist system". Article 50, Draft Constitution of the USSR as presented to the Constitutional Commission and approved by the Presidium of the USSR Supreme Soviet. (Text in *Pravda*, June 4, 1977, 1–4; *Current Digest of the Soviet Press* [hereafter, *CDSP*] 29(22):1–11).

46. As the following quotation indicates, the role of socialism in promoting legitimate human rights while forsaking the oppressive interests of capitalists is a recurrent theme in speeches by leaders of socialist states: "It was precisely socialist democracy that enabled the Soviet people to get rid of such 'freedoms' as the right to choose one's exploiter or to be unemployed, the right to starve or be a hired slave of capital. No it is not that way that our people conceive of freedom. We see in freedom the right of people to a dignified life without exploiters or exploitation, the right to a genuine political equality, the right to the use of all achievements of science and culture. We understand freedom as the liberation of the people from the horrors of unemployment and misery, from racial, national, and social oppression." N. Krushchev, "Pre-Election Speech," Moscow Radio Broadcast, March 14, 1958. (Text in *Soviet World Outlook*, Bureau of Intelligence and Research of U.S. Department of State, Washington, 1959.)

47. For examples of this view see, G. Ostroumov and V. Belenkov, "La Politique Exterieure du Socialism et des Droits de L'homme," *La Vie Internationale* 5 (1983):37–47; and W. Sokolewicz, "The Socialist Concept of Citizens' Basic Rights and Duties," *Polish Round Table* 9 (1979):107–132.

48. This phrase is borrowed from Robert Nozick, *Anarchy State and Utopia* (New York: Basic Books, 1974).

49. For discussions of the relationship between Marxist theory and the beliefs and practices of the power elite and the people of the Soviet Union, see Peter Reddaway, "The Theory and Practice of Human Rights in the Soviet Union," in *Human Rights and American Foreign Policy*, ed. Donald Kommers and Gilbert Loescher, 115–129; L. J. Macfarlane, "Marxist Theory and Human Rights," *Government and Opposition* 17(4):414–428; Roger Hamburg, "American and

Soviet Views of Human Rights," *Conflict* 2(2):163–175; and "Marksistsko-Leninskaja Koncepcija Prav Celoveka i Sovremennaja Ideologiceskaja Bor'ba," *Sovetskoe Gosudarstvo i Pravo* 7:3–12.

50. Richard Falk has argued that "a repressive government cannot be transformed by marginal, voluntary, remedial steps taken under pressure from without, of the sort associated with human rights initiatives." See "Theoretical Foundations of Human Rights," in Newberg, 70.

51. Warren Christopher "Human Rights: Principle and Realism," *U.S. Department of State Bulletin* 77(#1922):269–273, August 29, 1977; and Charles W. Maynes, "New Hopes for Human Rights," *U.S. Department of State Bulletin* 77(#2000):556–561, October 24, 1977. The inclusion of the needs-based rights to food, shelter, health care, and education within the Carter Doctrine conflicts with traditional liberal conceptions of human rights. Yet the extent of this conflict is minimal: At no point did the Carter Administration take any action with respect to either domestic policy or foreign policy to guarantee these rights for its own population, much less for foreign populations.

52. Christopher, 270. This discussion will only deal with the stated objectives of the Carter Doctrine, improving the protection of human rights around the world. For an argument that Carter's "real" goal was to regain U.S. prestige in the aftermath of Vietnam and Watergate, see Kurt R. Spillman, "Die Stadt auf dem Berge," *Schweizer Monatschrifte* 58(3):179–192, March, 1978; and Donald Fraser, "Freedom and Foreign Policy," *Foreign Policy* 26(1977):140–156. That Carter's objectives had more to do with domestic politics is also suggested by Daniel P. Moynihan, "The Politics of Human Rights," *Commentary* 64(2):14–26, August, 1977.

53. For critiques of Carter's human rights policy on the grounds that it involved interference with the internal affairs of other nations, see Ernest W. Lefever, "The Trivialization of Human Rights," *Policy Review* 3(1978):11–26; and T. E. Utley, "A Reappraisal of the Human Rights Doctrine," *Policy Review* 3(1978):27–34.

54. President Carter, "Address to the Representatives to the United Nations," on March 17, 1977. (Text in *Weekly Compilation of Presidential Documents*, March 21, 1977).

55. Harold Russell, "The Helsinki Declaration: Brobdingnag or Lilliput?" *American Journal of International Law* 70(2):242–271, 260.

56. 95th Congress, 1st Session Committee Print, "Human Rights in the International Community and in United States Foreign Policy, 1945–1976," prepared by the Foreign Affairs and National Defense Division, Congressional Research Service, Library of Congress. U.S. Government Printing Office, Washington, D.C., July 24, 1977, 3.

57. In contrast to Carter's reliance upon verbal and symbolic strategies, the U.S. Congress had attempted to use trade policies to reinforce concern for human rights, enacting legislation (Section 402 of the Trade Act of 1974, Public Law 93–618) intended to tie most favored nation (MFN) treatment for trade in products from nonmarket economies to the maintenance of freedom of emigration from those countries. It also established a Commission on Security and Cooperation in Europe (Public Law 94–304) to monitor actions of the signatories of the Helsinki Accord, especially actions dealing with Basket III provisions relating to cooperation in humanitarian fields and protection of human rights.

58. In "Bearing Witness and Human Rights," (Christian Century, August 31–September 7, 1977, 751–753) J. Patrick Dobel suggests that Carter's reliance upon verbal and symbolic strategies should be understood in the context of the evangelical Protestant tradition of "bearing witness to one's beliefs." As "an alternative to both self-righteous crusading and cynical realism," Dobel suggests that 'bearing witness' constitutes an important symbolic act precisely because it eschews violence and relies instead upon "persuasion by example." Although Dobel notes that the concept of human rights is an ambiguous one, he suggests that an international consensus concerning basic human rights does exist. Advancing a vision of this 'consensus' which incorporates both Liberal and Marxist conceptions of rights, Dobel suggests that to be maximally effective, Carter's rhetorical strategy of political witnessing requires that the Untied States overcome its "glaring deficiencies in the areas of substantive rights to food shelter, and health." Thus Dobel's article ends with a plea for the United States to reconcile its human rights rhetoric with its domestic policy. While Dobel's argument has the great virtue of demonstrating the manner in which human rights rhetoric can be used against the United States, it fails to take seriously the depth of differences which circumscribe the alternative conceptions of rights developed in the Liberal and Marxist traditions. Thus, Dobel's argument underestimates the scope of changes which would be required for the United States to accept notions of substantive rights.

59. Georgy Ratiani, "Sensationalism and Integrity," Prav-

da, January 1, 1977, 5; *CDSP* 29(1):16.

60. Editorial, "What Lies Behind the Furor over Human Rights?" *Pravda*, February 12, 1977, 4.; *CDSP* 29(6):1–5.

61. *Ibid.* The force of the Soviet rhetoric concerning the weakness of the United States conveyed in this series of quotes masks an ongoing debate in the Soviet Union about the precise degree of strength of the U.S., both militarily and economically, and the implications of this strength for detente, arms control, and peaceful existence. For a thorough explication of the historical development of this internal debate, see William B. Husband, "Soviet Perceptions of U.S. 'Positions of Strength' Diplomacy in the 1970s," *World Politics* 31(4):495–517, July 1979.

62. G. Shakhanazarov, "Peaceful Coexistence and Social Progress," *Pravda*, December 27, 1975, 4–5; *CDSP* 27(52):1–4.

63. Major General D. Volkonogov, "Ideological Struggles in the Conditions of Detente," *Kommunist Vooruzhennvkh Sil* 3(February 1977): 9–23, *CDSP* 29(5):5–7; and S. Popov, "Problems of Humanism in the Present Ideological Struggle," *Pravda*, August 16, 1975, 3–4, *CDSP* 28(33): 4–6.

64. V. Kuroyedov, "Religious Dignitaries for Stable Peace, Just Relations Among Nations," *Izvestia*, July 8, 1976, 5; *CDSP* 28(27): 19.

65. Popov, 4.

66. Yevgeny Grigoryev, "International Week," *Pravda*, June 19, 1977; *CDSP* 29(25):22.

67. I. Aleksandrov, "Concerning Freedoms, Real and Imaginary," *Pravda*, February 20, 1976; *CDSP* 28(7):1–8.

68. "Concerning Yet Another Anti-Soviet Furor," *Izvestia*, November 10, 1976; *CDSP* 28(45): 23.

69. The flavor of these accusations can be gleaned from the following quotations.
"In the United States itself, millions of Americans of various nationalities and skin colors are deprived of many human rights, above all the right to work, a fact to which the almost 8 million unemployed attest, as well as the right to free medical services, and the right to the security of the individual. Millions of Americans live in constant fear. Many of the civil liberties proclaimed in the United States Constitution exist only on paper, only as subjects for theoreti-

cal discourse while surveillance and wire-tapping have become daily practice." A. Petrov, "Senator Church is Meddling in Something that is None of His Business," *Pravda*, January 30, 1977, 4; *CDSP* 29(6):5.

"It is indicative that the 'fighters' for the political rights of the socialist countries' citizens at the same time play the role of suppressors of the self-same rights and liberties of their own countries' citizens. We know all about the continued persecution of communists and all democrats in the capitalist states which use a great variety of methods—from the fabrication of false accusations of lawbreaking and infringement of Constitutional procedures to restrictions on civil service employment, the deprivation of job opportunities, etc." Shakhanazarov, 5.

"The Wilmington 10 affair, as well as the persecution of many other dissidents in the U.S. exposes the hyprocrisy of the new administration's policy on human rights." "End Political Repressions," *Pravda*, April 8, 1977, 5; *CDSP* 29(14):19–20.

"Persecution for one's way of thinking has reached such proportions in the United States that many press organs—the weekly magazine *The Nation* for example—are writing with alarm of the growing danger that the U.S. will turn into a police state." "The All-Seeing Eye of the Police: Democracy Turned Inside Out," *Pravda*, February 7, 1977, 3; *CDSP* 29(6):5.

"While blowing up the manifestly far-fetched and nonexistent "jewish question" in the U.S.S.R., where citizens of all nationalities enjoy equal rights, the Republican and Democratic party leaders are deliberately closing their eyes to racial discrimination, lawlessness and violation of civil rights in the United States itself, these being an inherent attribute, as is well known all over the world, of the 'American way of life.'" A. Tolkunov, 'Strange Forgetfulness,' *Pravda*, September 18, 1976, 5; *CDSP* 28(38):16-17.

70. See, for example, Georgi Arbatov, Interview in *U.S. News and World Report*, March 14, 1977, 23; and V. Lapsky, "Whom is Washington Protecting?" *Izvestia*, August 24, 1977, 3; *CDSP* 29(34):18.

71. A. Tolkunov, 5. It should be noted that more than a year after Tolkunov's observation, President Carter did sign the International Covenants on Ecomonic, Social and Cultural Rights and on Civil and Political Rights at the UN on October 5, 1977.

72. V. Teplov, "Shouldn't Everyone Know?" *Pravda*, November 18, 1975, 5; *CDSP* 27(46):18–19; A. Petrov, "But What Does the Final

Act Say?" *Pravda*, March 6, 1977, 4; *CDSP* 29(10):4; and Gennady Gerasimov, "Lost Document," *Literaturnaya Gazeta*, April 17, 1977, 9; *CDSP* 29(17):16.

73. V. Alekseyev, "Crude Falsification," *Pravda*, December 19, 1975, 4; *CDSP* 27(52):4.

74. "Soviet Law and Freedom of Conscience," *Izvestia*, January 31, 1976, 5; *CDSP* 28(5): 1–4.

75. Mikhail Abelev, "One-Way Street," *Literaturnaya Gazeta*, September 22, 1976, 14; *CDSP* 28(43):27.

76. Yury Tsaplin, "Behind the Smoke Screen," *Pravda*, April 22, 1977, 5; *CDSP* 29(16): 22–23.

77. Mikhail Abelev, 14. The incident to which the article referred involved three American soldiers engaged in a mission for Army intelligence in Czechoslovakian territory near the West German border on October 17, 1975. The soldiers were arrested by Czech officials.

78. There have been numerous discussions of the U.S. human rights campaign as an infringement of the Soviet Union's right to determine its internal affairs. The following excerpts are representative of these discussions.

"It is impossible to ignore the actions of those circles in the West that from the very start tried to prevent the all-European Conference from succeeding and are now putting pressure on governments in an effort to poison the international atmosphere and turn the development of events back to the time of the cold war. With the aim of interfering with the internal affairs of the U.S.S.R. and other socialist countries, they are organizing propaganda campaigns about alleged 'violations' of certain of the Final Act's provisions by the Soviet Union and other socialist countries. It is time for the opponents of detente to understand once and for all that the Soviet people will not tolerate interference in their internal affairs from anyone, on any pretext." A. Shitikov, "Helsinki, Two Years Later: Fruitful Results," *Izvestia*, July 31, 1977, 3; *CDSP* 29(31):6.

"The establishment in the United States of a commission which includes representatives of the government to carry out the illegal function of control over the actions of states participating in the fulfillment of the Final Act of the CSCE . . . is essentially an attempt by the American side to assume the right arbitrarily and unilaterally to interpret the Final Act and on this basis to judge fulfillment of its provisions by other participating states. This contradicts the principle of non-interference in the internal affairs of other states—a fundamental principle of International Law recorded in the Final Act itself. . . . Any attempt to overemphasize certain provisions of the Final Act to the detriment of others would upset the current balance of agreements . . . Such a lopsided approach is absolutely illegal and contradicts the goal of implementing the decisions of the all-European conference in their entirety." "Representation to the United States State Department," *Pravda*, June 19, 1976, 5; *CDSP* 28(24): 16.

"The political atmosphere between the two countries (U.S. and U.S.S.R.) has changed for the worse. This is a direct result of a series of anti-Soviet propaganda campaigns following one after another in the United States and of attempts to interfere in the internal affairs of the U.S.S.R. and other socialist countries under the pretext of defending human rights. Attempts are made to justify such actions with claims that they involve no more than the usual ideological struggle, which the U.S.S.R. also finds entirely compatible with detente and peaceful coexistence. But ideological struggle is the comparison of ideas and facts and a dispute over the intrinsic value of a particular system and must not be turned into a conscious incitement of mistrust and hostility, the falsification of reality or, least of all, subversive activity. Ideological struggle should not develop into psychological warfare and should not be used as means of interference in the internal affairs of states and peoples or lead to political or military confrontations." G. Arbatov, "Soviet-American Relations Today," *Pravda*, August 3, 1977, 4–5; *CDSP* 29(31):1–3.

"The United States' President's human rights report is an attempt by the West to arrogate to itself the 'right' to interfere in our internal affairs. However, it is time to make clear to the report's authors as well as to authors of other such documents and statements that the Soviet Union will not allow anyone to assume the pose of mentor and teach it how to handle its internal affairs. As far as human rights and liberties in the socialist countries are concerned, we advise the Western champions of these rights to read the new draft of the U.S.S.R. Constitution." S. Vishnevsky, "Contrary to Logic and In Defense of Facts: Concerning the U.S. President's Human Rights Report," *Pravda*, June 11, 1977, 5; *CDSP* 29(31):5.

79. A. Sukharev, the First Deputy Minister of Justice, developed this point at length: "I want to stress that according to Soviet laws, citizens are not criminally or administratively liable for their beliefs. The Messrs. Propagandists know very well that this is a question not

of "dissent" but rather of specific concrete actions. A crime is recognized to be a dangerous action that infringes on the Soviet social or state system, the socialist economic system, socialist property, on the individual, or on the political, labor, property, or other rights of citizens. In certain cases, a socially dangerous act of omission is recognized to be a crime. . . . Systematic anti-state actions are recognized as crimes. . . . Activities of associations that under the guise of conducting religious rites harm citizens' health (a characteristic of fanatical sects), infringe on their persons or their rights or induce them to abjure socially useful activity or civic duties are being curbed and will continue to be. . . . Constructive criticism is encouraged . . . all attempts to suppress criticism are subject to severe penalties up to and including removal of guilty parties from their posts. But there is more than one kind of criticism. . . . There is criticism of another sort, in which the pen of the "accuser" is moved solely by the desire to present our reality in exceptionally gloomy light, in which an obvious lack of facts is made up for by outright fabrication. These are the sort of "accusers" whose services all your "liberties," "waves" and "voices" and their like rely upon. Naturally, the Soviet press and other mass media provide no rostrum for this kind of malevolence." "Guaranteed by Law: A. Sukharev, USSR First Deputy Minister of Justice Answers Questions from Literaturnaya Gazeta Correspondent, V. Aleksandrov," *Literaturnaya Gazeta*, October 27, 1976, 10; *CDSP* 28(44):1–4.

80. Editorial, "What Lies Behind the Furor over Human Rights?" *Pravda*, February 12, 1977, 4; *CDSP* 29(6):1–5.

81. Aleksandr Petrov (Agapov) "Liars and Pharisees," *Literaturnaya Gazeta*, February 2, 1977, 14; *CDSP* 29(4):3.

82. "Open Letter to the Presidium of the USSR Supreme Soviet from USSR Citizen and Candidate of Medicine S. L. Lipavsky," *Izvestia*, March 5, 1977, 3; *CDSP* 29(9):1–3.

83. "Furror over Human Rights," 4.

84. *Ibid.*

85. Popov, 3.

86. "New Draft USSR Constitution," *Pravda*, June 4, 1977, 1–4; *CDSP* 29(22):1–11.

87. V. Goncharov, "Mr. Brzezinski's Absurd Ultimatum," *Konsomolskava Pravda*, May 25, 1977, 3; *CDSP* 29(21):6–7.

CHAPTER 8

1. An earlier version of this chapter appeared as "Workfare and the Imposition of Discipline," *Social Theory and Practice* 11(2):163–181, Summer, 1985.

2. Rep. Paul Findley (R-Ill.), Letter to Members of Congress seeking cosponsors of his Workfare bill (December 22, 1980).

3. U.S. Comptroller General, *Insights Gained in Workfare Demonstration Projects*, CED–81–117 (Washington, D.C.: General Accounting Office, July 31, 1981), 12. Although workfare in its current form was instigated under the auspices of this 1977 legislation, this is not the first time in U.S. history that the poor have been required to work off their benefits. For discussions of earlier "work relief" programs, see Joel Handler, *Reforming the Poor* (New York: Basic Books, 1972); Sar Levitan, *Work and Welfare in the 1970s* (The Institute of Policy Sciences and Public Affairs, Duke University, 1977); and *Jobs Watch* Vol 1. No. 6 (September–October 1981).

4. P. L. 97–35, Sec. 2307–2308. For a detailed examination of a variety of workfare programs developed under this legislation, see Larry Glantz, *AFDC Workfare Proposals Being Planned by States* (National Employment Law Project, 1981).

5. By 1987, 37 states had initiated workfare programs applicable to some portion of their welfare recipients. In February 1987, the National Governor's Association issued a statement calling for the systematic extension of mandatory workfare.

6. Richard Schweiker, Secretary, United States Department of Health and Human Services, *Testimony Before the Subcommittee on Public Assistance and Unemployment Compensation*, U.S. Congress, House Committee on Ways and Means (97th Congress, March 11, 1981) 8.

7. This theme figured prominently in Ronald Reagan's 1970 campaign for Governor of California, as well as in his 1980 bid for the Presidency of the United States; cited in Harold Wilensky, *The Welfare State and Equality* (Berkeley: University of California Press, 1975) 33.

8. Lawrence Mead, "Social Programs and Social Obligations," *The Public Interest* 69(3):17–32; Fall, 1982, 20. To support this claim, Mead emphasizes that the proportion of low-income black males par-

ticipating in the workforce has dropped since 1960, allegedly because these men simply refuse to take the jobs available to them. It is important to note that he uses national aggregate statistics to make this point, and does not examine the relation between local and regional industrial closings, plant relocations, unemployment rates, and levels of workforce participation among both black and white low-income males. (In another essay in the same issue of *Public Interest*, Charles Murray notes that the crucial variable with respect to declining labor force participation rates is income not race: low-income white males have also been dropping out of the labor market. "The Two Wars on Poverty: Economic Growth and the Great Society," *Public Interest* 69(3):3–16.) To attribute this declining rate of participation in the labor force among low-income males to receipt of welfare benefits seems very odd in the light of the fact that most state welfare programs deny eligibility to able-bodied males. A more plausible explanation of the phenomenon might be based on both the variables associated with local and regional economic decline identified above and an examination of the effects of incarceration upon labor force participation.

9. Mead, 22.

10. *Ibid.*, 23.

11. *Ibid.*, 28. Mead provides a more detailed discussion of the relationship between authority, coercion, and the probable success of workfare programs in "Expectations and Welfare Work: WIN in New York City," *Policy Studies Review* 2(4):648–662; May 1983.

12. All of these arguments have surfaced during Congressional hearings and debates on workfare. For a helpful summary of these views, see Barbara Linden and Deborah Vincent, *Workfare in Theory and Practice* (Washington, D.C.: National Social Science and Law Center, 1982) 9–10.

13. Mildred Rein, *Dilemmas of Welfare Policy* (New York: Praeger, 1982) 154.

14. The phrase was also drawn from President Reagan's campaign rhetoric. See Wilensky, 33.

15. Nathan Glazer, "The Social Policy of the Reagan Administration: A Review," *The Public Interest* 75 (1984):76–98; 85.

16. This terminology is borrowed from Handler, 3.

17. For a more detailed discussion of this constellation of be-

liefs, see Michael Lewis' analysis of *The Culture of Inequality* (New York: New American Library, 1978); and William E. Connolly's analysis of the "ideology of sacrifice" in *Appearance and Reality in Politics* (Cambridge: Cambridge University Press, 1981).

18. Sheldon Danziger and Peter Gottschalk, "The Measurement of Poverty: Implications for Anti-Poverty Policy," *American Behavioral Scientist* 26(6):739–756; July–August, 1983, 751.

19. Mildred Rein, 123. It is interesting to note that Rein's study found that in direct contrast to popular stereotypes, black women receiving AFDC worked more often than did white women.

20. Linden and Vincent, 12.

21. Berkeley Planning Associates, Inc., *Evaluation Design: Assessment of Work-Welfare Projects* (Washington, D.C.: U.S. Department of Health and Human Services ,1980) 95.

22. *Ibid.*, 92. The quotation refers to the landmark study by Leonard Goodwin, *Do the Poor Want to Work? A Socio-Psychological Study of Work Orientations* (Washington, D.C.: The Brookings Institute, 1972). For other studies which confirm this view of the poor's commitment to work and the work ethic, see Bradley Schiller, "Empirical Studies of Welfare Dependency: A Survey," *Journal of Human Resources* 8(1973): Supplement; James Goodale, "Effects of Personal Background and Training on Work Values of the Hard-Core Unemployed," *Journal of Applied Psychology* 57(1973):1–9; Roy Kaplan and Curt Tausky, "Work and the Welfare Cadillac: The Function of the Commitment to Work Among the Hard Core Unemployed," *Social Problems* (Spring 1972):469–483; and Frank Levy, Clair Vickery, and Michael Wiseman, *The Income Dynamics of the Poor* (Berkeley: The Institute of Business and Economic Research, 1977).

23. Danziger and Gottschalk, 750.

24. In addition to the evaluation study conducted by Berkeley Planning Associates cited above, see U.S. Comptroller General, *Food Stamp Work Requirement—Ineffective Paperwork or Effective Tool,* CED–78–60 (Washington, D.C.: General Accounting Office, 1978); U.S. Comptroller General, *More Benefits to Jobless Can Be Attained in Public Service Employment,* HRD–77–53 (Washington, D.C.: General Accounting Office, 1977); James Koppel and Megan Murphy, *Final Report: A Study of General Assistance Workfare Programs* (Washington, D.C.: National Association of Counties, Inc., 1978);

U.S. Comptroller General, *Insights Gained in Workfare Demonstration Projects*, CED–81–117 (Washington, D.C.: General Accounting Office, 1981); U.S. Department of Labor, *Interim Report to Congress: Food Stamp Workfare Demonstration Projects* (Washington, D.C.: Office of Policy, Evaluation and Research, 1980); California, County of San Diego, *Workfare Demonstration Project: Final Report* (Sacramento: State Department of Public Welfare, 1980); California, State Employment Department, *Third Year and Final Report on the Community Work Experience Program* (Sacramento: Employment Development Department, 1976); Barry Friedman, Barbara Davenport, Robert Evans, Andrew Hahn, Leonard Hausman, and Cecile Paperno, *An Evaluation of the Massachusetts Work Experience Program* (Brandeis University: Center for Employment and Income Studies, 1980); Robert Mullinax, *The Current Status of Ohio's General Relief—Work Relief Program* (Chicago: Clearinghouse for Legal Services, #31, 355, 1981); and New York, State Department of Labor, *Work Programs for Welfare Recipients* (Albany: Legislative Commission on Expenditure Review, 1979). See also, Maurice Ensellem, *Work Requirements and Welfare: A Summary of Selected Literature* (Washington, D.C.: National Social Science and Law Center, 1981).

25. Joel Handler and Michael Sosin, *Last Resorts: Emergency Assistance and Special Needs Programs in Public Welfare* (New York: Academic Press, 1983) 156.

26. *Ibid.*, 130, 155.

27. Mildred Rein raises questions about both the discriminatory nature of these programs and their constitutionality in *Dilemmas of Welfare Policy*, 158.

28. The Omnibus Budget Reconciliation Act, P.L. 97—35 Section 2307, 409 (a)(1).

29. Koppel and Murphy, 8, 19.

30. Linden and Vincent, 33.

31. This point is made by Vernon M. Briggs, Brian Rungeling, and Lewis Smith, "Welfare Reform and the Plight of the Poor in the Rural South," *Monthly Labor Review* (April 1980):28–30; Richard Rosen, "Identifying States and Areas Prone to High and Low Employment," *Monthly Labor Review* (March 1980):22–24; and by Barry Friedman and Leonard Hausman, *Work and Welfare Patterns in Low Income Families* (Brandeis University: Heller Graduate

School For Advanced Studies in Welfare, 1975).

32. For a related discussion of a similar problem with the Work Incentive Program (WIN), see Leonard Goodwin, *The Work Incentive Program and Related Experiences* (Washington, D.C.: Employment Training Administration, U.S. Department of Labor, 1977).

33. Blanche Bernstein and Leonard Goodwin, "Do Work Requirements Accomplish Anything?" *Public Welfare* 32:(2):36–45; Spring, 1978.

34. Linden and Vincent, 38.

35. It is important to remember than in 1981, the year workfare was initiated as a full-scale welfare policy, the United States was experiencing the worst recession since the 1930s. Unemployment had climbed to twelve and one half percent, leaving some thirteen million Americans jobless.

36. Linda Demkovich, "Workfare—Punishment for Being Poor or An End to the Welfare Stigma," *National Journal* 12 (July 1981):1201–1205; 1204.

37. Ave Levine, "Administration of Public Welfare in the Case of AFDC," in Lester M. Salamon, ed., *Welfare: The Elusive Consensus* (New York: Praeger, 1978), 244.

38. Linden and Vincent, 16. For similar arguments, see Ensellem, 37; James Max Frendrich, "Race and Ethnic Relations: The Elite Policy Response in Capitalist Societies," *American Behavioral Scientist* 26(6):757–772, July–August 1983; and Frances Piven and Richard Cloward, *The New Class War (New York: Pantheon, 1982).*

39. Wilensky, 36; and Peter Taylor-Gooby, "Moralism, Self-Interest and Attitudes to Welfare," *Policy and Politics* 11(2): 145–160, April 1983.

40. The following analysis draws heavily upon the works of Michel Foucault, who reminds us that a "productive body" is also a "subjected body." *Discipline and Punish*, trans. Alan Sheridan (New York: Vintage Books, 1979), 26.

41. *Ibid.*, 189.

42. *Ibid.*, 201.

43. Michel Foucault, *The History of Sexuality*, vol. 1, trans. Robert Hurley (New York: Vintage Books, 1980), 85.

44. Foucault, *Discipline and Punish*, 257.

45. *Ibid.*, 294.

46. Foucault, *History of Sexuality*, 89.

47. William E. Connolly, "Discipline, Politics and Ambiguity," *Political Theory* 11(3):325–341, August, 1983.

48. Foucault, *Discipline and Punish*, 18.

49. L. Faucher, *De La Reforme des Prisons* (1838) 64; cited in Michel Foucault, *Discipline and Punish*, trans. Alan Sheridan (New York, Vintage Books, 1979), 242.

CHAPTER 9

1. For full discussion of these developments, see chapters 3 and 4.

2. For a discussion of these commonalities, see chapter 4, 80–92.

3. For a straightforward refutation of these views, see Douglas Amy, "Why Policy Analysis and Ethics Are Incompatible," *Journal of Policy Analysis and Management* 3(4): 573–591; and Bruce Jennings, "Interpretive Social Science and Policy Analysis," in *Ethics, the Social Sciences and Policy Analysis,* ed. D. Callahan and B. Jennings (New York: Plenum Press, 1983).

4. Amy, 580–591. Jennings adds an additional consideration, suggesting that the dissemination of positivist methods "ensures that normal scientific research will not have to rely on the availability of large numbers of gifted individuals, for within the confines of its method, large numbers of quite ordinary people can achieve extraordinary things." 20.

5. For concrete examples of the potential of such a reorientation of policy inquiry, see chapters 5, 6, 7, and 8.

6. The extent to which (and the mechanisms by which) scientific theories constrict the understanding of political possibility have not been adequately investigated. It would be fascinating to study the relationship between theories of policy making (e.g., the rational-comprehensive model, the organizational process model, the bureaucratic politics model) which are taught in MPA and MPP programs and the decision-making styles of politicians who graduate from

those programs, and of policy-makers who absorb these theories through the general dissemination of social science concepts. The dearth of attention to such issues is undoubtedly due in part to the positivist belief that science simply generates neutral descriptions of the given. Once that mistaken notion has been dispelled, whole new areas open up for investigation. Thus, post-positivist policy analysis suggests an expansive research agenda with important implications for contemporary political life. A full consideration of such issues takes us well beyond the scope of the present volume, and for this reason, must await development in another context.

Bibliography

Albert, Hans. (1985) *Treatise on Critical Reason*. Trans. Mary Varney Rorty. Princeton: Princeton University Press.

Allison, Graham. (1971) *Essence of Decision*. Boston: Little Brown and Company.

Amy, Douglas. (1983) "Teaching the Moral Analysis of Policy Issues." *News for Teachers of Political Science* 36:1,6.

———. (1984) "Why Policy Analysis and Ethics Are Incompatible." *Journal of Policy Analysis and Management* 4:573–591.

Anderson, Charles. (1979) "The Place of Principles in Policy Analysis." *American Political Science Review* 73:711–723.

Andrew, Edward. (1970) "Work and Freedom in Marcuse and Marx." *Canadian Journal of Political Science* 3(2):241–256.

Arendt, Hannah. (1958) *The Human Condition*. Chicago: University of Chicago Press.

Aristotle. (1958) *The Politics*. Trans. and ed. Ernest Barker. London: Oxford University Press.

Ayer, A. J., ed. (1959) *Logical Positivism*. New York: Free Press.

Backoff, Robert, and Barry Mitnick. (1986) "Reappraising the Promise of General Systems Theory for the Policy Sciences." In William Dunn, ed. *Policy Analysis: Perspectives, Concepts and Methods*. Greenwich Ct.: J.A.I. Press.

Barasch, F. K. (1973) "H.E.W., The University and Women." In Barry R. Gross, ed. *Reverse Discrimination*. New York: Prometheus Books.

Barron and Paul. (1977) *Murder of a Gentle Land*. Readers Digest Press.

Bay, Christian. (1965) "Politics and Pseudo-Politics: A Critical Evaluation of Some Behavioral Literature." *American Political Science Review* 59:39–51.

Beauchamp, Tom L., ed. (1975) *Ethics and Public Policy*. Englewood Cliffs, New Jersey: Prentice-Hall.

———. (1977) "The Justification of Reverse Discrimination." In William T.

Blackstone and Robert D. Heslep, eds. *Social Justice and Preferential Treatment*. Athens, Georgia: University of Georgia Press.

———. (1981) "The Moral Adequacy of Cost-Benefit Analysis As the Basis for Government Regulation of Research." In Norman Bowie, ed. *Ethical Issues in Government*. Philadelphia: Temple University Press.

Becker, Lawrence. (1982) "Individual Rights." In Tom Regan and Donald Van De Veer, eds. *And Justice For All*. Totowa, New Jersey: Rowman and Littlefield.

Bedau, Hugo. (1982) "International Human Rights." In Tom Regan and Donald Van De Veer, eds. *And Justice For All*. Totowa, New Jersey: Rowman and Littlefield.

Bellah, Robert. (1983) "Social Science as Practical Reason." In Daniel Callahan and Bruce Jennings, eds. *Ethics, The Social Sciences and Policy Analysis*. New York: Plenum Press.

Bellah, Robert, Richard Madsen, William Sullivan, Ann Swidler and Steven Tipton. (1985) *Habits of the Heart: Individualism and Commitments in American Life*. New York: Harper and Row.

Benhabib, Seyla. (1986) *Critique, Norm and Utopia*. New York: Columbia University Press.

Benveniste, Guy. (1984) "On a Code of Ethics for Policy Experts." *Journal of Policy Analysis and Management* 3:561–572.

Berkeley Planning Associates, Inc. (1980) *Evaluation Design: Assessment of Work-Welfare Projects*. Washington, D.C.: U.S. Department of Health and Human Services.

Bernstein, Blanche and Leonard Goodwin. (1978) "Do Work Requirements Accomplish Anything?" *Public Welfare* 32(2):36–45.

Bernstein, Richard. (1983) *Beyond Objectivism and Relativism: Science, Hermeneutics and Praxis*. Philadelphia: University of Pennsylvania Press.

———. (1976) *The Restructuring of Social and Political Theory*. Philadelphia: University of Pennsylvania Press.

Blackstone, William T. (1977) "Reverse Discrimination and Compensatory Justice." In William T. Blackstone and Robert D. Heslep, eds. *Social Justice and Preferential Treatment*. Athens, Georgia: University of Georgia Press.

Blackstone, William T. and Robert Heslep, eds. (1977) *Justice and Preferential Treatment*. Athens, Ga.: University of Georgia Press.

Bowie, Norman, ed. (1981) *Ethical Issues in Government*. Philadelphia: Temple University Press.

Briggs, Vernon M., Brian Rungeling, and Lewis Smith, (1980) "Welfare Reform and the Plight of the Poor in the Rural South." *Monthly Labor Review* (April):28–30.

Brown, Harold. (1977) *Perception, Theory and Commitment: The New Philosophy of Science*. Chicago: Precedent Publishing Company.

Brown, Peter. (1976) "Ethics and Policy Research." *Policy Analysis* 2:325–340.

———. (1978) "Ethics and Public Policy: A Preliminary Agenda." *Policy Studies Journal* 7(1):132–136.

Bulmer, Martin. (1982) *The Uses of Social Research: Social Investigation in Public Policy Making.* London: Allen and Unwin.

———. (1983) "The British Tradition of Social Administration." In Daniel Callahan and Bruce Jennings, eds. *Ethics, the Social Sciences and Policy Analysis.* New York: Plenum.

Burchett, Wilfred. (1981) *The China, Cambodia, Vietnam Triangle.* Chicago: Vanguard Books.

California, County of San Diego. (1980) *Workfare Demonstration Project: Final Report.* Sacramento: State Department of Public Welfare.

California, State Employment Department. (1976) *Third Year and Final Report on the Community Work Experience Program.* Sacramento: Employment Development Department.

Callahan, Daniel and Bruce Jennings, eds. (1983) *Ethics, The Social Sciences and Policy Analysis.* New York: Plenum Press.

Carley, Michael. (1980) *Rational Techniques in Policy Analysis.* London: Heineman.

———. (1986) "Into the Snakepit: Value Weighting Schemes in Policy Analysis." In William N. Dunn, ed. *Policy Analysis: Perspectives, Concepts and Methods.* Greenwich, Ct.: J.A.I. Press.

Carney, Timothy. (1977) *Communist Party Power in Kampuchea: Documents and Discussion.* Data Paper 106, Southeast Asia Program, Cornell University.

Cavell, Stanley. (1979) *The Claim of Reason.* New York: Oxford University Press.

Chambers, Erve. (1986) "The Cultures of Science and Policy." In William N. Dunn, ed. *Policy Analysis: Perspectives, Concepts and Methods.* Greenwich, Ct.: J.A.I. Press.

Chandler, David. (1979) "The Tragedy of Cambodian History." *Pacific Affairs* 52(3):410–419.

Chomsky, Noam, and Edward S. Herman. (1979) *After the Cataclysm: Post War Indochina and the Reconstruction of Imperial Ideology.* Boston: Southend Press.

Christopher, Warren. (1977) "Human Rights: Principle and Realism." *U.S. Department of State Bulletin* 77(1922):269–273.

Cohen, M., T. Nagel and T. Scanlon, eds. (1974) *Rights and Wrongs of Abortion.* Princeton: Princeton University Press.

———. (1974) *War and Moral Responsibility.* Princeton: Princeton University Press.

———. (1977) *Equality and Preferential Treatment.* Princeton: Princeton University Press.

Coleman, J. S. (1972) *Policy Research in the Social Sciences.* Morristown, N. J.: General Learning Press.

Comte, Auguste. (1974) *The Positive Philosophy.* New York: AMS Press.

Connolly, William E. (1974) "Toward Theoretical Self-Consciousness." In William E. Connolly and Glen Gordon, eds. *Social Structure and Political Theory.* Lexington, Ma.: D.C. Heath.

———. (1974) *The Terms of Political Discourse.* Lexington, Ma.: D.C. Heath.

———. (1981) *Appearance and Reality in Politics.* Cambridge: Cambridge University Press.

———. (1983) "Discipline, Politics and Ambiguity." *Political Theory* 11(3):325–341.

Cook, Thomas D. (1985) "Postpositivist Critical Multiplism," In R. Lance Shotland and Melvin M. Marks, eds. *Social Science and Social Policy.* Beverly Hills: Sage Publications.

Couch, W. T. (1960) "Objectivity and Social Science." In Helmut Schoek and James Wiggins, eds. *Scientism and Values.* Princeton: D. Van Nostrand Company.

Cunningham, Frank. (1973) *Objectivity in Social Science.* Toronto: University of Toronto Press.

Dallmayr, Fred. (1981) *Beyond Dogma and Despair.* Notre Dame: University of Notre Dame Press.

———. (1984) *Language and Politics.* Notre Dame: University of Notre Dame Press.

———. (1986) "Critical Theory and Public Policy." In William Dunn, ed. *Policy Analysis: Perspectives, Concepts and Methods.* Greenwich Ct.: J.A.I. Press.

Daneke, Gregory. (1983) "Ethics in Public Policy Education." In William N. Dunn, ed. *Values, Ethics and the Practice of Policy Analysis.* Lexington, Ma.: D.C. Heath.

Danziger, Sheldon and Peter Gottschalk. (1983) "The Measurement of Poverty: Implications for Anti-Poverty Policy." *American Behavioral Scientist* 26(6):739–756.

Davidson, James. (1979) *Indochina: Signposts in the Storm.* Singapore: Longman Malaysia.

Demkovich, Linda. (1981) "Workfare—Punishment for Being Poor or An End to the Welfare Stigma." *National Journal* 12:1201–1205.

Dobel, J. Patrick. (1977) "Bearing Witness and Human Rights," *Christian Century,* August 31–September 7: 751–753.

Donnelly, Jack. (1982) "Human Rights and Human Dignity: An Analytic Critique of Non-Western Conceptions of Human Rights." *American Political Science Review* 76(2):303–316.

Dror, Yehezkel. (1975) "Some Features of a Meta-Model for Policy Studies." *Policy Studies Journal* 3:245–250.

Dudman, Richard. (1971) *Forty Days with the Enemy.* New York: Liveright.

Dumont, Louis. (1965) "The Modern Conception of the Individual: Notes on Its Genesis and that of Concomitant Institutions." *Contributions to In-*

dian Sociology 8:13–61
———. (1970) *Homo Hierarchicus: The Caste System and Its Implications.* Trans. Mark Sainsbury. London: Weidenfeld and Nicolson.
Dunn v. Blumstein 405 U.S. 330 (1972).
Dunn, William N., A. Cahill, M. Dukes, and A. Ginsberg. (1986) "The Policy Grid: A Cognitive Methodology for Assessing Policy Dynamics." In William N. Dunn, ed. *Policy Analysis: Perspectives, Concepts and Methods.* Greenwich, Ct.: J.A.I. Press.
Dunn, William., ed. (1986) *Policy Analysis: Perspectives, Concepts and Methods.* Greenwich, Ct.: J.A.I. Press.
———. (1983) *Values, Ethics and The Practice of Policy Analysis.* Lexington, Ma.: D.C. Heath & Company.
———. (1981) *Public Policy Analysis.* Englewood Cliffs, N.J.: Prentice-Hall.
Dye, Thomas R. (1975) *Understanding Public Policy,* 2d edition. Englewood Cliffs, N.J.: Prentice Hall.
Einhorn, H. J., and W. McCoach. (1977) "A Simple Multi-attribute Procedure for Evaluation." *Behavioral Science* 22:270–282.
Eisenstein, Zillah. (1981) *The Radical Future of Liberal Feminism.* New York: Longman.
Ensellem, Maurice. (1981) *Work Requirements and Welfare: A Summary of Selected Literature.* Washington, D.C.: National Social Science and Law Center.
Euben, J. Peter. (1969) "Political Science and Political Silence." In Philip Greene and Sanford Levinson, eds. *Power and Community.* New York: Random House.
Falk, Richard. (1980) "Theoretical Foundations of Human Rights." In Paula Newberg, ed. *The Politics of Human Rights.* New York: New York University Press.
Fetscher, I. (1973) "Karl Marx on Human Nature." *Social Research* 40(3):443–467.
Fischer, Frank. (1980) *Politics, Values and Public Policy: The Problem of Methodology.* Boulder: Westview Press.
———. (1986) "Practical Discourse in Policy Argumentation." In William N. Dunn, ed. *Policy Analysis: Perspectives, Concepts, Methods.* Greenwich, Ct.: J.A.I. Press.
Fishkin, James. (1984) *Beyond Subjective Morality.* New Haven: Yale University Press.
Foucault, Michel. (1973) *The Order of Things: An Archaeology of the Human Sciences.* New York: Vintage Books.
———. (1979) *Discipline and Punish.* Trans. Alan Sheridan. New York: Vintage Books.
———. (1980) *The History of Sexuality,* vol. 1. Trans. Robert Hurley. New York: Vintage Books.
Fraser, Donald. (1977) "Freedom and Foreign Policy." *Foreign Policy* 26:140–156.
Frendrich, James Max. (1983) "Race and Ethnic Relations: The Elite Policy

Response in Capitalist Societies." *American Behavioral Scientist* 26(6):757–772.

Friedman, Barry and Leonard Hausman. (1975) *Work and Welfare Patterns in Low Income Families*. Brandeis University: Heller Graduate School For Advanced Studies in Welfare.

Friedman, Barry, Barbara Davenport, Robert Evans, Andrew Hahn, Leonard Hausman, and Cecile Paperno. (1980) *An Evaluation of the Massachusetts Work Experience Program*. Brandeis University: Center for Employment and Income Studies.

Fry, B. R., and M. E. Tompkins. (1978) "Some Notes on the Domain of Public Policy Studies." *Policy Studies Journal* 6(3):305–12.

Gallie, W. B. (1956) "Essentially Contested Concepts." *Proceedings of the Aristotelian Society* 56:167–199.

Garson, G. David. (1986) "From Policy Science to Policy Analysis: A Quarter Century of Progress." In William N. Dunn, ed. *Policy Analysis: Perspectives, Concepts and Methods*. Greenwich, Ct.: J.A.I. Press.

Geertz, Clifford. (1980) "Blurred Genres: The Refiguration of Social Thought." *American Scholar* 49:165–179.

George, Vic, and Paul Wilding. (1976) *Ideology and Social Welfare*. London: Routledge and Kegan Paul.

Gewirth, Alan. (1978) *Reason and Morality*. Chicago: University of Chicago Press.

Glantz, Larry. (1981) *AFDC Workfare Proposals Being Planned by States*. National Employment Law Project.

Glazer, Nathan. (1984) "The Social Policy of the Reagan Administration: A Review." *The Public Interest* 75:76–98.

Goldman, Alan H. (1976) "Affirmative Action." In Marshall Cohen, Thomas Nagel, and Thomas Scanlon, eds. *Equality and Preferential Treatment*. Princeton, New Jersey: Princeton University Press.

Goodale, James. (1973) "Effects of Personal Background and Training on Work Values of the Hard-Core Unemployed." *Journal of Applied Psychology* 57:1–9.

Goodin, Robert. (1982) *Political Theory and Public Policy*. Chicago: University of Chicago Press.

Goodwin, Leonard. (1972) *Do the Poor Want to Work? A Socio-Psychological Study of Work Orientations*. Washington, D.C.: The Brookings Institute.

———. (1977) *The Work Incentive Program and Related Experiences*. Washington, D.C.: Employment Training Administration, U.S. Department of Labor.

Gross, Barry R., ed. (1977) *Reverse Descrimination*. New York: Prometheus Books.

Guillemin, Jeanne and Irving Horowitz. (1983) "Social Research and Political Advocacy." In Daniel Callahan and Bruce Jennings, eds. *Ethics, The Social Sciences and Policy Analysis*. New York: Plenum Press.

Gunnell, John. (1986) *Between Philosophy and Politics.* Amherst: University of Massachusetts Press.

Gutmann, Amy, and Dennis Thompson, eds. (1984) *Ethics and Politics.* Chicago: Nelson-Hall Publishers.

Habermas, Jürgen. (1970) *Toward a Rational Society: Student Protest, Science and Politics.* Trans. Jeremy Shapiro. Boston: Beacon Press.

———. (1971) *Knowledge and Human Interests.* Trans. Jeremy Shapiro. Boston: Beacon Press.

———. (1975) *Legitimation Crisis.* Trans. Thomas McCarthy. Boston: Beacon Press.

———. (1979) *Communication and the Evolution of Society.* Trans. Thomas McCarthy. Boston: Beacon Press.

Hamburg, Roger. (1980) "American and Soviet Views of Human Rights." *Conflict* 2(2):163–175.

Handler, Joel and Michael Sosin. (1983) *Last Resorts: Emergency Assistance and Special Needs Programs in Public Welfare.* New York: Academic Press.

Handler, Joel. (1972) *Reforming the Poor.* New York: Basic Books.

Hanft, Ruth. (1983) "Use of Social Science Data for Policy Analysis and Policymaking." In Daniel Callahan and Bruce Jennings, eds. *Ethics, the Social Sciences and Policy Analysis.* New York: Plenum Press.

Harding, Sandra. (1986) *The Science Question in Feminism.* Ithaca: Cornell University Press.

Hare, R. M. (1952) *The Language of Morals.* London: Oxford University Press.

———. (1963) *Reason and Freedom.* Oxford: Clarendon Press.

Hartsock, Nancy. (1985) *Money, Sex and Power.* Boston: Northeastern University Press.

Hatry, Harry, et al. (1976) *Program Analysis for State and Local Government.* Washington, D.C.: The Urban Institute.

Hauser, Rita. (1979) "Human Rights: A First World View." In Donald Kommers and Gilbert Loescher, eds. *Human Rights and American Foreign Policy.* Notre Dame: University of Notre Dame Press.

Hayek, F. A. (1948) *Individualism and Economic Order.* Chicago: University of Chicago Press.

Healy, Paul. (1986) "Interpretive Policy Inquiry: A Response to the Limitations of the Received View." *Policy Sciences* 19:381–396.

Held, Virginia. (1975) "Reasonable Progress and Self-Respect," In Tom L. Beauchamp, ed. *Ethics and Public Policy.* Englewood Cliffs, New Jersey: Prentice-Hall.

Herson, Lawrence. (1984) *The Politics of Ideas: Political Theory and American Public Policy.* Homewood, Ill.: Dorsey Press.

Hesse, Mary. (1980) *Revolutions and Reconstructions in the Philosophy of Science.* Brighton: Harvester Press.

Herzog, Don. (1985) *Without Foundations: Justification in Political Theory.* Ithaca, N.Y.: Cornell University Press.

Hildebrand, George, and Gareth Porter. (1976) *Cambodia: Starvation and Revolution*. New York: Monthly Review Press.

Hoaglin, David, et al. (1982) *Data For Decisions: Information Strategies for Policymakers*. Cambridge, Ma.: ABT Books.

Hobbes, Thomas. (1958) *Leviathan*. New York: Bobbs-Merrill.

Hogwood, Brian and B. Guy Peters. (1985) *The Pathology of Public Policy*. Oxford: Clarendon Press.

Hook, Sidney. (1971) "The Bias of Anti-Bias Regulations," In Barry R. Gross, ed. *Reverse Discrimination*. New York: Prometheus Books.

Hoos, Ida. (1972) *Systems Analysis in Public Policy: A Critique*. Berkeley: University of California Press.

Horowitz, I. L., and J. E. Katz. (1975) *Social Science and Public Policy in the United States*. New York: Praeger.

Howe, Elizabeth, and Jerome Kaufman. (1983) "Ethics and Professional Practice." In William N. Dunn, ed. *Values, Ethics and the Practice of Policy Analysis*. Lexington, Ma.: D.C. Heath.

Hudson, W. D. (1970) *Modern Moral Philosophy*. New York: Anchor Books.

Hughes, Graham. (1975) "Reparation for Blacks." In Tom L. Beauchamp, ed. *Ethics and Public Policy*. Englewood Cliffs, New Jersey: Prentice-Hall.

Hume, David. (1975) *A Treatise on Human Nature*. L. A. Selby-Bigge, ed. Oxford: Clarendon Press.

———. (1927) *An Enquiry Concerning Human Understanding*. L. A. Selby-Bigge, ed. Oxford: Clarendon Press.

Humphreys, Willard C., ed. (1969) *Perception and Discovery*. San Francisco: Freeman, Cooper.

Husband, William B. (1979) "Soviet Perceptions of U.S. 'Positions of Strength' Diplomacy in the 1970s." *World Politics* 31(4):495–517.

Jackson, Karl. (1978) "Cambodia 1977: Gone to Pot." *Asian Survey* 18(1):76–90.

———. (1979) "Cambodia 1978: War, Pillage and Purge in Democratic Kampuchea." *Asian Survey* 19(1):72–84.

Jaggar, Alison. (1983) *Feminist Politics and Human Nature*. Totowa, New Jersey: Rowman and Allanheld.

Janowitz, M. (1972) *Sociological Models and Social Policy*. Morristown, N.J.: General Learning Systems.

Joergenson, J. (1951) *The Development of Logical Empiricism*. Vol. II, No. 9 of the *International Encyclopedia of Unified Science*. Chicago: University of Chicago Press.

Johanson, Robert. (1983) "Human Rights in the 1980s: Revolutionary Growth or Unanticipated Erosion." *World Politics* 35(2):286.

Johnson v. Transportation Agency, Santa Clara County, California. United States Law Week 55 LW 4379 (March 24, 1987).

Kaplan, Roy and Curt Tausky. (1972) "Work and the Welfare Cadillac: The Function of the Commitment to Work Among the Hard Core Unemployed." *Social Problems* 19(4):469–483.

Kariel, Henry. (1960) "Social Science as Autonomous Activity." In Helmut Schoek and James Wiggins, eds. *Scientism and Values*. Princeton, N.J.: D. Van Nostrand.

Katzner, Louis. (1982) "Reverse Discrimination." In Tom Regan and Donald Van de Veer, eds. *And Justice For All*. Totowa, New Jersey: Rowman and Littlefield.

Kearns, Kevin. (1986) "The Analytic Hierarchy Process and Policy Argumentation." In William N. Dunn, ed. *Policy Analysis: Perspectives, Concepts and Methods*. Greenwich, Ct.: J.A.I. Press.

Keat, R., and J. Urry. (1975) *Social Theory as Science*. London: Routledge and Kegan Paul.

Kelly, Rita Mae. (1986) "Trends in the Logic of Policy Inquiry: A Comparison of Approaches and a Commentary." *Policy Studies Review* 5:520–528.

Kershaw, Roger. (1980) "Multipolarity and Cambodia's Crisis of Survival: A Preliminary Perspective on 1979." *Southeast Asian Affairs 1980*.

Khanh, Huynh Kim. (1980) "Into the Third Indochina War." *Southeast Asian Affairs 1980*.

Kiernan, Ben. (1976) "Social Cohesion in Revolutionary Cambodia." *Australian Outlook* 30(3):371–386.

———. (1979) "Conflict in the Kampuchean Communist Movement." *Journal of Contemporary Asia* 10 (1–2):7–74.

Kirk, Donald. (1975) "Revolution and Political Violence in Cambodia 1970–1974." In Zasloff and Brown, eds. *Communism in Indochina*. Lexington, Ma.: D.C. Heath.

Koppel, James, and Megan Murphy. (1978) *Final Report: A Study of General Assistance Workfare Programs*. Washington, D.C.: National Association of Counties, Inc.

Korematsu v. United States 323 U.S. 214 (1944).

Kraft, Victor. (1952) *The Vienna Circle*. Trans. A. Pap. New York: Philosophical Library.

Kramer, Fred. (1975) "Policy Analysis as Ideology." *Public Administration Review* 35:509–517.

Kuhn, Thomas. (1970) *The Structure of Scientific Revolutions*, 2d enl. ed. Chicago: University of Chicago Press.

Ladd, John. (1973) "Policy Studies and Ethics." *Policy Studies Journal* 2:42–3.

———. (1975) "Ethics of Participation." In J. Roland Pennock and John W. Chapman, eds. *NOMOS XVI: Participation*. New York: Atherton Press.

Lane, Robert. (1966) "The Decline of Politics and Ideology in a Knowledgeable Society." *American Sociological Review* 31(5):649–662.

Lasswell, Harold. (1950) *Politics: Who Gets What, When, How*. New York: P. Smith.

———. (1951) "The Policy Orientation." In Harold Lasswell and Daniel Lerner, eds. *The Policy Sciences: Recent Developments in Science and Method*. Stanford: Stanford University Press.

———. (1963) *The Future of Political Science*. New York: Atherton.

_____ . (1971) *A Preview of Policy Science.* New York: Elsevier.

Lefever, Ernest W. (1978) "The Trivialization of Human Rights." *Policy Review* 3:11–26.

Leighton, Marion Kirsch. (1978) "Perspectives on the Vietnamese-Cambodian Border Conflict." *Asian Survey* 18(5):448–457.

Lenin, V. I. (1943) "Preliminary Draft of the Theses on the National and Colonial Questions." *Selected Works,* vol. X. Moscow: Foreign Languages Publishing House.

Lester, Richard. (1974) *Anti-Bias Regulations of Universities: Faculty Problems and Their Solutions.* New York: McGraw-Hill.

Levine, Ave. (1978) "Administration of Public Welfare in the Case of AFDC." In Lester M. Salamon, ed. *Welfare: The Elusive Consensus.* New York: Praeger.

Levitan, Sar. (1977) *Work and Welfare in the 1970s.* Duke University: The Institute of Policy Sciences and Public Affairs.

Levy, Frank, Clair Vickery, and Michael Wiseman. (1977) *The Income Dynamics of the Poor.* Berkeley: The Institute of Business and Economic Research.

Lewis, Michael. (1978) *The Culture of Inequality.* New York: New American Library.

Leys, Wayne. (1952) *Ethics for Policy Decisions: The Art of Asking Deliberative Questions.* New York: Prentice-Hall.

Lindblom Charles, and David Cohen. (1979) *Usable Knowledge: Social Science and Social Problem Solving.* New Haven: Yale University Press.

Linden, Barbara, and Deborah Vincent. (1982) *Workfare in Theory and Practice.* Washington, D.C.: National Social Science and Law Center.

Linder, Stephen. (1986) "Efficiency, Multiple Claims and Moral Values." In William N. Dunn, ed. *Policy Analysis: Perspectives, Concepts and Methods.* Greenwich, Ct.: J.A.I. Press.

Lipset, Seymour M., and William Schneider. (1977) "An Emerging National Consensus." *New Republic* 177(16):8–12.

Livingston, John. (1979) *Fair Game: Inequality and Affirmative Action.* San Francisco: W. H. Freeman.

Locke, John. (1947) *The Second Treatise of Civil Government.* New York: Hafner Press.

Lowi, Theodore. (1970) "Decision Making vs. Policy Making: Toward an Antidote for Technocracy." *Public Administration Review* 30:318–319.

_____ . (1972) "The Politics of Higher Education: Political Science as a Case Study." In George Graham and George Carey, eds. *The Post-Behavioral Era: Perspectives on Political Science.* New York: McKay Company.

Lukes, Stephen. (1973) *Individualism.* New York: Harper and Row.

Macfarlane, L. W. (1982) "Marxist Theory and Human Rights." *Government and Opposition* 17(4):414–428.

Machiavelli, Niccolo. (1950) *The Discourses.* Trans. and ed. Leslie J. Walker. London: Routledge and Kegan Paul.

MacIntyre, Alasdair. (1979) "Utilitarianism and Cost/Benefit Analysis: An Essay on the Relevance of Moral Philosophy to Bureaucratic Theory." In Tom Beauchamp and Norman Bowie, eds. *Ethical Theory and Business.* Englewood Cliffs, N.J.: Prentice-Hall.

_____. (1981) *After Virtue.* Notre Dame, In: University of Notre Dame Press.

Macpherson, C. B. (1962) *The Political Theory of Possessive Individualism.* Oxford: Clarendon Press.

_____. (1977) *The Life and Times of Liberal Democracy.* London: Oxford University Press.

MacRae, Duncan. (1976) *The Social Function of Social Science.* New Haven: Yale University Press.

MacRae, Duncan and James Wilde. (1979) *Policy Analysis for Public Decisions.* N. Scituate, Ma.: Duxbury.

Marx, Karl and Friedrich Engels. (1974) *Selected Works.* New York: International Publishers.

Maynes, Charles W. (1977) "New Hopes for Human Rights." *U.S. Department of State Bulletin* 77(2000):556–561.

Mazor, Allan. (1977) "Science Courts." *Minerva* 17:2–4.

McCarthy, Thomas. (1978) *The Critical Theory of Jürgen Habermas.* Cambridge, Ma.: M.I.T. Press.

McCormack, Gavan. (1979) "The Kampuchean Revolution 1975-1978: The Problem of Knowing the Truth." *J. Contemporary Asia* 10(1–2):75–118.

McCoy, Charles and John Playford, eds. (1967) *Apolitical Politics.* New York: Thomas Crowell.

McPherson, Michael. (1983) "Imperfect Democracy and the Moral Responsibilities of Policy Advisors." In Daniel Callahan and Bruce Jennings, eds. *Ethics, The Social Sciences and Policy Analysis.* New York: Plenum Press.

Mead, Lawrence. (1982) "Social Programs and Social Obligations." *The Public Interest* 69(3):17–32.

_____. (1983) "Expectations and Welfare Work: WIN in New York City." *Policy Studies Review* 2(4):648–662.

Meehan, Eugene. (1973) "Philosophy and Policy Studies." *Policy Studies Journal* 2:43–44.

Meltsner, Arnold. (1976) *Policy Analysts in the Bureaucracy.* Berkeley: University of California Press.

Merriam, Charles. (1945) *Systematic Politics.* Chicago: University of Chicago Press.

Michalos, Alex. (1986) "Technology Assessment, Facts and Values." In William N. Dunn, ed. *Policy Analysis: Perspectives, Concepts and Methods.* Greenwich, Ct.: J.A.I. Press.

Moon, Donald. (1975) "The Logic of Political Inquiry: A Synthesis of Opposed Perspectives." In Fred Greenstein and Nelson Polsby, eds. *Handbook of Political Science,* vol. I. Reading, Ma.: Addison-Wesley.

Moore, Mark. (1983) "Social Science and Policy Analysis: Some Fundamental

Differences." In Daniel Callahan and Bruce Jennings, eds. *Ethics, The Social Sciences and Policy Analysis*. New York: Plenum Press.

Moynihan, Daniel P. (1977) "The Politics of Human Rights." *Commentary* 64(2):14–26.

Mullinax, Robert. (1981) *The Current Status of Ohio's General Relief—-Work Relief Program*. Chicago: Clearinghouse for Legal Services, #31, 355.

Murray, Charles. (1982) "The Two Wars on Poverty: Economic Growth and the Great Society." *Public Interest* 69(3):3–16.

Murray, Thomas. (1983) "Partial Knowledge." In Daniel Callahan and Bruce Jennings, eds. *Ethics, The Social Sciences and Policy Analysis*. New York: Plenum Press.

Nagel, Ernest. (1979) *The Structure of Science*, 2d ed. Indianapolis: Hackett.

Nagel, Stuart. (1983) *Public Policy: Goals, Means and Methods*. New York: St. Martins.

———. (1984) *Contemporary Public Policy Analysis*. Tuscaloosa: University of Alabama Press.

Nagel, Thomas. (1986) *The View From Nowhere*. London: Oxford University Press.

Nehamas, Alexander. (1985) "Untruth as a Condition of Life." *Nietzsche: Life As Literature*. Cambridge, Ma.: Harvard University Press.

Nelson, John S., Allan Megill, and Donald McCloskey, eds. (1987) *The Rhetoric of the Human Sciences*. Madison: University of Wisconsin Press.

Newberg, Paula., ed. (1980) *The Politics of Human Rights*. New York: New York University Press.

New York, State Department of Labor. (1979) *Work Programs for Welfare Recipients*. Albany: Legislative Commission on Expenditure Review.

Nieburg, H. L. (1969) *Political Violence: The Behavioral Process*. New York: St. Martins Press.

Nielsen, Kai. (1983) "Emancipatory Social Science and Social Critique." In Daniel Callahan and Bruce Jennings, eds. *Ethics, The Social Sciences and Policy Analysis*. New York: Plenum Press.

Nieva, Veronica, and Barbara Gutek. (1980) "Sex Effects on Evaluation." *Academy of Management Review* 5(2):267–276.

Nisbet, Lee. (1977) "Affirmative Action—A Liberal Program?" In Barry R. Gross, ed. *Reverse Discrimination*. New York: Prometheus Books.

Nozick, Robert. (1974) *Anarchy, State and Utopia*. New York: Basic Books.

Ono, Shin'ya. (1967) "Limits of Bourgeois Pluralism." In Charles McCoy and John Playford, eds. *Apolitical Politics*. New York: Thomas Crowell Company.

O'Rourke, J. J. (1974) *The Problem of Freedom in Marxist Thought*. Dordrecht: D. Reidel.

Okin, Susan Moller. (1979) *Women in Western Political Thought*. Princeton: Princeton University Press.

Osborne, Martha Lee. (1979) *Women in Western Thought.* New York: Random House.

Ostrooumov, G. and Belenkov, V. (1983) "La Politique Exterieure du Socialism et des Droits de L'homme." *La Vie Internationale* 5:37–47.

Paris, David C. and James F. Reynolds. (1983) *The Logic of Policy Inquiry.* New York: Longman.

Paul, Ellen and Philip Russo, eds. (1982) *Public Policy: Issues, Analysis and Ideology.* Chatham, N.J.: Chatham House.

Pinkard, Terry. (1980) "Models of the Person." *Canadian Journal of Philosophy* 10(4):623–635.

Pitkin, Hannah. (1972) *Wittgenstein and Justice.* Berkeley: University of California Press.

Piven, Frances, and Richard Cloward. (1982) *The New Class War.* New York: Pantheon.

Polanyi, Michael. (1958) *Personal Knowledge.* Chicago: University of Chicago Press.

Pollack, John. (1986) "A Theory of Moral Reasoning." *Ethics* 96:506–523.

Pollis, A., and P. Schwab, eds. (1980) *Human Rights: Cultural and Ideological Perspectives.* New York: Praeger.

Ponchaud, Francois. (1977) *Year Zero.* New York: Holt, Rinehart and Winston.

Poole, Peter. (1976) "Cambodia 1975: The GRUNK Regime." *Asian Survey* 16(1):23–30.

———. (1975) "Communism and Ethnic Conflict in Cambodia 1960–1975." In Zasloff and Brown eds. *Communism in Indochina.* Lexington, Ma.: D.C. Heath.

Popper, Karl. (1950) *The Open Society and Its Enemies,* 2 vols. rev. ed. Princeton: Princeton University Press.

———. (1957) *The Poverty of Historicism.* Boston: Beacon Press.

———. (1959) *The Logic of Scientific Discovery.* New York: Basic Books.

———. (1972) *Conjectures and Refutations: The Growth of Scientific Knowledge,* 4th rev. ed. London: Routledge and Kegan Paul.

———. (1972) *Objective Knowledge: An Evolutionary Approach.* Oxford: Clarendon Press.

Pottinger, J. Stanley. (1971) "Come Now, Professor Hook." *New York Times* CXXI:29. Saturday, December 18.

Pottinger, J. Stanley. (1972) "The Drive Toward Equality." In Barry R. Gross, ed. *Reverse Discrimination.* New York: Prometheus Books.

Prewitt, Kenneth. (1983) "Subverting Policy Premises." In Daniel Callahan and Bruce Jennings, eds. *Ethics, the Social Sciences and Policy Analysis.* New York: Plenum Press.

Price, Philip B., James N. Richards, Calvin W. Taylor, and Tony L. Jacobsen. (1964) "Measurement of Physician Performance." *Journal of Medical Education* 39:203.

Quade, Edward. (1982) *Analysis for Public Decisions.* New York: Elsevier.

Raemer, Frederic G. (1986) "Principles of Ethics and the Justification of Policy." In William N. Dunn, ed. *Policy Analysis: Perspectives, Concepts, Methods.* Greenwich, Ct.: J.A.I. Press.

Rawls, John. (1971) *A Theory of Justice.* Cambridge, Ma.: Belknap Press.

_____. (1975) "Fairness to Goodness." *Philosophical Review* 84:536–554.

Reddaway, Peter. (1979) "The Theory and Practice of Human Rights in the Soviet Union." In Donald Kommers and Gilbert Loescher, eds. *Human Rights and American Foreign Policy.* Notre Dame: University of Notre Dame Press.

Regan, Tom and Donald Van de Veer, eds. (1982) *And Justice for All.* Totowa, N.J.: Rowman and Littlefield.

Regents of the University of California v. Bakke 438 U.S. 265 (1978).

Reid, Herbert and Ernest Yanarella. (1975) "Political Science and the Postmodern Critique of Scientism and Domination." *Review of Politics* 37:286–316.

Rein, Martin. (1976) *Social Science and Public Policy.* New York: Penguin.

_____. (1983) "Value Critical Policy Analysis." In Daniel Callahan and Bruce Jennings, eds. *Ethics, the Social Sciences and Policy Analysis.* New York: Plenum Press.

Rein, Mildred. (1982) *Dilemmas of Welfare Policy.* New York: Praeger.

Riesman, David. (1979) "Human Rights: Competing Ideals." In Barry Rubin and Elizabeth Spiro, eds. *Human Rights and U.S. Foreign Policy.* Boulder, Co.: Westview Press.

Rhoads, Steven., ed. (1980) *Valuing Life: Public Policy Dilemmas.* Boulder, Co.: Westview Press.

Ripley, Randall. (1985) *Policy Analysis in Political Science.* Chicago: Nelson-Hall Publishers.

Rosen, Richard. (1980) "Identifying States and Areas Prone to High and Low Unemployment." *Monthly Labor Review* (March): 22–24.

Rousseau, Jean Jacques. (1950) "A Discourse on the Origin of Inequality." *The Social Contract and Discourses.* New York: E.P. Dutton & Co.

Rowe, William., ed. (1979) *Energy Risk Management.* New York: Academic Press.

Runciman, W.G. (1963) *Social Science and Political Theory.* Cambridge: Cambridge University Press.

Russell, Harold. (1976) "The Helsinki Declaration: Brobdingnag or Lilliput?" *American Journal of International Law* 70(2):242–271.

Sagoff, Mark. (1986) "Values and Preferences." *Ethics* 96:301–316.

Schaff, Adam. (1970) *Marxism and the Human Individual.* New York: McGraw Hill.

Schiller, Bradley. (1973) "Empirical Studies of Welfare Dependency: A Survey." *Journal of Human Resources* 8:Supplement.

Scoble, Harry, and Laurie Wiseberg. (1981) "Problems of Comparative Research on Human Rights." In V. Nanda, J. Scarritt, and G. Shepherd, eds. *Global Human Rights.* Boulder, Co.: Westview Press.

Schoek, Helmut, and James Wiggins. (1960) *Scientism and Values*. Princeton: D. Van Nostrand Company.

Schrader-Frechette, Kristin. (1980) *Nuclear Power and Public Policy*. Dordrecht: D. Reidel.

Scott, R. A., and A. R. Shore. (1979) *Why Sociology Does Not Apply: A Study of the Use of Sociology in Public Policy*. New York: Elsevier.

Seidelman, Raymond, and Edward Harpham. (1985) *Disenchanted Realists: Political Science and the American Crisis 1884–1984*. Albany: SUNY Press.

Sellars, Wilfred. (1963) *Science, Perception and Reality*. New York: Humanities Press.

Sennett, Richard, and Jonathan Cobb. (1972) *The Hidden Injuries of Class*. New York: Alfred A. Knopf.

Shawcross, William. (1979) *Sideshow: Nixon, Kissinger and the Destruction of Cambodia*. New York: Simon and Schuster.

Shils, Edward. (1980) *The Calling of Sociology and Other Essays on the Pursuit of Learning*. Chicago: University of Chicago Press.

Shotland, R. Lance, and Melvin Marks, eds. (1985) *Social Science and Social Policy*. Beverly Hills: Sage.

Sihanouk, Norodom. (1980) *War and Hope: The Case for Cambodia*. New York: Pantheon Books.

Simon, Sheldon. (1975) "The Khmer Resistance: External Relations, 1973–1974." In Zasloff and Brown, eds. *Communism in Indochina*. Lexington, Ma.: D.C. Heath.

———. (1978) "Cambodia: Barbarism in a Small State Under Seige." *Current History* 75(442):197–201.

Sleeth, Boyd C., and Robert Mishell. (1977) "Black Underrepresentation in United States Medical Schools." *New England Journal of Medicine* 297(21):1146–1148.

Smith, Adam. (1948) *Moral and Political Philosophy*. H. W. Schneider, ed. New York: Hafner.

———. (1976) *An Inquiry into the Causes of the Wealth of Nations*. R. H. Campbell and A. S. Skinner, eds. Oxford: Clarendon.

Sohn-Rethel, A. (1974) "Mental and Manual Labor in Marxism." In P. Walton and S. Hall, eds. *Situating Marx*. London: Human Context Books.

Sokolewicz, W. (1979) "The Socialist Concept of Citizens' Basic Rights and Duties." *Polish Round Table* 9:107–132.

Sorzano, José. (1975) "David Easton and the Invisible Hand." *Amercian Political Science Review* 69:91–106.

Sowell, Thomas. (1976) "'Affirmative Action' Reconsidered." In Barry R. Gross, ed. *Reverse Discrimination*. New York: Prometheus Books.

Spillman, Kurt R. (1978) "Die Stadt auf dem Berge." *Schweizer Monatschrifte* 58(3):179–192.

Starling, Grover. (1979) *The Politics and Economics of Public Policy*. Homewood, Ill.: The Dorsey Press.

Steelworkers v. Weber 443 U.S. 193 (1979).

Stevenson, Charles L. (1944) *Ethics and Language.* New Haven: Yale University Press.

———. (1963) *Facts and Values.* New Haven: Yale University Press.

Stockman, Norman. (1983) *Anti-Positivist Theories of the Sciences: Critical Rationalism, Critical Theory and Scientific Realism.* Dordrecht: D. Reidel.

Stokey, Edith, and Richard Zeckhauser. (1978) *A Primer for Policy Analysis.* New York: Norton.

Strong, Tracy. (1980) "Taking Rank With What Is Ours: American Political Thought, Foreign Policy and the Question of Rights." In Paula Newberg, ed. *The Politics of Human Rights.* New York: New York University Press.

Suppe, Frederick., Ed. (1977) *The Structure of Scientific Theories,* 2d ed. Urbana: University of Illinois Press.

Svobgo, Eddison J. M. (1979) "Human Rights: A Third World View." In Donald Kommers and Gilbert Loescher, eds. *Human Rights and American Foreign Policy.* Notre Dame: University of Notre Dame Press.

Taylor, Charles. (1978) "Neutrality in Political Science." In Peter Laslett and W. G. Runciman, eds. *Philosophy, Politics and Society,* 3d. series. London: Basil Blackwell.

Taylor-Gooby, Peter. (1983) "Moralism, Self-Interest and Attitudes to Welfare." *Policy and Politics* 11(2):145–160.

Thompson, Judith Jarvis. (1977) "Preferential Hiring." In Marshall Cohen, Thomas Nagel, and Thomas Scanlon, eds. *Equality and Preferential Treatment.* Princeton, New Jersey: Princeton University Press.

Todorovich, Miro M. and Howard Glickstein. (1977) "Discrimination in Higher Education: A Debate on Faculty Employment." In Barry R. Gross, ed. *Reverse Discrimination.* New York: Prometheus Books.

Tong, Rosemarie. (1986) *Ethics in Policy Analysis.* Englewood Cliffs, N.J.: Prentice-Hall.

Torgerson, Douglas. (1986) "Between Knowledge and Politics: Three Faces of Policy Analysis." *Policy Sciences* 19:33–59.

Tribe, Laurence. (1972) "Policy Science: Analysis or Ideology." *Philosophy and Public Affairs* 2:66–110.

Tribe, Laurence, Corrine Schelling, and John Voss. eds., (1976) *When Values Conflict: Essays on Environmental Analysis, Discourse and Decision.* Cambridge: Ballinger.

Tucker, Robert C., ed. (1978) *The Marx-Engels Reader,* 2d ed. New York: W. W. Norton.

Unger, Roberto. (1975) *Knowledge and Politics.* New York: Free Press.

U.S. Comptroller General. (1977) *More Benefits to Jobless Can Be Attained in Public Service Employment.* HRD-77–53. Washington, D.C.: General Accounting Office.

U.S. Comptroller General. (1978) *Food Stamp Work Requirements—Ineffec-*

tive Paperwork or Effective Tool. CED-78–60. Washington, D.C.: General Accounting Office.

U.S. Comptroller General. (1981) *Insights Gained in Workfare Demonstration Projects.* CED–81–117. Washington, D.C.: General Accounting Office.

U.S. Department of Labor. (1980) *Interim Report to Congress: Food Stamp Workfare Demonstration Projects.* Washington, D.C.: Office of Policy, Evaluation and Research.

United States v. Iron Workers Local 86 443 F.2d 544 (9th Circuit, 1971) cert. denied. 404 U.S. 984.

Utley, T. E. (1978) "A Reappraisal of the Human Rights Doctrine." *Policy Review* 3:27–34.

Vacarro, Vincent. (1981) "Cost Benefit Analysis and Public Policy Formulation." In Norman Bowie (ed.) *Ethical Issues in Government.* Philadelphia: Temple University Press.

Van den Daele, W. (1977) "The Social Construction of Science." In E. Mendelsohn, P. Weingart, R. Whitley (eds.) *The Social Production of Scientific Knowledge.* Dordrecht: D. Reidel.

Van der Kroef, Justus. (1979) "Cambodia: From Democratic Kampuchea to People's Republic." *Asian Survey* 19(8):731–750.

———. (1979) "Political Ideology in Democratic Kampuchea." *Orbis* 22(4):1007–1032.

Vivas, Eliseo. (1960) "Science and the Studies of Man." In Helmut Schoek and James Wiggins, eds. *Scientism and Values.* Princeton, N.J.: D. Van Nostrand Company.

Walton, P., A. Gamble, and J. Coulter. (1971) "The Image of Man in Marx." *Social Theory and Practice* 1(2):69–84.

Warwick, David. (1980) *The Teaching of Ethics in the Social Sciences.* Hastings-on Hudson, N.Y.: Institute of Society, Ethics and the Life Sciences.

Warwick, Donald, and Thomas Pettigrew. (1983) "Toward Ethical Guidelines for Social Science Research in Public Policy." In Daniel Callahan and Bruce Jennings, eds. *Ethics, The Social Sciences and Policy Analysis.* New York: Plenum.

Weale, Albert. (1983) *Political Theory and Social Policy.* London: MacMillan.

Weaver, Mark. (1980) "The Concept of Mind in Political Theory." Ph.D. Dissertation, University of Massachusetts (Amherst).

Weaver, Richard. (1960) "Concealed Rhetoric in Scientistic Sociology." In Helmut Schoek and James Wiggins, eds. *Scientism and Values.* Princeton: D. Van Nostrand Company.

Weber, Max. (1946) "Politics as a Vocation." in Hans Gerth and C. Wright Mills, trans. and eds. *From Max Weber: Essays in Sociology.* New York: Oxford University Press.

———. (1949) *The Methodology of the Social Sciences.* Edward Shils and Henry Finch, trans. and eds. New York: Free Press.

Weiss, Carol. (1977) *Using Social Research in Public Policy Making.*

Lexington, Ma.: D.C. Heath.

——— . (1983) "Ideology, Interests and Information: The Basis of Policy Decisions." In Daniel Callahan and Bruce Jennings, eds. *Ethics, the Social Sciences and Policy Analysis.* New York: Plenum Press.

Werkmeister, W. H. (1960) "Social Science and the Problem of Value." In Helmut Schoek and James Wiggins, eds. *Scientism and Values.* Princeton: D. Van Nostrand Company.

White, M., et al. (1980) *Managing Public Systems: Analytic Techniques for Public Administration.* N. Scituate, Ma.: Duxbury.

Wildavsky, Aaron. (1979) *Speaking Truth to Power: The Art and Craft of Policy Analysis.* Boston: Little, Brown.

Wilensky, Harold. (1975) *The Welfare State and Equality.* Berkeley: University of California Press.

Williams, Bernard. (1985) *Ethics and the Limits of Philosophy.* Cambridge, Ma.: Harvard University Press.

Winter, Gibson. (1966) *Elements for a Social Ethic: Scientific and Social Perspectives on Social Process.* New York: Macmillan.

Wolin, Sheldon. (1981) "Max Weber: Legitimation, Method and the Politics of Theory." *Political Theory* 9:401–424.

Wood, Ellen. (1972) *Mind and Politics.* Berkeley: University of California Press.

Wright, John T. (1980) "Human Rights in the West: Political Liberties and the Rule of Law." In Pollis and Schwab, eds. *Human Rights: Cultural and Ideological Perspectives.* New York: Praeger.

Wygant v. Jackson Board of Education. In *United States Law Week* 54 LW 4479 (May 19, 1986).

Young, Robert. (1978) "Dispensing with Moral Rights." *Political Theory* 6(1):63–74.

Index

PAUS -8911 - 5216 -(MF)
PAUS 9141 -4866
ECON 8100 -4799

HPM 522   2313 call /hr